LAW AND PHILOSOPHY

LAW AND PHILOSOPHY

A SYMPOSIUM

Edited by Sidney Hook

New York University Press   1964

The contents of this volume comprise the proceedings of the sixth annual New York University Institute of Philosophy, held at Washington Square, New York, May 10–11, 1963. Previous volumes in the series, also edited by Sidney Hook are:

Determinism and Freedom in the Age of Modern Science
Psychoanalysis, Scientific Method, and Philosophy
Dimensions of Mind
Religious Experience and Truth
Philosophy and History

Contents

Contents

Preface

IF ANYONE were to wonder in this "age of analysis" about the relevance of philosophy to human concern, he could find it without difficulty in the history, theory, and practice of law. Almost every major philosopher has written either on the philosophy of law or on themes that have a direct bearing on it. There is an obvious reason for this. The kinds of questions one naturally raises *about* law and even some questions *within* law are intimately related to questions philosophers have discussed in their professional capacity. The ends of law, the relation of law to justice, the role of law in preserving order, insuring stability in human transactions, and furthering human welfare are themes that raise ethical issues as profound as they are complex. These ethical issues are among the few intellectual interests in the tradition of the West which provide threads of continuity in the philosophical enterprise from Socrates to Dewey. At any definite time one can discover substantive provisions of the law, as well as principles of procedure, that embody philosophical assumptions of an earlier era, and are coming under the critical fire of contemporary prophets, reformers, or philosophers. Sometimes the influence of religious traditions on law is even more conspicuous than that of explicit philosophy. But since religion and morality are so intertwined in social life, a consideration of the first usually involves the second. In consequence, the challenge to a philosophical evaluation of the law is as perennial as the recurring challenges to the moral, social, and religious order.

There is a second major aspect of the law which exemplifies a type of philosophical activity even when philosophers have not been aware of it. The intellectual life of the law largely consists in the analysis of questions concerning the meaning and proper use of key terms, and especially in the legitimate extension or modification of the meaning and use of terms in new contexts. There is hardly a topic in Anglo-American as well as Continental law which does not call for distinctions and refinements in the light of new situations and new problems. Long before Wittgenstein appeared on the philosophical scene, without benefit of meta-legal theory, jurists were attempting to liberate themselves from linguistic traps and rigidities which their own abstractions created. As a discipline, the law is a pre-eminent illustration of the fact that linguistic analysis affects much more than language and linguistic use, that it reflects and sometimes even redetermines the development of institutions.

For many years the philosophy of law in America was pursued more by practicing jurists than by professional philosophers. Happily, our own time has been marked by a marked growth of interest among philosophers in problems concerned with the philosophy of law. Although it is hardly proper to speak of a renaissance of interest, its expression, quantitatively and qualitatively, is already impressive. The theme of this volume is an indication of its character.

Three major topics, suggested by contemporary issues, were taken as a focus of the discussion at the sessions of the New York University Institute of Philosophy on "Law and Philosophy." The first concerned itself with the moral grounds of obligation to obedience of law. The phenomenon of mass movements of civil disobedience in this country has given an edge of urgency to even recondite discussions of this theme. Professor John Rawls submitted the opening essay as "a working paper" for discussion rather than as a statement of his final, considered views on the subject. It served its purpose well. I am informed that he is now at work on a fuller version that will remedy "expository difficulties and over-brevity in parts of the argument" disclosed in part in the course of the interesting and provocative exchange to which it gave rise.

The second topic provided an opportunity for one more attempt to come to grips with the doctrine of natural law. In reaction to certain historical events in the twentieth century which have outraged the moral consciences of men, the number who profess allegiance to natural law are now legion. It seemed desirable, with what success the reader can judge for himself, to discover what were the necessary and/or sufficient conditions of allegiance to natural law, and to assess the validity of its doctrines.

The third topic on the nature of judicial reasoning was an attempt to clarify the process by which judicial conclusions are reached, and to throw some light on such apparently strange phenomena as the fact that the same set of words (e.g. in the American Constitution) in situations where the facts themselves are not in dispute can be taken as premises for diametrically opposed conclusions. That judicial reasoning and decision must to some extent be legislative seemed evident: how they could escape being arbitrary and subjective, less so. The echoes of the stimulating sessions devoted to this theme will remain in the memory of the participants for a long time.

Sidney Hook

LAW AND PHILOSOPHY

LAW AND THEOSOPHY

PART I

Law and Ethics

A

Legal Obligation and the Duty of Fair Play

JOHN RAWLS
Harvard University

1. THE SUBJECT of law and morality suggests many different questions. In particular, it may consider the historical and sociological question as to the way and manner in which moral ideas influence and are influenced by the legal system; or it may involve the question whether moral concepts and principles enter into an adequate definition of law. Again, the topic of law and morality suggests the problem of the legal enforcement of morality and whether the fact that certain conduct is immoral by accepted precepts is sufficient to justify making that conduct a legal offense. Finally, there is the large subject of the study of the rational principles of moral criticism of legal institutions and the moral grounds of our acquiescence in them. I shall be concerned solely with a fragment of this last question: with the grounds for our moral obligation to obey the law, that is, to carry out our legal duties and to fulfill our legal obligations. My thesis is that the moral obligation to obey the law is a special case of the prima facie duty of fair play.

I shall assume, as requiring no argument, that there is, at least in a society such as ours, a moral obligation to obey the law, although it may, of course, be overridden in certain cases by other more stringent obligations. I shall assume also that this obligation must rest on some general moral principle; that is, it must depend on some principle of justice or upon some principle of social utility or the common good, and the like. Now, it may appear to be a truism, and let us suppose

3

it is, that a moral obligation rests on some moral principle. But I mean to exclude the possibility that the obligation to obey the law is based on a special principle of its own. After all, it is not, without further argument, absurd that there is a moral principle such that when we find ourselves subject to an existing system of rules satisfying the definition of a legal system, we have an obligation to obey the law; and such a principle might be final, and not in need of explanation, in the way in which the principles of justice or of promising and the like are final. I do not know of anyone who has said that there is a special principle of legal obligation in this sense. Given a rough agreement, say, on the possible principles as being those of justice, of social utility, and the like, the question has been on which of one or several is the obligation to obey the law founded, and which, if any, has a special importance. I want to give a special place to the principle defining the duty of fair play.

2. In speaking of one's obligation to obey the law, I am using the term "obligation" in its more limited sense, in which, together with the notion of a duty and of a responsibility, it has a connection with institutional rules. Duties and responsibilities are assigned to certain positions and offices, and obligations are normally the consequence of voluntary acts of persons, and while perhaps most of our obligations are assumed by ourselves, through the making of promises and the accepting of benefits, and so forth, others may put us under obligation to them (as when on some occasion they help us, for example, as children). I should not claim that the moral grounds for our obeying the law is derived from the duty of fair-play except insofar as one is referring to an obligation in this sense. It would be incorrect to say that our duty not to commit any of the legal offenses, specifying crimes of violence, is based on the duty of fair play, at least entirely. These crimes involve wrongs as such, and with such offenses, as with the vices of cruelty and greed, our doing them is wrong independently of there being a legal system the benefits of which we have voluntarily accepted.

I shall assume several special features about the nature of the legal order in regard to which a moral obligation arises. In addition to the generally strategic place of its system of rules, as defining and relating the fundamental institutions of society that regulate the pursuit of substantive interests, and to the monopoly of coercive powers, I shall suppose that the legal system in question satisfies the concept of the *rule of law* (or what one may think of as justice as regularity). By this I mean that its rules are public, that similar cases are treated similarly, that there are no bills of attainder, and the like. These are all features of a legal system insofar as it embodies without deviation the notion of a public system of rules addressed to rational beings for the organization of their conduct in the pursuit of their substantive interests. This concept imposes, by itself, no limits on the *content* of legal rules, but only on their regular administration. Finally, I shall assume that the legal order is that of a constitutional democracy: that is, I shall suppose that there is a constitution establishing a position of equal citizenship and securing freedom of the person, freedom of thought and liberty of conscience, and such political equality as in suffrage and the right to participate in the political process. Thus I am confining discussion to a legal system of a special kind, but there is no harm in this.

3. The moral grounds of legal obligation may be brought out by considering what at first seem to be two anomalous facts: first, that sometimes we have an obligation to obey what we think, and think correctly, is an unjust law; and second, that sometimes we have an obligation to obey a law even in a situation where more good (thought of as a sum of social advantages) would seem to result from not doing so. If the moral obligation to obey the law is founded on the principle of fair play, how can one become bound to obey an unjust law, and what is there about the principle that explains the grounds for forgoing the greater good?

It is, of course, a familiar situation in a constitutional democracy that a person finds himself morally obligated to obey an unjust law. This will be the case whenever a member of the minority, on some legislative proposal, opposes the majority view for reasons of justice. Perhaps the standard case is where the majority, or a coalition sufficient to constitute a majority, takes advantage of its strength and votes in its own interests. But this feature is not essential. A person belonging to the minority may be advantaged by the majority proposal and still oppose it as unjust, yet when it is enacted he will normally be bound by it.

Some have thought that there is ostensibly a paradox of a special kind when a citizen, who votes in accordance with his moral principles (conception of justice), accepts the majority decision when he is in the minority. Let us suppose the vote is between two bills, A and B each establishing an income tax procedure, rates of progression, or the like, which are contrary to one another. Suppose further that one thinks of the constitutional procedure for enacting legislation as a sort of machine that yields a result when the votes are fed into it—the result being that a certain bill is enacted. The question arises as to how a citizen can accept the machine's choice, which (assuming that B gets a majority of the votes) involves thinking that B ought to be enacted when, let us suppose, he is of the declared opinion that A ought to be enacted. For some the paradox seems to be that in a constitutional democracy a citizen is often put in a situation of believing that both A and B should be enacted when A and B are contraries: that A should be enacted because A is the best policy, and that B should be enacted because B has a majority—and moreover, and this is essential, that this conflict is different from the usual sort of conflict between prima facie duties.

There are a number of things that may be said about this supposed paradox, and there are several ways in which it may be resolved, each of which brings out an aspect of the situation. But I think the simplest thing to say is to deny straightway that there is anything different in this situation than in any other situation where there is a conflict of prima facie principles. The essential of the matter seems to be as follows: (1) Should A or B be enacted and implemented, that is, admin-

istered? Since it is supposed that everyone accepts the outcome of the vote, within limits, it is appropriate to put the
enactment and implementation together. (2) Is *A* or *B* the
best policy? It is assumed that everyone votes according to
his political opinion as to which is the best policy and that the
decision as to how to vote is not based on personal interest.
There is no special conflict in this situation: the citizen who
knows that he will find himself in the minority believes that,
taking into account only the relative merits of *A* and *B* as
prospective statutes, and leaving aside how the vote will go,
A should be enacted and implemented. Moreover, on his own
principles he should vote for what he thinks is the best policy,
and leave aside how the vote will go. On the other hand, given
that a majority will vote for *B*, *B* should be enacted and implemented, and he may know that a majority will vote for *B*.
These judgments are relative to different principles (different
arguments). The first is based on the person's conception of
the best social policy; the second is based on the principles on
which he accepts the constitution. The real decision, then, is
as follows: A person has to decide, in each case where he is
in the minority, whether the nature of the statute is such that,
given that it will get, or has got, a majority vote, he should
oppose its being implemented, engage in civil disobedience, or
take equivalent action. In this situation he simply has to balance his obligation to oppose an unjust statute against his
obligation to abide by a just constitution. This is, of course, a
difficult situation, but not one introducing any deep logical
paradox. Normally, it is hoped that the obligation to the
constitution is clearly the decisive one.

Although it is obvious, it may be worthwhile mentioning,
since a relevant feature of voting will be brought out, that
the result of a vote is that a rule of law is enacted, and although
given the fact of its enactment, everyone agrees that it should
be implemented, no one is required to believe that the statute
enacted represents the best policy. It is consistent to say that
another statute would have been better. The vote does not
result in a statement to be believed: namely, that *B* is superior,

on its merits, to A. To get this interpretation one would have
to suppose that the principles of the constitution specify a
device which gathers information as to what citizens think
should be done and that the device is so constructed that it
always produces from this information the morally correct
opinion as to which is the best policy. If in accepting a constitution it was so interpreted, there would, indeed, be a serious
paradox: for a citizen would be torn between believing, on his
own principles, that A is the best policy, and believing at the
same time that B is the best policy as established by the constitutional device, the principles of the design of which he
accepts. This conflict could be made a normal one only if one
supposed that a person who made his own judgment on the
merits was always prepared to revise it given the opinion constructed by the machine. But it is not possible to determine
the best policy in this way, nor is it possible for a person to
give such an undertaking. What this misinterpretation of the
constitutional procedure shows, I think, is that there is an important difference between voting and spending. The constitutional procedure is not, in an essential respect, the same
as the market: Given the usual assumptions of perfect com-
petition of price theory, the actions of private persons spending
according to their interests will result in the best situation, as
judged by the criterion of Pareto. But in a perfectly just constitutional procedure, people voting their political opinions on
the merits of policies may or may not reflect the best policy.
What this misinterpretation brings out, then, is that when
citizens vote for policies on their merits, the constitutional
procedure cannot be viewed as acting as the market does,
even under ideal conditions. A constitutional procedure does
not reconcile differences of opinion into an opinion to be taken
as true—this can only be done by argument and reasoning—
but rather it decides whose opinion is to determine legislative
policy.

4. Now to turn to the main problem, that of understanding how a person can properly find himself in a position where,
by his own principles, he must grant that, given a majority

vote, *B* should be enacted and implemented even though *B* is unjust. There is, then, the question as to how it can be morally justifiable to acknowledge a constitutional procedure for making legislative enactments when it is certain (for all practical purposes) that laws will be passed that by one's own principles are unjust. It would be impossible for a person to undertake to change his mind whenever he found himself in the minority; it is not impossible, but entirely reasonable, for him to undertake to abide by the enactments made, whatever they are, provided that they are within certain limits. But what more exactly are the conditions of this undertaking?

First of all, it means, as previously suggested, that the constitutional procedure is misinterpreted as a procedure for making legal rules. It is a process of social decision that does not produce a statement to be believed (that *B* is the best policy) but a rule to be followed. Such a procedure, say involving some form of majority rule, is necessary because it is certain that there will be disagreement on what is the best policy. This will be true even if we assume, as I shall, that everyone has a similar sense of justice and everyone is able to agree on a certain constitutional procedure as just. There will be disagreement because they will not approach issues with the same stock of information, they will regard different moral features of situations as carrying different weights, and so on. The acceptance of a constitutional procedure is, then, a necessary political device to decide between conflicting legislative proposals. If one thinks of the constitution as a fundamental part of the scheme of social cooperation, then one can say that if the constitution is just, and if one has accepted the benefits of its working and intends to continue doing so, and if the rule enacted is within certain limits, then one has an obligation, based on the principle of fair play, to obey it when it comes one's turn. In accepting the benefits of a just constitution one becomes bound to it, and in particular one becomes bound to one of its fundamental rules: given a majority vote in behalf of a statute, it is to be enacted and properly implemented.

The principle of fair play may be defined as follows. Suppose } f.p def

over

there is a mutually beneficial and just scheme of social cooperation, and that the advantages it yields can only be obtained if
everyone, or nearly everyone, cooperates. Suppose further that
cooperation requires a certain sacrifice from each person, or
at least involves a certain restriction of his liberty. Suppose
finally that the benefits produced by cooperation are, up to a
certain point, free: that is, the scheme of cooperation is un-
stable in the sense that if any one person knows that all (or
nearly all) of the others will continue to do their part, he
will still be able to share a gain from the scheme even if he
does not do his part. Under these conditions a person who
has accepted the benefits of the scheme is bound by a duty of
fair play to do his part and not to take advantage of the free
benefit by not cooperating. The reason one must abstain from
this attempt is that the existence of the benefit is the result of
everyone's effort, and prior to some understanding as to how
it is to be shared, if it can be shared at all, it belongs in fairness
to no one. (I return to this question below.)

Now I want to hold that the obligation to obey the law, as
enacted by a constitutional procedure, even when the law
seems unjust to us, is a case of the duty of fair play as defined.
It is, moreover, an obligation in the more limited sense in that
it depends upon our having accepted and our intention to continue accepting the benefits of a just scheme of cooperation
that the constitution defines. In this sense it depends on our
own voluntary acts. Again, it is an obligation owed to our fellow citizens generally: that is, to those who cooperate with us
in the working of the constitution. It is not an obligation owed
to public officials, although there may be such obligations.
That it is an obligation owed by citizens to one another is
shown by the fact that they are entitled to be indignant with
one another for failure to comply. Further, an essential condition of the obligation is the justice of the constitution and the
general system of law being roughly in accordance with it.
Thus the obligation to obey (or not to resist) an unjust law
depends strongly on there being a just constitution. Unless one
obeys the law enacted under it, the proper equilibrium, or

balance, between competing claims defined by the constitution
will not be maintained. Finally, while it is true enough to say
that the enactment by a majority binds the minority, so that
one may be bound by the acts of others, there is no question
of their binding them in conscience to certain beliefs as to
what is the best policy, and it is a necessary condition of the
acts of others binding us that the constitution is just, that we
have accepted its benefits, and so forth.

5. Now a few remarks about the principles of a just constitution. Here I shall have to presuppose a number of things
about the principles of justice. In particular, I shall assume that
there are two principles of justice that properly apply to the
fundamental structure of institutions of the social system and,
thus, to the constitution. The first of these principles requires
that everyone have an equal right to the most extensive liberty
compatible with a like liberty for all; the second is that inequalities are arbitrary unless it is reasonable to expect that they
will work out for everyone's advantage and provided that the
positions and offices to which they attach or from which they
may be gained are open to all. I shall assume that these are
the principles that can be derived by imposing the constraints
of morality upon rational and mutually self-interested persons
when they make conflicting claims on the basic form of their
common institutions: that is, when questions of justice arise.

The principle relevant at this point is the first principle,
that of equal liberty. I think it may be argued with some
plausibility that it requires, where it is possible, the various
equal liberties in a constitutional democracy. And once these
liberties are established and constitutional procedures exist,
one can view legislation as rules enacted that must be ostensibly compatible with both principles. Each citizen must decide
as best he can whether a piece of legislation, say the income
tax, violates either principle; and this judgment depends on a
wide body of social facts. Even in a society of impartial and
rational persons, one cannot expect agreement on these matters.

Now recall that the question is this: How is it possible that a person, in accordance with his own conception of justice, should find himself bound by the acts of another to obey an unjust law (not simply a law contrary to his interests)? Put another way: Why, when I am free and still without my chains, should I accept certain a priori conditions to which any social contract must conform, a priori conditions that rule out all constitutional procedures that would decide in accordance with my judgment of justice against everyone else? To explain this (Little has remarked),[1] we require two hypotheses: that among the very limited number of procedures that would stand any chance of being established, none would make my decision decisive in this way; and that all such procedures would determine social conditions that I judge to be better than anarchy. Granting the second hypothesis, I want to elaborate on this in the following way: the first step in the explanation is to derive the principles of justice that are to apply to the basic form of the social system and, in particular, to the constitution. Once we have these principles, we see that no just constitutional procedure would make my judgment as to the best policy decisive (would make me a dictator in Arrow's sense).[2] It is not simply that, among the limited number of procedures actually possible as things are, no procedure would give me this authority. The point is that even if such were possible, given some extraordinary social circumstances, it would not be just. (Of course it is not possible for everyone to have this authority). Once we see this, we see how it is possible that within the framework of a just constitutional procedure to which we are obligated, it may nevertheless happen that we are bound to obey what seems to us to be and is an unjust law. Moreover, the possibility is present even though everyone has the same sense of justice (that is, accepts the same principles of justice) and everyone regards the constitutional procedure itself as just. Even the most efficient constitution cannot prevent the enactment of unjust laws if, from the complexity of the social situation and like conditions, the majority decides to enact them. A just constitutional procedure cannot foreclose all injustice; this depends on those who carry out the procedure. A constitutional procedure is not like a market reconciling interests to an optimum result.

6. So far I have been discussing the first mentioned anomaly of legal obligation, namely, that though it is founded on justice, we may be required to obey an unjust law. I should now like to include the second anomaly: that we may have an obligation to obey the law even though more good (thought of as a sum of advantages) may be gained by not doing so. The thesis I wish to argue is that not only is our obligation to obey the law a special case of the principle of fair play, and so dependent upon the justice of the institutions to which we are obligated, but also the principles of justice are absolute with respect to the principle of utility (as the principle to maximize the net sum of advantages). By this I mean two things. First, unjust institutions cannot be justified by an appeal to the principle of utility. A greater balance of net advantages shared by some cannot justify the injustice suffered by others; and where unjust institutions are tolerable it is because a certain degree of injustice sometimes cannot be avoided, that social necessity requires it, that there would be greater injustice otherwise, and so on. Second, our obligation to obey the law, which is a special case of the principle of fair play, cannot be overriden by an appeal to utility, though it may be overriden by another duty of justice. These are sweeping propositions and most likely false, but I should like to examine them briefly.

I do not know how to establish these propositions. They are not established by the sort of argument used above to show that the two principles, previously mentioned, are the two principles of justice, that is, when the subject is the basic structure of the social system. What such an argument might show is that, if certain natural conditions are taken as specifying the concept of justice, then the two principles of justice are the principles logically associated with the concept when the subject is the basic structure of the social system. The argument might prove, if it is correct, that the principles of justice are incompatible with the principle of utility. The argument might establish that our intuitive notions of justice must sometimes conflict with the principle of utility. But it leaves unsettled what the more general notion of right requires when this conflict occurs. To prove that the concept of justice should have an absolute weight with respect to that of utility would require a deeper argument based on an analysis of the concept of right, at least insofar as it relates to the concepts of justice and utility. I have no idea whether such an analysis is possible. What I propose to do instead is to try out the thought that the concept of justice does have an absolute weight, and to see whether this suggestion, in view of our considered moral opinions, lead to conclusions that we cannot accept. It would seem as if to attribute to justice an absolute weight is to interpret the concept of right as requiring that a special place be given to persons capable of a sense of justice and to the principle of their working out together, from an initial position of equality, the form of their common institutions. To the extent that this idea is attractive, the concept of justice will tend to have an absolute weight with respect to utility.

7. Now to consider the two anomalous cases. First: In the situation where the obligation requires obedience to an unjust law, it seems true to say that the obligation depends on the principle of fair play and, thus, on justice. Suppose it is a matter of a person being required to pay an income tax of a kind that he thinks is unjust, not simply by reference to his interests. He would not want to try to justify the tax on the ground that the net gain to certain groups in society is such as to outweigh the injustice. The natural argument to make is to his obligation to a just constitution.

But in considering a particular issue, a citizen has to make two decisions: how he will vote (and I assume that he votes for what he thinks is the best policy, morally speaking), and, in case he should be in the minority, whether his obligation to support, or not obstruct, the implementation of the law enacted is not overridden by a stronger obligation that may lead to a number of courses including civil disobedience. Now in the sort of case imagined, suppose there is a real question as to whether the tax law should be obeyed. Suppose, for example, that it is framed in such a way that it seems deliberately calculated to undermine unjustly the position of certain social or religious groups. Whether the law should be obeyed or not depends, if one wants to emphasize the notion of justice, on such matters as (1) the justice of the constitution and the real opportunity it allows for reversal; (2) the depth of the injustice of the law enacted; (3) whether the enactment is actually a matter of calculated intent by the majority and warns of further such acts; and (4) whether the political sociology of the situation is such as to allow of hope that the law may be repealed. Certainly, if a social or religious group reasonably (not irrationally) and correctly supposes that a permanent majority, or majority coalition, has deliberately set out to undercut its basis and that there is no chance of successful constitutional resistance, then the obligation to obey that particular law (and perhaps other laws more generally) ceases. In such a case a minority may no longer be obligated by the duty of fair play. There may be other reasons, of course, at least for a time, for obeying the law. One might say that disobedience will not improve the justice of their situation or of their descendants' situation; or that it will result in injury and harm to innocent persons (that is, members not belonging to the unjust majority). In this way, one might appeal to the balance of justice, if the principle of not causing injury to the innocent is a question of justice; but, in any case, the appeal is not made to the greater net balance of advantages (irrespective of the moral position of those receiving them). The thesis I want to suggest then, is that in considering whether we are obligated to obey an unjust law, one is led into no absurdity if one simply throws out the principle of utility altogether, except insofar as it is included in the general principle requiring one to establish the most efficient just institutions.

Second: Now the other sort of anomaly arises when the law is just and we have a duty of fair play to follow it, but a greater net balance of advantages could be gained from not doing so. Again, the income tax will serve to illustrate this familiar point: The social consequences of any one person

(perhaps even many people) not paying his tax are unnotice-
able, and let us suppose zero in value, but there is a noticeable
private gain for the person himself, or for another to whom he
chooses to give it (the institution of the income tax is subject
to the first kind of instability). The duty of fair play binds us
to pay our tax, nevertheless, since we have accepted, and intend to continue doing so, the benefits of the fiscal system to
which the income tax belongs. Why is this reasonable and not
a blind following of a rule, when a greater net sum of advantages is possible?—because the system of cooperation consistently followed by everyone else itself produces the advantages generally enjoyed and in the case of a practice such as
the income tax there is no reason to given exemptions to anyone so that they might enjoy the possible benefit. (An analogous case is the moral obligation to vote and so to work the
constitutional procedure from which one has benefited. This
obligation cannot be overridden by the fact that our vote
never makes a difference in the outcome of an election; it may
be overridden, however, by a number of other considerations,
such as a person being disenchanted with all parties, being
excusably uninformed, and the like.)

There are cases, on the other hand, where a certain number of exemptions can be arranged for in a just or fair way;
and if so, the practice, including the exemptions, is more efficient, and when possible it should be adopted (waiving problems of transition) in accordance with the principle of establishing the most efficient just practice. For example, in the
familiar instance of the regulation to conserve water in a
drought, it might be ascertained that there would be no harm
in a certain extra use of water over and above the use for
drinking. In this case some rotation scheme can be adopted
that allots exemptions in a fair way, such as houses on opposite sides of the street being given exemptions on alternate
days. The details are not significant here. The main idea is
simply that if the greater sum of advantages can effectively
and fairly be distributed amongst those whose cooperation
makes these advantages possible, then this should be done. It

would indeed be irrational to prefer a lesser to a more efficient just scheme of cooperation; but this fact is not to be confused with justifying an unjust scheme by its greater efficiency or excusing ourselves from a duty of fair play by an appeal to utility. If there is no reason to distribute the possible benefit, as in the case of the income tax, or in the case of voting, or if there is no way to do so that does not involve such problems as excessive costs, then the benefit should be foregone. One may disagree with this view, but it is not irrational, not a matter of rule worship: it is, rather, an appeal to the duty of fair play, which requires one to abstain from an advantage that cannot be distributed fairly to those whose efforts have made it possible. That those who make the efforts and undergo the restrictions of their liberty should share in the benefits produced is a consequence of the assumption of an initial position of equality, and it falls under the second principle. But the question of distributive justice is too involved to go into here. Moreover, it is unlikely that there is any substantial social benefit for the distribution of which some fair arrangement cannot be made.

8. To summarize, I have suggested that the following propositions may be true:

First, that our moral obligation to obey the law is a special case of the duty of fair play. This means that the legal order is construed as a system of social cooperation to which we become bound because: first, the scheme is just (that is, it satisfies the two principles of justice), and no just scheme can ensure against our ever being in the minority in a vote; and second, we have accepted, and intend to continue to accept, its benefits. If we failed to obey the law, to act on our duty of fair play, the equilibrium between conflicting claims, as defined by the concept of justice, would be upset. The duty of fair play is not, of course, intended to account for its being wrong for us to commit crimes of violence, but it is intended to account, in part, for the obligation to pay our income tax, to vote, and so on.

Second, I then suggested that the concept of justice has an

absolute weight with respect to the principle of utility (not necessarily with respect to other moral concepts). By that I meant that the union of the two concepts of justice and utility must take the form of the principle of establishing the most efficient just institution. This means that an unjust institution or law cannot be justified by an appeal to a greater net sum of advantages, and that the duty of fair play cannot be analogously overridden. An unjust institution or law or the overriding of the duty of fair play can be justified only by a greater balance of justice. I know of no way to prove this proposition. It is not proved by the analytic argument to show that the principles of justice are indeed the principles of justice. But I think it may be shown that the principle to establish the most efficient just institutions does not lead to conclusions counter to our intuitive judgments and that it is not in any way irrational. It is, moreover, something of a theoretical simplification, in that one does not have to balance justice against utility. But this simplification is no doubt not a real one, since it is as difficult to ascertain the balance of justice as anything else.

NOTES

1. The metaphor of being free and without one's chains is taken from I. M. D. Little's review of K. Arrow's book *Social Choice and Individual Values*, (New York, 1951) which appeared in *Journal of Political Economy*, LX (1952). See p. 431. My argument follows his in all essential respects, the only addition being that I have introduced the concept of justice in accounting for what is, in effect, Arrow's non-dictatorship condition.

2. See Arrow, *opus cit. supra*.

B

Civil Disobedience and the Duty of Fair Play

MILTON R. KONVITZ
Cornell University

I

Professor Rawls has constructed a model that contains the legal order of a constitutional democracy in which all citizens enjoy the equal right to vote, equal security of the person, and freedom of thought and conscience, and which embodies the rule of law. In this political order, it is assumed (1) that each citizen has an opportunity, in some institutional way, to approve or disapprove laws before they are enacted, and (2) that bills that win majority support shall be enacted and enforced. The minority who have opposed the measure while it was pending are morally obligated to obey its terms when their objections are overridden and the bill becomes a statute. Citizens are in and out of shifting majorities and minorities, and the rule of fair play requires that I must accept the will of the majority when the vote goes against my position, just as I expect that my neighbor will accept the majority decision when the vote goes my way and against his judgment. "In accepting the benefits of a just constitution one becomes bound to it," says Professor Rawls, "and in particular one becomes bound to one of its fundamental rules: given a majority vote in behalf of a statute, it is to be enacted and properly implemented."

This principle of fair play obtains, says Professor Rawls, even when the dissenting citizen believes that the law is unjust; for his obligation to abide by the just constitution overrides his moral obligation to oppose an unjust law. There are, however, a number of provisos:

First, Professor Rawls excludes from consideration laws against acts that are inherently wrong, such as crimes of violence and "vices of cruelty and greed." I think that Professor Rawls has in mind what the law calls wrongs that are *malum in se* and that do not need the denouncement of a statute. Such wrongs, says Professor Rawls, are condemned "independently of there being a legal system the benefits of which we have voluntarily assumed."

Second, a citizen may conclude that on balance he has a duty to disobey an unjust law when the enactment is outside "certain limits," left undefined. The closest Professor Rawls comes to stating the case for civil disobedience is in the following passage: "Certainly, if a social or religious group reasonably (not irrationally) and correctly supposes that a permanent majority, or majority coalition, has deliberately set out to undercut its basis and that there is no chance of successful constitutional resistance, then the obligation to obey that particular law (and perhaps other laws more generally) ceases. In such a case a minority may no longer be obligated by the duty of fair play." There may be, then, the duty of civil disobedience, and this duty, Professor Rawls thinks, runs counter to the duty of fair play and overrides it. "An unjust institution or law or the overriding of the duty of fair play," he says in his conclusion, "can be justified only by a greater balance of justice." He adds that he knows of no way to prove this proposition.

The main thrust of Professor Rawls's argument, however, seems to be on the necessary coexistence of obedience and the duty of fair play.

II

First, I find it difficult to see that the argument of fair play is connected intimately only with constitutional democracy. Perhaps I can make this point by referring to the argument of Socrates in the *Crito* when his friends tried to persuade him to escape from prison. He put his arguments into the mouth of the Laws and Constitution of Athens, who essentially said that by running away Socrates would not be acting in accordance with the rules of fair play. "Do you imagine," said the Constitution and Laws, "that a city can continue to exist and not be turned upside down, if the legal judgments which are pronounced in it have no force but are nullified and destroyed by private persons? . . . Was there provision for this in the agreement between you and us, Socrates?" The argument continues that it was by the laws that Socrates' parents were married and that he was their legitimate son; that by them his parents were compelled to give him a decent upbringing and an education. "Are you not grateful for those of us Laws which were instituted for this end?" The tenor of the Socratic argument for obedience of the laws is in the spirit of Professor Rawls, yet Socrates does not try to base the argument of fairness on the proposition that it somehow flows out of the logic of constitutional democracy. It flows perhaps out of the fact that one lives in a society, regardless of its political form.

The duty of obedience, I think, must be based on another foundation, the essence of which must be found in human nature rather than in any adventitious political form that is historically conditioned.

The duty of fair play, in the sense in which Socrates may have used it, can be as convincing to a citizen of the U.S.S.R. or of Spain as to a citizen of the United States.

Taking, then, the duty of fair play as the basis of the duty of obedience, I would say that I do not see how, philosophically, it can be restricted to constitutional democracies; for what men may feel universally cannot be explained by the character of a social order that is by no means universal. The link between (1) the duty of obedience and (2) the duty of fairness and constitutional democracy may be justified ideologically, but I doubt if it can be justified philosophically.

III

Secondly, I find it difficult to accept the restriction of fair play to laws that punish acts that are only *malum prohibitum* —acts that are wrong *because* they are prohibited, acts that are not inherently immoral but which have become so only because of a majority vote forbidding them. As to wrongs that are inherently evil, Professor Rawls says that one should not commit them "independently of there being a legal system the benefits of which we have voluntarily accepted." Thus some acts I ought not to do because they are inherently evil, and some acts I ought not to do because of the duty of fair play. The former duty obtains everywhere, the latter obtains only where there is a constitutional democracy.

But just as a constitutional democracy has laws that are directed at both kinds of wrongs, so has any other kind of social order. There are traffic laws in Spain under Franco and in the U.S.S.R.; also income tax laws, compulsory school-attendance laws, and thousands of other laws over the justice or reasonableness of which reasonable minds may differ. Does Professor Rawls mean that where a constitutional democracy does not exist—as in Egypt or Spain or the U.S.S.R.—there is no duty of fair play compelling obedience of laws that relate to wrongs that are *malum prohibitum*? I trust not, for every social order depends for its existence on men obeying such laws, even primitive societies that have never heard of constitutional democracy.

The temptation to resort to civil disobedience is felt not because of the laws that relate to acts that are wrong only because they are prohibited by the government, but because governments have legalized what some men would call murder or other acts of violence, or acts that degrade human beings or that deprive them of personal freedom or liberty of conscience, and that violate the ideal of the rule of law. It is such laws that normally give rise to the duty of civil disobedience; yet Professor Rawls has put them all beyond our consideration by limiting his model to situations in which the law is somehow "unjust" yet is a law that makes an act wrong only because a majority has declared it to be that.

Professor Rawls uses the tax laws as his primary example. Let us consider some cases of civil disobedience as directed at such laws.

Before the April 15th deadline a clergyman in California sent a letter to the Internal Revenue Service saying that he refused to pay 61 per cent of his federal income tax because, he said, this portion would go for "carefully planned machinery to kill millions of human beings." He added that he would be glad to pay the withheld money if it would be devoted to peaceful ways of solving international differences instead of going for military purposes.

Now, we should note that in the mind of this taxpayer the income tax law is not itself unjust. He is not objecting to this law. His objection is to the use to which most of his tax money would be put. He really objects to the national budget and to the government's military expenditures. And as to these acts of government, he reacts as if the government had legalized what he considers murder and other acts of violence, in which he has no will to participate. He means to practice civil disobedience directed against wrongs that are *malum in se*.

This was equally the case with Thoreau. He did not question the duty to pay taxes in general, regardless of how the money would be used by the government, and regardless, too, whether the taxes would support a constitutional democracy or any other kind of government.

> If the injustice is part of the necessary friction of the machine of government, let it go, let it go. . . . If the injustice has a spring, or a pulley, or a rope, or a crank, exclusively for itself, then perhaps you may consider whether the remedy will not be worse than the evil; but if it is of such a nature that it requires you to be the agent of injustice to another, then, I say, break the law. Let your life be a counter friction to stop the machine. What I have to do is to see, at any rate, that I do not lend myself to the wrong which I condemn.

The wrong that Thoreau condemned was the government's support of the slave owners and the slave states, as well as our war on Mexico. By refusing to pay the poll tax, Thoreau was expressing his protest, not against the tax itself, but against the government and the nation for robbing the Negro and the Mexican of their human rights. He was saying, in effect—as he said, too, in *Walden*, in a broader context:—"Stop the world! I want to get off!" His civil disobedience was of a law that he considered a matter of moral indifference, but this act of civil disobedience was aimed at injustices that transcended the poll tax law. The civil disobedience was aimed at a wrong that was *malum in se*.

Indeed, it is perhaps almost impossible to engage in civil disobedience against a tax law as an end in itself, for usually the state will find a way to collect the tax. The citizen might be fined or imprisoned, but his property can be taken to satisfy the tax judgment, and the tax in fact gets paid. This is quite different from the more usual case of civil disobedience, as that of the conscientious objector to war who is an absolutist: if he refuses to recognize the draft laws, although vicarious registration might be accomplished for him, nothing beyond that could be done that would involve him in subjecting himself to those laws, which remain disobeyed.

These examples illustrate the proposition that the distinction between inherent wrongs and acts that are wrong only because the government declares them to be wrong is often insufficient to the conscience of the citizen as a basis for his decision on the duty of obedience or civil disobedience, for the latter type of wrongs are often seen as perhaps innocent means to immoral ends.

This situation is aggravated by the fact that what may appear to the legislator to be conduct subject to regulation—like the compulsory flag salute—may appear to the citizen to be inherently evil and to be resisted regardless of personal consequences.

A further aggravation is illustrated by Sophocles' *Antigone*, in which the ruler declares an act, otherwise innocent, to be inherently evil because of special circumstances, so that the burial of a corpse becomes a seditious or treasonable act; but to Antigone the failure to bury her brother appeared to be an enormity that her conscience could not accept.

The play illustrates three different judgments of the same act: (1) to Creon the burial of Polyneices had to be a capital crime; (2) to Antigone the burial of Polyneices was so important that she was willing to die for performing this duty to her brother; and (3) to Ismene the whole business was incomprehensible and unimportant—she was only a woman, she thought, and therefore felt not called upon to deal with matters she could not understand or with events she could not control.

IV

Finally, I wish to explore briefly the question whether civil disobedience can be said to be an overriding of fair play, as Rawls says it is. The citizen who disobeys a law when moved to do so by principles of civil disobedience must feel deeply that what the law demands of him is inherently evil; for he must be ready—and even willing—to suffer the penalty for his disobedience, and this he is not likely to want to do if he feels that the act is not inherently evil. Acts of civil disobedience are directed against deeply felt evils, which a man will not do even if he faces imprisonment or death for his disobedience.

Thus, in the classic cases, Thoreau chose to go to jail rather than help perpetuate slavery or help the aggressor in an unjust war; and Antigone chose death rather than fail to perform the required burial rites for her brother. They did not try to hide their violations of the law but, on the contrary, they openly invited the punishment. In the case of Gandhi there are other considerations that we have no time to explore, but on this limited point Gandhi, too, may be cited. In 1922, when he faced the British judge in Ahmedabad, after the indictment was read, Gandhi rose and declared: "I am here

. . . to invite and cheerfully submit to the highest penalty
that can be inflicted upon me for what in law is a deliberate
crime and what appears to me to be the highest duty of a
citizen." Time and again Gandhi stressed the idea that civil
disobedience entails "suffering in your own person by inviting
the penalty for the breach of the law." Voluntary—and even
willing—assumption of the legal punishment for violation of
the law is an essential characteristic of civil disobedience.

This is, I think, important, for Thoreau and Gandhi used
civil disobedience not, as Professor Rawls seems to put it, as
an overriding of the principles of fair play, but rather as *a way
of winning a place for these principles or as a vindication of
them.* When the Negro was denied his liberty, it meant that
the majority was putting the Negro beyond the reach of the
principles of fairness, as if he were a stone or a piece of wood;
and the Negro slave had no political or legal voice of his own.
Thoreau, then, by his act of civil disobedience, acted out sym-
bolically what Professor Rawls acknowledges to be the right
of a minority against whom the majority have ganged up and
who are left without a "chance of successful constitutional
resistance."

In the same way, Gandhi's acts need to be interpreted as
symbolic or vicarious acts of civil disobedience staged by the
group—for example, the untouchables—which, spiritually, he
felt he represented. So, too, I think, the absolutist among conscientious objectors to war feels that by inviting imprisonment
he acts vicariously for all humanity whom he would save from
military slaughter. In this way the act of civil disobedience is
an affirmation of the prisoner's brotherhood with all men on
the other side of the prison bars. The intention of his act is
not to override the principles of fair play but to achieve their
vindication in the wills and institutions of men; and I believe
that fair play requires that we do justice to this intention in our
attempt to formulate the moral principles that are the under-
pinnings of obedience and disobedience. Such men cannot be
in any way charged with trying to be "free riders." They try,
through civil disobedience and paradoxically, to affirm, rather

than to breach, the agreement between themselves and the Laws of which Socrates spoke.

I would note that by recognizing the duty of civil disobedience even in a constitutional democracy, Professor Rawls stands with Thoreau, though Professor Rawls might not accept the following significant passage from Thoreau's "Civil Disobedience":

> Even voting *for the right* is *doing* nothing for it. It is only expressing to men feebly your desire that it should prevail. A wise man will not leave the right to the mercy of chance, nor wish it to prevail through the power of majority. . . . When the majority shall at length vote for the abolition of slavery, it will be because they are indifferent to slavery, or because there is but little slavery left to be abolished by their vote.

What Thoreau said, and what Professor Rawls is saying, is that the moral judgment must be given priority over the political or any other judgment. When pressed far enough, this means that the individual conscience must have the last word: If that last word means civil disobedience, which entails the penalty of the law, then the penalty must be imposed, and in this way both conscience and law are vindicated. Socrates could not and would not accept as binding on his conscience the majority vote of the jury that tried him, but he willingly submitted to the penalty. So, too, a citizen may not accept as binding on his conscience the majority vote of the legislature, though he will willingly submit to the penalty for his civil disobedience of that law. In this way civil disobedience may render unto Caesar what is Caesar's and unto God what is God's.

There may be rare cases where a person may be justified in disobeying a law and yet refusing to take the penalty for the breach. This type of situation may be illustrated by the case of Zola. After he was convicted of criminal libel and sentenced to imprisonment by judges who were pledged to maintain the "honor" of the French military apparatus rather than to maintain justice, Zola's friends urged him to run away to England. Like Socrates, he refused, arguing that his flight would

itself be an act of injustice and dishonor. But his friends re-
joined that if he were to go to a French prison, he would be
silenced and Dreyfus would continue to languish in prison,
whereas if he were to find refuge in England, he could continue the fight he had started with *J'accuse* as champion of
justice for Dreyfus. Zola agreed, and when he reached London
resumed his struggle—not on his own behalf, but on behalf of
the prisoner on Devil's Island. Zola's case was obviously different from that of Socrates in a way that made Zola's flight a
justified act.

By looking exclusively at the act of disobedience, one sees
only half of the event. The punishment is the other half, which
is just as essential to the person as the act of disobedience;
for even as he breaks the law, he means at the same time to
restore its wholeness. He does not act as an outlaw; he is no
free rider. He may be mistaken in what he does, but he ought
not to be blamed for wrongs that are entirely beyond his intention. "What will you have? quoth God; pay for it and take
it." This Emersonian rule is the measure by which he who
breaks the law in civil disobedience acts. He takes and pays,
and thus affirms, rather than overrides, the duty of fair play.

C

The Problem of Mr. Rawls's Problem

JOHN COURTNEY MURRAY, S.J.
Woodstock College

NO ONE will question the permanent validity of the issue to which Professor Rawls addresses himself. In one or another state of the question, as influenced by one or another cultural context, it has long been argued; and it will need continually to be argued, since it is central to the public philosophy. Is our social existence, as structured by law, based only on force and fear or also somehow on morality and conscience? Is civil obedience a form of moral action or merely a matter of expediency and interest? Is it a free response to a moral obligation whose grounds are grapsed by intelligence, or is it no more than a craven conformism effected by coercion? Is the political obligation also a moral obligation, and, if so, why? The issue can be stated in all sorts of ways.

Professor Rawls's dominant intention is to remedy the defects and inadequacies of utilitarian theory. In its application, the rule of the greater happiness of the greater number results in inequities that are visited on a minority, whose happiness is the price at which the greater happiness is bought. This result appears prima facie as a social surd; and its appearance casts doubt on the theory.

The major question is whether the concept of fair play, which Rawls advances as his principle of solution, will bear the theoretical and practical weight he wishes to thrust upon it.

There is, however, the preliminary issue of the manner in which he states the problem. He takes his start from "two anomalous facts," and he chooses to argue the "hard case" of the obligation of civil obedience to an unjust law. It is, however, normally perilous to argue from perplexed cases, as they are technically called. The danger is a distortion of theory. Moreover, the question "Why am I obliged to obey the law in the hard case?" is subsumed under, and supposes a solution to, the more general classic question "Why am I obliged to obey the law at all?" I do not therefore see the advantage of stating the problem in terms of the hard case.

Furthermore, I find two conceptual difficulties in the statement of the problem. First, I fail to grasp the exact meaning intended in the phrase "unjust law." Is it a question of legal enactments that are violative of certain demonstrable rights of man and citizen or of enactments that are merely damaging to certain interests of a minority? Is the question simply political —a question of the prudence of legislation and its effective relation to the furtherance of the common good? Or is the question properly moral—a question of legislative trespass on the order of rights whose ultimate roots are in the sacredness of the human person? A minority might complain that a tax bill, for instance, is unjust, meaning that it is contrary to the interests of the income bracket in which the minority finds itself. This, however, is to use the word "unjust" in a loose sense. The justice of the bill might still be sustained on the ground that it distributes equitably the social burden of taxation and precisely to this end contravenes the interests of a particular social group.

On the other hand, a minority—or a single man, for that matter—might complain against the injustice of a statute enforcing euthanasia on certain classes of the population judged by the state to be useless. Here the word "unjust" would be used with full propriety; the right to life is inherent in the human person, inalienable in the face of the state. There is no moral case to be made for a statute enforcing euthanasia (so, at least, we commonly think at the moment). Moreover, in the characterization of laws as unjust, attention would have to be paid to the classic distinction between *malum quia prohibitum* and *prohibitum quia malum.* The first question therefore concerns the sense in which Rawls speaks of an "unjust" law.

I should add here that, in my view, no moral issue of civil obedience rises in the case of a legal enactment that is unjust in the proper sense. To the question "Why am I obliged to obey an unjust law?" the only answer is that I am not obliged to obey it. I cannot be bound in conscience to comply with a legislative act that does violence to my rights as a man. Failure to comply may indeed result in my being coerced by the power of the state, but the coercion is doubly injurious. I take it that this position furnishes the basis for the classic right of resistance to unjust rule, which is one of the Germanic components of the liberal tradition of politics.

My second question concerns the use of the word "obligation." Again I fail to grasp Rawls's meaning. In its classic sense, the concept of obligation exhibits two notes. There is, first, the note of necessity, stated in the word "ought." Second, there is the note of freedom, implied in the word "ought." Obligation asserts a necessity of the moral, not the physical, order; therefore my response to it must be a free act of obedience. To pay a just debt at the point of a gun, and only because the gun is pointed, is not to act as a moral agent consciously responding to a sense of obligation. I am not quite sure that Rawls is using the word "obligation" in its full sense or in some attenuated sense. Something seems to be missing with regard to the note of "necessity."

In any event, his problem is to know the reason for the obligation—the rational and moral necessity—of obeying legislative prescriptions or prohibitions of human enactment (I put the question in its full mode of generality). The solution is sought in the concept of fair play. By a voluntary act I once chose to accept the benefits accruing to me from the social cooperation whose organization and maintenance are effected by the legal order of society. This voluntary act is prolonged in the intention to continue to accept these benefits. This act and this intention create an obligation to play fair. And this obligation comes to bear on me in the hard case from the law (and also, I should think, in any case of encounter with the social fact of law). So, at least, I understand the solution, though my understanding may be clouded by the difficulties already noted.

The first question concerns the problematic—the problem of the problem. Are we once more back in the problematic created by the will to remove from human law all manner of transcendental reference, and indeed any note of heteronomy, in the name of a morality of perfect personal autonomy? This problematic is usually associated with the name of Rousseau, but in one or other form it is common within the secularistic tradition of the autonomous man, derivative from the Enlightenment, which has transposed the state of the question in all the great issues of philosophy, politics, and law. How shall it be brought about that in society I shall obey only myself—is this the problem behind Rawls's problem? Have we here another speculative effort to find in personal freedom the final root of moral obligations in and toward society? Does this direction of effort command the appeal to something that looks very like the celebrated "state of nature" of rationalist theory —what the author calls the "original position of equal liberty," which seems at least to have some sort of natural priority over the social consensus, which in turn seems to be no more than contractual? Or am I doing the unpardonable thing, which is to indulge in exegesis? Not, at any rate, willfully. The fact is that I do not clearly see what Rawls's problematic is. And an understanding of it would have to be the first step toward a judgment on his mode of positing and solving his problem.

I might perhaps note here that I myself stand within the older tradition, derivative from the Old and New Testaments and developed by the schools in the wake of Augustine, which constructs the problematic of the political obligation in the light, for instance, of Romans 13:1. The issue is how shall it be brought about, in theory and in practice, that in society a man should, in the end, obey only God? Even if one believes in God as Pantocrator, some nice argument, of considerable complexity, is required to elaborate the solution.

Under precision from larger issues, it would be only fair to consider Rawls's solution in its own terms. From this point of view, it is not without some fragilities.

First, there is the issue of the inference from the decision to be a societal man to the obligation of playing fair. It is by no means evident that the inference is valid in itself or that it terminates in a proper obligation, a rational and moral necessity to keep the rules on all occasions. Unless some other moral factor is introduced into the argument, the conclusion might well be qualified by the famous scientific proviso: Having agreed to be a societal man, I am obliged to play fair, other things being equal. Other things, however, are not always equal, as we so well know. But an obligation that is only hypothetical does not satisfy the exigencies of the problem. From another point of view, the conclusion from the premise might merely be that, since I will to participate in society, it would be a good thing for me to keep the rules. It would be only fair for me to play fair. Thus I would display my social virtue— and also stay out of trouble. The difficulty is that the good and the obligatory are not conceptually identical. The moral order and the juridical order are not to be divorced in some sort of Kantian style; but they are to be differentiated. Moreover, against any supposed obligation to play fair I could always, in the particular instance, appeal to an "ethic of the situation" and transcend any a priori demand in the name of some higher personal value, perhaps even some higher social value, that would accrue, if I were to break the rules. Finally, it is not possible to prove that the order of society, from which benefits derive to the individual, requires that everybody should always play fair. In the perspectives of Aquinas' realist view of the human likelihood of virtuous behavior, it is sufficient that a minority behave well out of a motive of virtue and that a just system of coercive law obtain that will constrain and restrain the *maior pars* who, as he says, are "not perfect in virtue." But if it is not necessary that everybody should play fair, why should I? Whence comes the necessity? I should indeed be the gentleman who plays fair. However, as Newman

pointed out, being a gentleman has *per se* little to do with
morality. And in the climactic hard case, which is that of the
famous gentleman of the "Gentleman's Psalm" (number 15 in
Hebrew), who "swears to his own hurt and does not change,"
the reason for his fidelity to his word was not a prior decision
to accept the benefits of Hebrew society. It was the fear of the
Lord, the desire to sojourn in his tent, to dwell on his holy hill.

1

Equality and Obedience to Law

MONROE C. BEARDSLEY
Swarthmore College

THE ARGUMENT that John Rawls has given for his main thesis seems to me sound at heart, but perhaps some of the complexities in his way of developing it can be avoided. I should like, in a cooperative as well as critical spirit, to see whether the argument cannot be simplified and rendered less exposed to attack. My plan is to outline a case for obedience to law, and along the way comment comparatively on a few parallel points in Rawls's paper.

I begin with the Principle of Equality, which I take in the form of an injunction: "All persons are to be treated alike, except where circumstances require different treatment." The built-in qualification is, of course, indispensable, and makes the Equality Injunction peculiarly innocuous. There are so many unspecified ways in which the second clause can cancel the first. Yet it is certainly not null. It has full force when applied to the simplest of distribution-situations (as when candy is to be divided among children, none of whom can allege any differences between them that would be ground for giving one a larger share than the others). And in complex distribution-situations, where inequalities are justified, the Equality Injunction remains the underlying presupposition and defines the starting point for calculations of fairness. The word "treatment" is the most general available. It can include particular actions as well as general practices, or modes of treatment. It covers all distributions of goods and ills, and all rules and regulations. And it is meant to bridge the customary transition from Sub-

stantive Equality to Methodic Equality, when in certain sorts
of situation goods themselves cannot be equally distributed
but fairness requires at least an equal opportunity to possess
them.

What is the status of the Equality Injunction? It can be
stated as an ethical proposition ("should be," or "ought to be,"
replacing "are to be"), and in that form it requires either to
be justified in argument or to be accepted as basic, without justification. Both of these consequences can be avoided by adopting the alternative view: that the Equality Injunction is not
itself a positive rule of ethics, but a rule for adopting rules—
somewhat in Kant's sense, a metamoral maxim. The reference
to circumstances is really a reference to reasons, and the injunction is most explicitly stated in this way: "All persons are to be
treated alike, unless good reasons can be given for treating
them differently." It is still hollow, of course, until filled in with
criteria for deciding what reasons are to count as good. But the
feature of it that I hope to emphasize and clarify first is that
its full and sole force consists in stating where the burden of
proof belongs, in disputes about fairness.

Consider a simple situation in which two men stumble
on a buried treasure. A says, "I claim half of it." B says, "Give
me a good reason why you should have half." The Equality
Injunction rules B's request out of order. A is not required to
give any reason why he should have half; it is up to B to give
a reason (if he can) why A should *not* have half, and then it
would be proper for A to reply to B. But it is not up to A to
defend his claim to half. The question of defending a claim
does not arise until someone makes a claim to an unequal
share; it is that which requires a reason.

I think this notion of the ultimate burden of proof is very
useful in other philosophical areas as well, but I do not know
how to give general criteria for deciding where the burden
lies. It cannot be self-evident; it is not even obvious to some
legal systems that the burden of proof in a criminal trial rests
on the prosecution rather than on the defense. One might say
that in any conflict of contradictory propositions, the burden

of proof rests on him who asserts the existential proposition; in some primitive sense, he is saying more, going out on a limb. (It is not that there is an a priori antecedent probability that things do not exist.) As for equality, there is a sense in which the person who asks for equal shares is not asking anything— not "anything special," as we say. By being willing to accord to *B* an exact equivalent of what he takes for himself, *A* achieves a kind of neutrality of claim, which has the same effect as a zero claim, such as he would make by tossing the whole treasure into the sea. (*B* might object strenuously to this action and say that *A* was being "unfair;" but *A*'s action would not produce an unfair distribution of the treasure. It seems to me important not to smuggle into the concept of fairness the notion of maximizing the values involved, as some recent writers on justice have tended to do.)

Obviously I am straining to avoid saying about the Equality Injunction what Rawls says about his principle of Fair Play —namely, that it expresses a "prima facie obligation." There is, strictly speaking, no (moral) obligation to treat people equally, but only a (logical) requirement to supply a good reason for treating people unequally. Moral considerations will often enter into the reasons given to justify differential treatment, but there does not need to be a *special* moral principle about equality. The question as to what is to count as a good reason, why certain properties are "relevant" and others "irrelevant," is one of the hard ones, of course. Rawls's requirement that inequalities can only be justified when it is reasonable to expect that they will work out to everyone's advantage seems to be too strict, for example. Even the most valuable act of Congress, favoring some industry or section of the country (farm subsidies, TVA), may not benefit everyone, but it may not be unfair.

It may be argued that this analysis really begs the question, that what makes it seem evident that claims to equal shares require no justification is just the tacit assumption that equality is morally right. I do not think so. The proposition that men are born equal means only that no one carries into this world with him a prior duty to treat other people differently from the way he treats himself, and so any demands by others are void until they are instituted and justified.[1] It is true that sometimes the demand for equal rights has to be forcefully stated and vigorously pressed, but that is only when inequalities have been so firmly institutionalized or ingrained in custom that they seem to many people natural and inevitable—if, indeed, they are noticed at all. This does not mean that the demand for equal rights must be supported by ethical premises or asserted as a basic ethical principle. This point is tacitly acknowledged by people even in moments of anger and fear. When a Negro family moves into a previously all-white neighborhood and (as still occasionally happens, though with decreasing frequency) his neighbors-to-be riot and throw stones, even some of the rioters will realize that the Negro has said all he needs to say when he says to reporters, "All we want to do is live in a nice house in the suburbs, like any other family," and they feel they must counter this appeal to equality somehow, no matter by what wild accusations of deceit, conspiracy, and block-busting. When women demanded the vote, the attack on them did not, after all, consist in requiring them to justify equality, but in trying to show (very unsuccessfully) that sex is a relevant basis for distinguishing those who deserve suffrage from those who do not.

The obligation to obey the law seems to me to derive directly from the Equality Injunction (I refer here to what I shall call the "primary" obligation to obey a particular law as such). For to demand of others conformity to a rule without being prepared to conform to it oneself is a simple violation of the injunction. Now, a person does not contradict himself when he merely refuses to follow a custom that everyone else follows, for he does not deny them the freedom to abandon the custom if they wish. There has to be, on his part, some explicit or implicit call upon others, in order for him to be obliged similarly to call upon himself. In some cases, this is *assent*. When four players begin a game and call it "Chicago bridge," or whatever, there is certainly a clear announcement that each

expects the others to follow certain rules, and hence a clear
obligation, based on the Equality Injunction, for each to follow
them. In the case of statutory rules passed by a state legislature
or city council, there is the rather tenuous form of assent involved in the election of representatives. In the case of the
State Department's passport regulations, it is hard to find assent at all. In any case, how binding the rule is depends on
one's behavior. In so far as we give evidence of expecting and
wanting other people to abide by the law, then we are ourselves obliged to expect and want (hence, to resolve) to do
the same. It is not our knowledge of the origin of the law (the
conditions of its enactment) or our hopes for its utility that
makes obedience obligatory, but simply our acceptance of it
as a general rule for others. This acceptance may be signified
by receiving the benefits of other people's obedience—or by
failing to make a protest when the law is applied to others.

To this it may be replied that we cannot, as individuals,
divest ourselves of the obligation to obey a particular law that
we happen to dislike simply by announcing that we do not care
whether others obey it or not—or even by urging others to disobey it. But this is because we cannot easily divest ourselves of
the benefits that accrue to us from general obedience or ex-
tricate ourselves from the web of relationships in which the
particular law is involved. It is true that some people feel justified in illegal betting on horses because they have no objection if others do the same, and would make no effort to have
others arrested and punished for betting. Let us make this example stronger by ruling out considerations of utility; let it be
assumed that the general welfare would be promoted if betting
were legalized and regulated by government. Then, if I am
prepared to allow others to bet illegally, why should I feel
obliged to obey this law myself?

First, it might be argued that if the police successfully
prevent many people from betting illegally, but I manage to
get away with it, then I am taking unfair advantage of others.
This consideration could no doubt trouble a man of tender
conscience, but it does not seem to be required by the Equality

Injunction. For I cannot make it easier for others to bet illegally by refraining from doing so myself when I can get away with it, and so my illegality does not deprive others of equal rights. All that can be required of me is that I grant everyone else the right to bet whenever he has a safe opportunity—exactly what I am granting myself.

Second, it might, of course, be argued that I ought not to bet illegally because this will tend to undermine and weaken the whole fabric of the law—by setting a bad example, by encouraging criminals, by promoting the corruption of law-enforcement officers, and so forth. This argument is, of course, extremely powerful. I am inclined to think that it is the only argument that can be effectively given. But it does not show that I have any primary obligation to obey the betting law as such, only that my obligation to obey it derives from a general interest in law and order and an interest in the flourishing of other laws.

If I am correct, then, the obligation of a particular individual to obey a particular law derives from his express or tacit invitation of others to like behavior. And this primary obligation does not depend on the utility of the law or on the manner in which it originated (it does not, for example, presuppose a constitutional democracy, as Rawls seems to imply). But it does depend on the form and nature of the law itself: the law must genuinely embody the Equality Injunction, in treating all individuals in the same manner, or in containing (or resting upon) a justification of differential treatment. And this consequence defines the limit of that primary obligation. When a law itself, regardless of its origin or social effects, violates the Equality Injunction by imposing arbitrary discriminations, then there can be no obligation to obey it, as such. Neither he who is discriminated against nor he who benefits from the discrimination has such an obligation. Indeed, both of them have a moral obligation to disobey the law (when some desirable end can be obtained thereby), since to obey it is to violate the Equality Injunction. Certainly, there is room for much dispute as to whether a particular law does in fact impose such arbitrary discriminations; a fairly pure and undeniable case is a statute (or, in some states, a constitutional provision[2]) forbidding white females to marry Negro males but permitting Negro females to do this. But it is hard to be sure, in many cases, that the inequalities introduced by a law (for example, subsidies to producers of certain crops but not others) are really indefensible, and under some circumstances the presumption is that they are not.

But of course the obligation to ignore an unfair law does not settle the question what is to be done in a particular case. Every individual's general stake in the whole legal structure must always count heavily against disobeying a particular law on a particular occasion. Suppose it is a local segregation ordinance that would be disobeyed by a sit-in. The initial primary obligation is to pay no attention to the law, since it is patently discriminatory and therefore unjust. No one can claim any primary obligation to support such a law or to acknowledge its legitimacy. The second, and very strong, counterobligation is certainly to obey the law—considered now, not in itself, but in relation to the whole set of local ordinances, the structure of government and law enforcement, and the possible consequences of blunting the prevailing respect for lawfulness. Out of the conflict between these two obligations, some resultant must be found. Other considerations enter in. For example, the obligation to obey may be strengthened by the reflection that, since the law was arrived at by constitutional methods, there is hope of repealing it in the same way, and repealing the law is preferable to flouting it. On the other hand, the obligation to obey may be weakened by the reflection that, political conditions being what they are, the only possible chance of getting rid of the law is to disobey it, and appeal a conviction to a higher court, in which more fundamental constitutional principles can be brought to bear and the deeper conscience of the nation may be heard. Throughout all deliberation, it seems to me, the interest in general lawfulness remains so strong that every deliberate decision to disobey a law (to engage in civil disobedience, in the broad sense) must be undertaken solemnly

and regretfully—and with a determination to act in every way
so as at the same time to sustain the general respect for law.[3]

NOTES

1. This meaning is even more evident in George Mason's significant alternative phrase, "equally free and independent," which appears in a number of state constitutions (I take this information,
but no conclusions, from R. Carter Pittman, "Equality *v.* Liberty:
the Eternal Conflict," reprinted by the Virginia Commission on Constitutional Government from the *Journal of the American Bar Association* [August, 1960]).

2. See Jack Greenberg, *Race Relations and the American Law,*
(New York: Columbia University Press, 1959), pp. 397–98.

3. Compare Stuart Brown, "Civil Disobedience," *Journal of
Philosophy,* LVIII (1961), 669–81.

Utility and the Obligation to Obey the Law

RICHARD C. BRANDT
University of Michigan

VARIOUS WRITERS have suggested in recent years that a closer look will show that considerations of welfare consequences have much less to do with our moral rights and obligations than is usually supposed. Professor Rawls, in his paper, appears to hold this view. These writers are undoubtedly correct in thinking that the traditional utilitarians oversimplified matters. Nevertheless one can easily go too far in criticizing the utilitarian position. In what follows I shall argue that the utility of consequences is of more importance for our obligation to obey the law than Rawls appears to think. I am not sure, however, that I am arguing against anything Rawls really asserts, for his paper is highly condensed and often allows of different interpretations, as I shall indicate in due course. Perhaps the points I shall make will be of some interest, however, irrespective of whether they contradict anything Rawls means to assert.

It may be helpful if I begin by outlining the essential points of Rawls's theory.

1. Rawls asserts that if a person is living in a constitutional democracy with a just constitution and in which the majority of the laws are constitutional, then if any action, *A*, were to be that person's legal duty (be required by law), he would on that account have a prima facie moral Obligation (I explain the capitalization in a moment) to do *A*. I assume Rawls supposes one has a legal duty to do something if the statutes or

court decisions either explicitly affirm or imply that one has
(perhaps by specifying some penalty for failure to do *A*).

In what sense of "Obligation"? Rawls says he is using this
term in "its more limited sense" in which it "has a connection
with institutional rules." One might question whether the term
has any such special sense; but when I think I am using it in
Rawls's special sense, I shall capitalize the word. I think Rawls
means to use the word in such a way as to imply that whenever
we have an Obligation we have an Obligation *to* someone;
hence when he says we have an Obligation to obey the law,
he means we have an Obligation to our fellow citizens to obey
the law. This use contrasts with a broader use in which "is
morally obligated to do" implies that witting and unjustified
failure to do renders the agent subject to reasonable disapproval, but not necessarily that the action is owed *to* anyone.
(One might say that the United States is morally obligated to
do something about conditions in South Africa and not imply
that something is *owed to* anyone in the way we think it is
when someone has performed an important service for us.)
Thus Rawls is saying not merely that people have a moral obligation in *some* sense to do whatever is their legal duty, but
that they have a moral Obligation in this narrow sense. This
fact has a dual effect: that his thesis is a stronger one than it
would otherwise be and, on the other hand, that it is more
plausible that any moral Obligation in this sense derives from
considerations of fair play.

Rawls asserts merely a *prima facie* Obligation to do one's
legal duty. What does he mean by "prima facie"? Philosophers
usually say there is a prima facie obligation to do something
only if one is absolutely bound to do it, morally, *unless* there
is a counterobligation of superior weight.[1] Rawls's contention
is somewhat stronger than this: he thinks there is a prima facie
Obligation to act that is absolutely binding unless considerations of justice override it.

2. Rawls holds that the prima facie Obligation to do one's
legal duty is a special case of the duty of fair play. That is, he
holds that as a sound general moral principle one is Obligated

not to enjoy the benefits of cooperative undertakings without making one's own contribution; and he thinks that from this principle, plus a description of the situation of a person living under a constitutional democracy (and so forth), it follows that a person has a prima facie moral Obligation to do his legal duty. Furthermore, this Obligation derives *only* from the duty of fair play, in the sense that there is *no other* acceptable moral principle from which, taken with a description of the situation of a person in a constitutional democracy, it follows that a person has a prima facie Obligation to do his legal duty. Rawls does not, of course, deny that there are other principles from which it follows that I have a prima facie Obligation to do what happens also to be my legal duty, such as supporting my children; nor does he deny that there are other principles from which it follows that I have a prime facie obligation (wider sense) to do my legal duty. He only holds that the duty of fair play is the duty from which it follows that a person in a constitutional democracy has a moral Obligation to do his legal duty as such.

3. Where the constitution is unjust [2] or where many laws do not conform to a just constitution, the general duty of fair play does not have this implication; hence one has no moral Obligation to do one's legal duty, since one has this Obligation only as a case of the duty of fair play.

4. Unjust institutions cannot be justified by their utility. Thus, given an unjust constitution, no utilitarian considerations can bring about an obligation to do one's legal duty, since this derives from the duty of fair play.

5. The prima facie Obligation to do one's legal duty cannot be overridden by any appeal to utility. This follows from point one above, given his conception of "prima facie" Obligation.

I

The first question I wish to raise is whether one has a prima facie obligation (broad sense) to do one's legal duty just as such. I am not merely asking whether one has a prima facie (in Rawls's strong sense) Obligation to do one's legal duty; although, if one has no prima facie (usual weaker sense) obligation, a fortiori one has no prima facie (Rawls's stronger sense) Obligation. I tend to think the answer to this question is "No." I suggest that being my legal duty can make a certain action a prima facie moral obligation only when some other property is present. Which other property I will discuss later.

Lest this denial sound shocking, let me hasten to add that a prima facie obligation is different from a presumption of obligation. To make the distinction clear, consider promises. If I know only that someone has promised to do A, I am entitled to presume that he has a prima facie obligation to do A. But this presumption can be rebutted, for example, by information that the promise was made on the basis of deliberately falsified information offered with the intent of inducing a promise. Not every kind of promise is sufficient to sustain a prima facie obligation to perform. Now, I suggest, if I know that something is my legal duty, that does create a presumption of a prima facie obligation to perform: just as the appearance of a statement in a textbook creates a presumption that there is evidence behind it, so knowledge that something is my legal duty creates a presumption of an obligation to perform, for it creates a presumption that there is substantial moral reason behind requiring people to do that sort of thing. Most laws ought to be obeyed most of the time, and have good reasons behind them. Since a known legal duty creates a presumption of a prima facie moral obligation to perform accordingly, it would be wrong to fail to perform without serious reflection. But it does not follow that reflection will sustain the utility of prima facie obligation to perform.

How might one support the view that being a legal duty alone is not sufficient to support a prima facie moral obligation? Obviously, if we can find even a single case of a legal duty without a corresponding prima facie moral obligation, that will be sufficient, for this would show that legal duty *as such* is not sufficient for prima facie moral obligation.

Consider, as possible examples, laws restricting personal behavior that does not affect other people, such as the laws about sexual behavior that were criticized in H. L. A. Hart's recent *Law, Liberty, and Morality*. Doubtless many of these are dead letters,[3] but some are not. Or consider the Connecticut law forbidding physicians to give birth-control information or the Pennsylvania law (recently declared unconstitutional) requiring teachers to begin the day's work with certain religious exercises. Physicians and teachers might obey these laws from fear of the consequences of infraction, but it seems dubious to say they had a prima facie moral obligation to obey, much less an Obligation to their fellow citizens so strong that it could be overcome only by some consideration of justice!

II

It is always a bit unconvincing to support a thesis merely by parading some moral convictions as counterexamples, even when the thesis being questioned implies the absence of counterexamples. Therefore I shall now approach the status of such laws from another angle: that of questioning whether the duty of fair play implies a prima facie Obligation (or obligation) to do one's legal duty in a constitutional democracy. I concede that a negative answer will not quite show that there is no prima facie obligation to do one's legal duty, since this might be a case of some other general moral principle. But a negative answer will have some force; and in any case it will be pertinent to Rawls's second thesis, that the prima facie Obligation to do one's legal duty is a special case of the duty of fair play.

Most people will probably agree with Rawls that there is an obligation not to free ride, meaning by "free riding" the enjoyment of the benefits of a cooperative enterprise—benefits that would be unavailable but for the cooperation of the vast majority—without making a fair contribution to the success of the common enterprise, at least provided the benefits are worth the cost. One might, then, consider disobedience to law a case of free riding. For the benefits of a secure and ordered life are available only because almost everyone obeys the law. These benefits are available to everyone, irrespective of whether they are law-abiding themselves. A person who does not obey a law is to that extent free riding. So, if one is obligated (fair play) not to free ride, one is obligated to obey the law. And since this obligation may be said with some plausibility to be *to* the individuals who produce the benefits of law and order, it might be said that one is Obligated to one's fellow citizens in a constitutional democracy, Obligated to obey the law. But is this reasoning sound?

First, the benefits of a secure and ordered life are produced by general obedience to some laws, not others. One would be quite content to live in a society in which no one obeys laws like those I have argued involve no prima facie obligation to obey. Second, there is a social gain in discriminating people refusing to obey some laws at their personal peril. Even in a constitutional democracy the members of the legislature are often ill educated, prejudiced, and self-interested. The meekness of the citizens in abiding faithfully by any law the legislature passes is an invitation to the legislators to promulgate their prejudices. The fact that many people will refuse to obey a law that the legislature has no business passing is itself a force that helps maintain a tolerable standard of thoughtfulness in law, since legislators know that passage of a law that people will refuse to obey merely brings discredit on the law and on themselves. Third, a person who refuses to obey a given law may not himself be enjoying any particular benefit from that action, and hence is not taking any advantage of the law-abidingness of others. For instance, a physician who insists on giving birth-control information, at risk to his own professional status, is in this position. Finally, before a charge of "free riding" can be made out, it would seem necessary to show that one's own total contribution or sacrifice to an institution in question is unfairly low, perhaps below that of the average individual. If so, then in the present case there is no free riding unless many or most individuals obey the law with more care

than the individual who refuses on occasion. But, in fact, the individual who refuses to submit himself to some laws may be the very individual who is most scrupulous about obeying laws that are justified and have a point. Further, this same individual may be the one who makes the greatest sacrifice to promote the ends of government in general.

The plausibility of the view that disobedience to any law is a case of free riding arises from the apparent analogy with some institutions in which refusal to obey the rules really is a case of free riding. Consider, for instance, one facet of the institution of the family. Part of this institution is (or was) the fact that parents are obligated to care for and educate their children, and children in their turn are obligated to care for and support parents in illness or old age. I think we would agree—although there is a good deal to be said about the matter—that there is a strong prima facie obligation for a child to play his role when it comes his turn, even at pretty heavy cost, given that the institution is just and that he has accepted its benefits. If he refuses, he is a free rider, to mention only one thing. But the analogy with refusal to obey any law is far from exact, as one can see by comparing the situations for the points just mentioned above. To take just one difference, if the child does not do his part someone else stands to lose heavily. But this need not be true for the case of law; disobedience in some cases does no harm at all—or at least, if harm is done it is indirect, through such effects as lowering the general standards of law-abidingness. But, as Professor Pennock shows, it is far from made out that such an effect is certain to take place.

More argument, then, is needed to show that the duty of fair play implies a prima facie obligation to do one's legal duty as such, whatever it may happen to be in a particular case.

III

I have questioned whether there is a prima facie moral obligation to do one's legal duty as such, in every type of case,

and whether the duty of fair play implies that there is such a prima facie obligation. On the other hand, it is quite clear that there is a prima facie obligation to do some things that would not have been had not the law prescribed them: for example, driving on the right-hand side of the road or reporting one's income to the government. So evidently in some conditions the content of the law makes a difference to one's prima facie obligations. What are some of these conditions?

One such condition is that the law in question has some function in what Professor Pennock outlines as the general business of government: preservation of security of the person and property, justice, the general welfare, and protection of the rights of the individual generally. Several of these items, although I think not all of them, may be regarded as concerned with maintaining utility, or the social welfare, at the highest possible level. It follows that I am saying that if a law has a function in maintaining the social utility at the highest possible level, there is a prima facie obligation to obey that law. In that sense utility seems to be important for our obligation to obey the law.

Since I am not suggesting that only the best possible (the ideally most utility-producing) laws deserve obedience, but only that, to deserve obedience, it is sufficient that a law have a utility-producing function and be part of the going concern of laws, my suggestion is only mildly utilitarian, and perhaps critics of utilitarianism would not object to it. My suggestion does not, for instance, imply that a person is free of obligation to report his income just because there could be a more utility-producing, or more just, income-tax law. It is clear that the collection of an income tax has a function, since some form of tax of this general sort seems required to provide for the defense and welfare functions of government, among others. A law forbidding the dissemination of birth-control information is in a very different position.

It is worth noticing that, according to Rawls's view, utility is also a necessary condition of a prima facie Obligation to do one's legal duty: the obligation to fair play arises only when

an institution produces benefits for its members that a person can enjoy although making no contribution. Thus there can be no obligation of fair play to obey the rules of an institution that provides no benefits. Rawls holds that the utility of the legal system as a whole is a necessary condition of the prima facie obligation to do one's legal duty; but he thinks it unnecessary for any particular law to have a function in the proper business of government for there to be a prima facie Obligation to obey that law.

IV

In the course of arguing that "the principles of justice are absolute with respect to the principle of utility," Rawls argues that the prima facie Obligation to do one's legal duty cannot be overriden by an appeal to utility. Taken literally, this claim is insupportable, as I shall show. But this is one of the points at which I think the condensed nature of Rawls's statement prevents his formulation from doing justice to his actual view.

To see the indefensibility of the position stated, consider the following real-life example. In the Commonwealth of Pennsylvania it is unlawful to operate a motor vehicle that has not been inspected. The penalty is not high—perhaps $25, more or less, depending on the whims of the magistrate. But the action *is* unlawful. Now suppose an uninspected car is the only vehicle available for transporting an ill person to a hospital for urgently needed care. The position stated implies that such an emergency would not provide a moral justification for breaking the law. It might be argued that there is a "duty of justice" in the present case, but it is not easy to see how. To take a more serious case, it is surely arguable that, for considerations of euthanasia, it is sometimes morally permissible to break laws forbidding homicide. Here again there seems to be an appeal to utility.

It might be argued that such breaches are in fact not breaches of the law. The courts excuse, as justified, certain breaches of the letter of the law when the specific action was of a kind that the legislators did not intend to prevent. Perhaps what this shows, however, is that even the courts recognize that avoidance of harm is often a justification for infraction of the actual statutes. So, again, it seems, considerations of utility are important to our obligation to obey the law.

V

The contention that "unjust institutions cannot be justified by an appeal to the principle of utility" is, despite the fact that the judgment presumably is intended to apply to unjust laws, hardly central to Rawls's paper. But the inherent interest of the issue is so great that some comments may be in order.

We must get clear first what the issue is. The word "unjust" is sometimes used in a condemning sense. Used in this sense, it implies "is wrong, everything considered." In this sense of the word, any demonstration that an institution is not wrong would automatically require withdrawal of description of it as unjust. Now, if an institution is unjust in this sense, obviously it cannot be justified by appeal to utility or anything else, for to say it is unjust *is* to say that it is to be condemned in view of every type of reasonable appeal, utility not excepted. But "unjust" is not always used in this sense. We may say of a piece of legislation that it "will work some injustice" or of a faculty rule that it is "unjust to" certain classes of students. In such cases we do not mean to exclude the possibility of justifying it on other grounds. In fact, we use this mode of speech, very often, precisely because we think this *can* be done.

As I understand it, however, Rawls's contention above is rather more specific than a claim about institutions that might be said to be unjust in either of these ordinary senses. I believe he is speaking of institutions that are "unjust" in the sense of infringing one or the other of Rawls's two principles of justice, as formulated above. Let us speak of an institution that is unjust in this sense as being "unjust$_R$."

Our question, then, is whether an institution (law) that is unjust$_R$ can be justified (shown to be right) by appeal to utility. Rawls says it cannot, although he is on the brink, at one point, of the opposite position when he says that an unjust$_R$ institution may be "tolerable" if "social necessity requires it." He is only on the brink, however, for he goes on to explain that he means by "social necessity requiring it" that "there would be greater injustice otherwise." I believe, however, that utility can sometimes justify as being right a law that is unjust$_R$.

I shall confine attention to the second of his principles. My comment will consist in describing a possible law that seems to infringe this principle but that seems justified by the utilities involved. Later, I shall sketch an alternative to his second principle, an alternative that permits appeals to utilities and that I think conforms more closely to our sense of justice.

For our example, let us first suppose the discovery of a sure method of determining which women are carriers of hemophilia. This disease we recall, is carried only by women as a defect in their chromosomes, whereas only men suffer from it. Let us suppose, further, that any male child of an average carrier of the defective chromosomes has a 50-50 chance of developing severe hemophilia. Now it would seem to me not obviously wrong for women, known to be carriers, to be prohibited by law from having children. I believe, however, that a law to this effect would be unjust$_R$ by Rawls's second principle. Evidently women consider it a sacrifice not to have children even at this risk (known carriers often continue to enlarge their families). Such a law would not have the effect of making the position of carriers of hemophilia better than it is; it would in no way be to their self-interest.

It might be argued that in the above case the appeal is not to utility but to justice, since what is being prevented is harm to others. Until this argument is presented in detail, however, there is much to be said for thinking that an assessment of such a law is primarily a matter of balancing the risk of hemophilia against the satisfaction to women of having their own children.

But there are other possible cases. Suppose the Chinese

were to place a severe crop tax on farmers that would require
the next generation of farmers to live at the subsistence level
or below, on the ground that this is necessary in order to get
industrialization well started. Would such a law necessarily be
wrong? And if not, would the reason not be the expected benefits to future generations? Much the same could be said for a
free-trade agreement that would throw thousands of workers
out of the jobs for which they have been trained, on the ground
that in the long run free trade is of benefit to all (except those
who are hit by it at the outset).

If one concludes from such examples that part of Rawls's
proposal needs modification, one has a choice whether to modify his dictum that an unjust$_R$ institution cannot be justified
by appeal to utility, perhaps by outlining appeals to utility that
are acceptable, or to modify his definition of "unjust," corre-
spondingly affirming, then, that an institution unjust in a new
sense cannot be justified by appeal to utility. It is questionable
whether one of these moves is more helpful than the other, but
I shall conclude with a proposal along the latter line.

Rawls's suggestion is that one condition for a just institution is that it provide equality in positions except for those
inequalities it is reasonable to expect will work out for the
advantage of every individual. On this proposal, any inequality
must be justified by a gain for each individual concerned, as
compared with some "base" position. I suggest that an inequality may be justified if a somewhat different condition is met.
This condition is that the total gains from the inequality be
such that anyone in the disfavored minority who was sympathetic enough not to resent his disfavored position in view of
the general gain would also, if he were in the majority, not feel
obligated to work for a removal of that inequality—provided
there were a full and vivid knowledge of the facts. I suggest
that we say an institution is unjust if it involves unjust inequalities in the sense suggested. Thus unjust inequalities are a sufficient condition for an unjust institution, although not, perhaps,
a necessary one.

This formulation leaves room for what seems a proper appeal to utility in the determination of what is just. Presumably, a sympathetic person will balance hardships to the few against benefits to the many. I do not suggest how heavily the advantage of the many will weigh. I am prepared to believe that it will not weigh very heavily—in the sense that almost any amount of positive satisfaction for the many will hardly balance pain, insecurity, or loss of life to the few. But that it does not weigh at all is hard to believe.

NOTES

1. Some philosophers think that a weak prima facie obligation may be overweighed by a strong personal interest of the agent. This seems correct. Suppose I have promised to attend a tea to which hundreds are invited and at which my absence will not even be noticed. There is *some* Obligation to attend, but a chance to go to the theater might well be sufficient grounds for it to be right to go to the theater instead.

2. I have so far not indicated that Rawls is using "unjust" also in a special sense. From henceforth we should keep in mind that he *means*, by saying that an institution is unjust, that either (a) it does not provide equal rights to the most extensive liberty compatible with a like liberty for all or (b) it fails to provide equality in positions except for those inequalities it is reasonable to expect will work out for the advantage of everyone.

3. Rawls does not say whether there is a prima facie Obligation to obey laws which are on the books, but no longer enforced.

3

Law, Justice, and Obedience

SIDNEY HOOK
New York University

"SHOULD ONE obey an unjust law?" is a question that cannot be answered intelligently unless a whole host of specifications is added to it. It may make a difference to our answer whether the unjust law is a traffic law or one involving freedom of agitation. It may make a difference whether the burden of the injustice is suffered by most citizens in the community or by a few, singled out on grounds of prejudice rather than reason. Whether the unjust law denies a moral right that is regarded as unabridgeable, like the freedom to worship God; whether the law is one of a series or stands alone; whether it is a law of a democratic government we are discussing or of a totalitarian regime; whether one is a democrat or hostile to democracy; whether the consequences of disobedience will help abolish the unjust law or provoke abominable excesses—these are some additional considerations that may be pertinent to answering the question.

Some of these additional specifications may be construed from what Professor Rawls says; others, from what he implies. It is a pity, however, in view of the current civil disobedience movement and of the historical significance of the refusal to obey and/or enforce laws like the Fugitive Slave Laws, that Professor Rawls did not take his concrete point of departure from some specific contemporary issue. This would have enabled him to develop his argument more clearly.[1] As it stands, the strategy of his working paper seems to me to be tantalizingly obscure, as if he were scratching his left ear with his right hand. That is to say, his discussion appears in some places needlessly complicated; in others, truistic. What is most challenging about his position is the thesis, not entailed by his other views, that "justice has an absolute weight with respect to the principle of utility," and that an "unjust" law can never be justified by social utility, but only by "a greater balance of justice."

Rawls specifies that the question "should one obey an unjust law?" is raised in a constitutional democracy. The presupposition clearly is that the question is posed for democrats, for those who are committed to belief that democracy is preferable to other alternatives. Now in one sense anyone who accepts democracy as a form of government is rejecting anarchy and despotism, which are its generic alternatives. Anyone who proclaims "I shall obey the law only when I believe it is just," and who presumably generalizes the principle to hold for others, "No one should obey the law unless he believes it is just," would be taken to hold an anarchistic position. Anarchism is not the belief that government is unnecessary but rather that the state as an institution involving coercion is unnecessary. If citizens in a democracy were permitted to act on the maxim that only those laws were to be obeyed that individual citizens deemed just, disobedience would not be punished and human affairs would run out into chaos. The democrat who rejects anarchism and despotism does so *not* because he believes that the laws in a democracy will not be unjust but because he believes that, where discussion is open and intelligence is pooled, the likelihood of unjust laws being passed is much less than under the rule of anarchy or despotism. The obligation to obey an unjust law in a democracy is political and not directly moral. It may be compared, perhaps not too misleadingly, to the obligation to accept as valid the unjust decision of the umpire in a game, where agreement to bring in an umpire has resulted from the realization that the game cannot be properly played without rules or with one side or both interpreting the rules. The umpire, it is presumed, is calling the plays as he honestly sees them even when his decisions occasionally seem outrageous to us. Yet we prefer to chance this eventuality than to forego the game altogether or spend more time arguing than playing, as is the case when one or both teams interpret the rules.

There is no paradox whatsoever when a *democrat* accepts the decision of the majority when he is in a minority. After all, unless decisions are to be taken only by unanimous vote, there must be a minority; and the normal assumption of sincere debate on any issue is that each side believes its position is justified. The obligation to obey an unjust law, subject to some qualifications to be considered below, on the part of a democrat who finds himself in the minority does not follow from any special principles of fair play. Such a commitment is what it means to be a democrat in the sense that if anyone proclaimed himself to be a democrat but indicated that he was not going to abide by a "well-formed" decision of the majority (that is, a decision made after vigorously exercised rights to agitate, educate, plead, and the like, on the part of the minority) or actually repudiated the decision of the majority (such as the forcible liquidation of the Constituent Assembly by the Russian Communists in 1918, after they had failed to win more than 19% of the seats) we would be entitled to say that he either did not understand the meaning of constitutional democracy or, more likely, that he was no democrat at all.

However, only an absolutist and apriorist would contend that in a democracy the well-formed decision of the majority should always be obeyed. Democracy in the first instance is a political mechanism of government, justified by the reasonable hope that under certain conditions it will make for greater justice and human welfare than other systems of government. The truth of this is an empirical matter. Conditions may exist in which it would be foolish to expect a democratic system to give these results. And it is perfectly conceivable that even after a democracy is established, after free, fair, and prolonged debate in which members of the minority participate on the same terms as all their fellow citizens, the majority may legislate some barbaric policy or practice like the proscription of a religious minority, the confiscation of their estates, or their imprisonment and torture. On moral grounds, it might be obligatory to disobey the law even if, in contradistinction to passive nonviolent resistance, such resistance might result in revolutionary action. One cannot, of course, intelligibly call oneself a democrat while encouraging or leading a revolt against the democratic majority. Even Lincoln, in an address that comes perilously close to advocating democratic absolutism,[2] stated that bad laws should be religiously observed while they are in force, but adds an escape clause: "if they are not too intolerable."

In several places Rawls indicates that the obligation of a democrat to obey an unjust law of a democracy ceases when certain limits have been transcended. Unfortunately, he does not explore the question of the circumstances in which, in the interests of morality, we are justified in disobeying a law and how far that disobedience can go. It is in this field that most of the interesting questions of our time fall. But Rawls tells us little more than that if these limits are not transcended, our obligation to obey an unjust law remains intact. More important, in determining these limits, it is not clear whether or not, and if so, to what extent, the fact that the unjust law leads to unnecessary human suffering—the violation of the principle of utility—enters into the consideration. Apparently, "our obligation to obey the law cannot be overridden by an appeal to utility." Our overriding of an unjust law or institution "can be justified only by a greater balance of justice." There is no absurdity, Rawls suggests, in the thesis that one can disregard completely the principle of utility in considering whether we are obligated to obey an unjust law.

This seems to me to be a grave mistake unless justice is so defined as to go beyond formal equality of distribution and include reference to human weal or woe. The very considerations that have led to approval of a bill that falls short of justice may also constitute sufficient grounds for observing it faithfully when it becomes a law. Even if this were not the case, say for those who opposed the bill in the first place, the social consequences of violating an unjust law may be so grave that, compared with it, the injustice involved appears a mere bagatelle. To refuse to balance utility, the happiness and suffering of mankind, against justice may have the virtue of a theoretical simplification, but it is much more likely to lead to grotesqueries of moral judgment, to the dangerous oversimplification, of Kantian formalism and the attitude of *fiat justitia pereat mundus*. To take such a view is to refuse to recognize that sometimes justice and human happiness do conflict, that this conflict cannot always be resolved by proposals that permit all relevant interests to be equally satisfied, and that the necessary sacrifice of one or the other is an expression of man's tragic estate. Sometimes we may obey an unjust law on grounds that a greater injustice will be compounded by violating it. But sometimes this cannot be established. In such situations it may be perfectly valid to argue for obedience to an unjust law on the grounds of social utility. It all depends on the magnitude of the injustice and the dimensions of human suffering involved.

NOTES

1. I have tried to follow this course in Chapter III, "Intelligence, Conscience and the Right to Revolution," in my *The Paradoxes of Freedom* (Berkeley: University of California Press), 1962.

2. *Ibid.*, p. 114ff.

4

Law and Morality: Internalism vs. Externalism

JOHN LADD
Brown University

THE QUESTION with which I shall be concerned is "Why ought we to respect and obey the law as such?" I shall assume that there are moral reasons for doing what the law requires us to do simply because the law requires it, and that these moral reasons make it our duty to obey the law not only when what it requires conflicts with our self-interest, but also, sometimes, when what it requires conflicts with other requirements of morality itself; for, indeed, moral questions connected with civil disobedience, resistance, and revolution are genuine moral questions only on the assumption that in the case of conflict with other moral principles, sometimes we must give precedence to our legal duties, although, of course, at other times we ought not.

Accordingly, I shall assume that there is a prima facie duty to obey the law as such, a prima facie duty that sometimes may override other duties and that itself may sometimes be overridden by them. My question, then, is "Why do we have such a duty and how does it arise?"

Two easy replies to the question of why we ought to obey the law may be immediately dismissed as failing to meet the conditions of the problem as I have formulated it. The first is that we ought to obey the law simply because it prohibits actions that are morally wrong, *mala in se*, like murder and stealing. This, of course, is often a perfectly good reason for obeying a law, but it fails to explain why we ought to obey those laws that concern acts morally indifferent in themselves and that become wrong only because prohibited by law, *mala quia prohibita*. Obviously the requirements of law and of morality do not always coincide, and our answer must relate to cases in which our moral duty to obey the law extends beyond the other ordinary requirements of morality. The important point, however, is that this reply does not really answer our question at all, for it supposes that it is not the lawfulness of the required conduct that makes it right, but some other moral quality possessed by it. Our question, on the other hand, is "Why does the mere lawfulness of an action make it right?"

The other easy reply to the question "Why obey the law?" is that we ought to do so to avoid evil, in the form of sanctions, either to ourselves or to others. Again, we have what is often a very good reason for obeying the law, but it is not an answer to our question, since it implies that it is simply the consequences of being caught breaking the law, rather than its lawfulness, that makes conduct in conformity with the law right.

Let us return to our original question, "Why does the bare fact that certain actions are required by law give us a prima facie duty for performing them?" There are, I submit, basically two different ways of answering this question: the first appeals directly to the nature of law itself for the answer, whereas the second bases its answer on moral considerations outside the law. I shall call these two ways of answering our question *internalism* and *externalism*, respectively.

An internalist holds that law itself is intrinsically a moral conception, or at least that it necessarily includes certain moral elements. This position is most obviously represented by the Aristotelian-Thomistic natural law theory, since it maintains that the human law is part of the moral law, that is, is a determination of the natural law and that any human law departing from the law of nature is "no longer a law but a perversion of law." There are, however, other versions of internalism besides the natural law theory. For example, Fuller's conception of the internal morality of the law, if I understand it correctly, is internalist, and so is the theory set forth by Kant in his *Meta-*

physical Elements of Justice. At the end of this paper I shall briefly describe and defend another internalist theory.

An externalist, on the other hand, asserts that our duty to obey laws comes from a nonlegal source of some kind or other, for example, from the principle of utility or from a social contract. Legal positivism in its many varieties, including Hart's, illustrates this position. Socrates' arguments in the *Crito* for obeying the Athenian laws are also externalist, since he appeals to nonlegal considerations such as the wrongness of breaking an implicit agreement and the principles of obedience to one's parents and teachers. Rawls is also, I believe, an externalist, inasmuch as he grounds our duty to obey the law on the principle of fairness. A distinctive feature of externalist theories is that, to preserve the logical separation of law and morality, they have to use a morally neutral concept of law. This, of course, explains why the analytical school of jurisprudence, with its various neutral definitions of law, provides us with the most typical externalist theories.

In this paper I shall try to show that no externalist theory can provide a satisfactory answer to our question, and that we must therefore adopt an internalist theory of some sort. (The other alternative, of course, is to reject the question entirely by denying its presuppositions. I cannot discuss this position here.) The version of internalism that I shall advance is not, I believe, open to the usual objections to the natural law theory. Like many other philosophers, I find the natural law theory objectionable on metaphysical and epistemological grounds. It also seems to me to present many difficulties from the point of view of the philosophy of law—in particular, with regard to the distinction between law as it is and law as it ought to be, actual and ideal law.

The internalist theory I want to propose, in contrast to natural law theories, holds that our duty to obey the law comes from the formal nature of law, its lawfulness, rather than from its content, that is, the kind of acts enjoined or their consequences. By "its formal nature" I mean the formal legal and judicial procedures that define "law," "due process," or what is

often called the "rule of law." By making the distinction between the form and the content of law, I hope to allow for the
possibility of bad and unjust laws that, nevertheless, we ought
to obey simply because they are lawful.

The arguments I shall give here are, for the most part,
ethical rather than jurisprudential. Consequently, I shall only
incidentally examine the concept of law itself in the way in
which it is discussed in the well-known Hart-Fuller debate.
Let us begin by considering more closely the externalist view
of the relation of law and morality.

The main point on which I wish to focus attention is that
externalist theories characteristically seek to explain our duty
to obey the law in particular situations by reference to the
legal system as a whole. We ought to obey particular laws and
particular decisions, they maintain, because they are parts of a
system, they are derived from a basic constitution, or they
come from a single source of legislative power or authority,
and so on, and it is by virtue of their belonging to a legal
system with a unity of this sort that we are bound to obey
them. Our duty thus emanates from, and is dependent on, a
prior commitment to the system and, other moral considerations being equal, it is the legal system as a whole that determines the ground, the extent, and the limits of our duty to obey
the law.

Two examples of how externalist theories employ the concept of a legal system as a whole to explain why we ought to
obey particular laws will suffice for the present purpose. The
first, a version of utilitarianism, argues that we ought to obey
the law because the existence of a stable legal system has
public utility and our particular acts of obedience are instru-
mental to building up, as our acts of disobedience are to destroying the stability of the system as a whole. On a utilitarian
analysis of this kind, then, our duty to obey laws is derivative
from the general value of the system as a whole.

A second example is provided by contract theories.
Locke's theory, for example, bases our duty to obey particular

laws on our commitment to the sovereign legislature, so that "all obedience, which by the most solemn ties anyone can be obliged to pay, ultimately terminates in this supreme power." [1] Thus our obligation to obey laws is derivative from, and dependent upon, our general obligation vis à vis the whole system. (It may be noted in passing that for both the utilitarian and the contractarian the character of the system as a whole determines when we are released from the duty to obey particular laws as well as when we are bound to obey them; thus, if the system is bad or illegitimate or oversteps its authority, we are no longer bound to obey the particular laws derived from it.)

Externalism, then, predicates the existence of a legal system, a monolithic legal order, as a basis for explaining why we have a moral duty to obey particular laws and legal decrees. It is this assumption that I regard as the Achilles' heel of externalism, for, as I shall try to show, it has disastrous consequences for any view of the relation between law and morality. The fact that they are parts of a legal system is, in my opinon, neither necessary nor sufficient to explain why we should obey particular laws. It is the lawfulness of laws and decrees, rather than their being parts of a legal system, that constitutes the ground of our duty to respect and and obey them.

For brevity's sake, I shall skip over utilitarianism and consider the more typical externalist view that we have a moral obligation to obey the law, a view represented, although not exclusively, by the contract theory. To sharpen the issue before us, I shall take for granted that the term "obligation" is used here in its strict and narrow sense in which it refers to a special kind of moral tie between persons and one that is assumed, created, or incurred by a special circumstance of some sort or other, normally a voluntary act of some kind. (The obligation incurred through making a promise is the paradigm of obligation in the strict sense intended here.) An obligation will thus be differentiated from and contrasted with other kinds of duty.

It is no accident that most externalist theories of the relation of law and morals should seize on the concept of obligation to explain this relationship, since obligation itself is a kind of external, adventitious moral relation conferring a new moral quality (of rightness or wrongness) on acts that in themselves are morally indifferent. Obligations, as such, bind us to perform or to refrain from acts to which we were not previously and would not ordinarily be bound; for example, as the result of a promise I must now do something that I previously did not have to do. In this sense of obligation, it is probably impossible to incur an obligation to do something that is already right in itself (such as to tell the truth) or to avoid doing something that is already wrong in itself (such as not to hurt others). If this is so, then it follows that the externalist view that we ought to obey the law because of an obligation implies that there is nothing right or wrong in itself about obeying the law itself. This is a consequence that I find absurd. Indeed, I find it as absurd to suppose that we have a moral obligation to fulfill our legal obligations as it is to suppose that we have a moral obligation to fulfill our moral obligations.

But there are further objections to the notion that we have an obligation to obey the law. To begin with, obligations are ordinarily incurred as the result of a free, voluntary act of some kind or other, and consequently it is fair to assume that a person who is under an obligation had some kind of option—to assume or to avoid the obligation. The customary objection to the contract theory, namely, that most of the subjects of a government actually never have any choice in agreeing to the contract, applies more generally to the notion of an obligation to obey the law. This is a point clearly seen by Socrates when, in the *Crito*, as part of the proof that he had an obligation to obey the Athenian laws, he cites the fact that he could have left Athens and taken up residence in another city-state. By implication, then, he assumes that having an option is a necessary condition of acquiring an obligation. In the modern world, needless to say, the option of residence is a condition that is rarely fulfilled; hence, one might conclude, having an *obliga-*

tion to obey laws is just as rare. It is true that we might incur the obligation to obey the laws of a country as a result of free choice, as we do when we visit a foreign country and agree to abide by its laws. But in the end this is as artificial a condition of our obedience to the laws as is the notion of an original social contract. (And yet, it must be said, it is a condition that is presupposed by Rawls's analysis.)

Suppose, however, that we play along with the fanciful idea that somehow through some act of our own we have incurred the obligation to obey the laws, to my mind there are still two more serious objections to the obligation-model, objections that arise from the assumption that our obligation to obey particular laws comes from their being parts of a legal system.

To begin with, although we may sometimes have an option to obey or not to obey particular laws, it is quite fantastic to suppose that we have an option with regard to the whole legal system. Nevertheless, it is easy for someone espousing the obligation-model to slip into the error of supposing that we do have such an option as a result of construing our relation to the law as merely one of obedience. Whether the ground for obedience is sanctions, utility, a moral commitment arising from a contract or from the principle of fairness, or whatever it may be, to conceive of the problem as simply whether or not to obey distorts the whole issue of the relation of morality and law. (This error reminds one of Hart's gunman model, which is a somewhat less respectable member of the same family of errors.) It is a distortion because law is much more than simply a system of mandatory rules of behavior. Indeed, as Hart points out, one of the principal functions of law is to create powers that enable us to do things that we are not obliged to do at all. For example, it is only through law and by its means that we are able to get married, draw up a will, transfer property, or run for office, and yet, obviously, we are under no obligation to do any of these. Law, whether we like it or not, is part of our way of life, and we simply have to act through it; indeed, it is only through law that social life, not

to mention civilized life, is feasible at all. Hence the question
whether or not to obey the law as a whole, that is, whether or
not to accept the legal system, is entirely academic. Even
under a totalitarian dictatorship this question does not and
cannot arise, nor has there ever been a revolution which over-
turned the existing legal system in its entirety and in all its
parts.

From an ethical point of view, an even more damaging
objection to linking the question of obedience to law to the acceptance of the legal system as a whole is that it misconstrues
and distorts the whole issue of rightful disobedience. There
are, of course, circumstances in which we ought not to do what
the law says we ought to do, but the externalist is forced to
maintain that disobedience is justified only when moral (nonlegal) considerations override our obligation to obey, that is,
when the prima facie duty to obey the law is overridden by
some other prima facie duty, say the duty of nonmaleficence.

Not only does this answer make our relation to the law
quite equivocal by introducing a new and undesirable element
of uncertainty, since the concept of prima facie duty makes
the determination of one's actual duty indeterminate in the
case of conflict, but it oversimplifies the realities. For as a matter of fact, when we examine actual cases in which we think
it right to disobey a law, we see that they cannot simply be
construed as conflicts of law with morality; they are, rather,
conflicts of law with law, in the broader sense. Most, if not
all, conflicts in which we ought to disobey a law arise, at least
partly, from the consideration that the law involved is poor law,
that it lacks certain essential ingredients of law.

For example, the justification generally given of the sit-ins
and freedom rides in the South is that the Negroes are being
deprived of their legal rights, and that these measures are designed to procure what is their legal due, in other words, that
the segregation laws are considered to be poor laws in the light
of the U.S. Constitution. Similarly, Hitler's *Katastrophenedikt*,
which required the summary execution of suspected traitors,
may be considered to be poor law because it deprived the ac-

cused of a judicial trial and required executions without due process.

Our duty to obey the law is, I suggest, a function of the juridical character of the laws themselves rather than, as the externalist maintains, purely a moral (nonlegal) question. It is not the fact of a moral duty as such that overrides the duty to obey the law, but the fact that the treatment accorded by actual law is not in conformity with what legal processes should be, that is, with the rule of law. This explains why disobedience is justified only if all the legal processes have been exhausted and the legal remedies are inadequate—if, in other words, there has been a breakdown in the rule of law. (Incidentally, only a principle such as the one just stated can be used to support the kind of limited disobedience practiced by Thoreau and Gandhi, which, indeed, might even be described as a lawful disobedience, for their disobedience was more of a resistance to authority than it was to law as such, since they were willing to respect the law and peacefully go to prison for their disobedience.)

In sum, externalism, and in particular the notion that we have an obligation to obey the law, goes wrong because it ties our duty to act conformably to law to our relation to the legal system as such (for example, to the Constitution) rather than to the character of the particular laws and legal decisions concerned. Let us now see whether internalism can do better. I can only briefly suggest the lines along which a satisfactory internalist theory should be developed.

Law is not, I submit, internally related to morality through an identity of content, that is, the kind of conduct that it prescribes, nor is positive law moral only by virtue of its derivation from a higher law, which functions as a kind of superconstitution (perhaps divinely instituted). It is clear, I think, that any definition of law must fasten on some formal aspect of the law. In this respect, the classical definitions of law in the Austinian tradition of legal positivism are surely on the right track. The Austinian type of definition, however, goes wrong in choosing coercion as the central factor in law. Because of this

undue emphasis on coercion, from Austin to Kelsen, I think we
have become blind to other aspects of law that link it more
closely to morality.

In our attempts to understand law we would do well to
consider other kinds of law besides municipal law—international law, for instance. If we do so, I think we will see that
the heart of any kind of law consists of the legal procedures
that it provides for settling disputes and laying down norms
of conduct. Thus we might say that it is the legal method that
distinguishes and defines lawfulness, and this method must
be rational in some sense or other. There are, of course, indefi-
nitely many variations in legal procedure and processes, but
they all involve, as Hart points out, rules for adjudication,
identification, and changing laws, and these, in turn, involve
legal reasoning and legal argument, which demand the citing
of accepted facts, rules and principles, the practice of advocacy and defense, hearing both sides, impartiality on the part
of the person or agency rendering the decision, and so forth.
In other words due process, in some form or other, is an essential element in law.

The legal procedures that I have in mind relate not only
to judicial decisions, that is, decisions involving individual
cases, but also to legislative enactments. It is sometimes said
that judges make the law, but it could also be said that the
legislators find the law, that is, act as judges with reference to
proposed legislation, and that such enactments, like legal decisions, are lawful only insofar as they follow rules and procedures. Hence we may say that due process is a requirement
of the legislative process as well as of the judicial process.

The legal processes, procedure, and method, which I hold
to be essential to the nature of law, are also, of course, to be
found in international law and primitive law, as well as in
municipal law and constitutional law; the question of whether
there is an enforcing agency or monopoly of power is not the
crucial one. Furthermore, it is the absence of legal processes
thus conceived that is one of the distinguishing features of
tyranny and that makes us hesitate to call its decrees law.

Obviously the kind of procedures that I have in mind exist

to a varying extent in different societies and under different legal system. Indeed, within a single body of law, the requirement is met to different degrees in different parts; for example, Hitler's *Katastrophenedikt* clearly failed to fulfill the requirements of due process, although under Hitler there obviously were many judicial decisions in private civil law that adhered to these requirements as fully as the decisions in our own courts.

Let us now turn to the question of the relationship of law so conceived to morality. The connection should be obvious. From the point of view of morality, the essential element in law is the idea of due process, the rule of law; for the duty to demand, respect, and observe the requirements of law conceived as due process is a direct application of the principle of treating men as ends in themselves and not as mere means, that is, the categorical imperative. The dignity of man requires that any measures affecting his basic interests, in particular, his moral interests, must be adopted only after a reasonable airing of all the issues, and this involves reference to accepted rules and principles, a fair, public hearing, and all the elements of what could be called "due process" and that characterize the "rule of law."

It follows that the concept of law that I am advocating is a moral concept, since it sets forth what ought to be rather than what, frequently, is. But it sets forth only what ought to be as far as procedures are concerned, not content. We have a duty to respect and adhere to these procedures even though the outcome may not be to our liking, or indeed, even though we may morally disapprove of it. Thus our prima facie duty to obey the law comes from our duty to treat others as ends and not merely as means, since acting conformably to law is one way, perhaps the main way, of fulfilling this duty.

NOTE

1. John Locke, *Second Treatise*, paragraph 134.

5

Fair Play and Civil Disobedience

ERNEST NAGEL

Columbia University

THE QUESTION to which Professor Rawls devotes his carefully reasoned paper is a straightforward one. On the assumption that in certain societies there is a prima facie obligation to obey the law and the further assumption that this obligation must rest on some general moral principle, his problem is to identify this principle. His paper tries to show that the required principle is the principle of fair play. However, despite the importance Professor Rawls ostensibly attaches to the problem, it is difficult to see why the problem as he formulates it is not trivial, and how he arrives at his proposed answer to it.

Professor Rawls maintains not only that the moral obligation to obey the law may be overridden by more stringent duties, but also that this obligation exists only in a special type of society. Although he says relatively little about the circumstances under which, according to him, civil disobedience is morally justifiable, he does make explicit a number of necessary conditions that must be satisfied if obedience to the law is to be morally obligatory. It is in fact his account of these conditions that is the source of my difficulties in appreciating his problem and in understanding his solution of it. First, the moral duty to obey the law is said to exist only in a constitutional democracy satisfying two general principles of justice, so that the society must have a "just constitution." Second, though the legal order is on the whole a just one, some of the laws enacted in it may nevertheless be unjust. Third, the continued existence of the legal order (and therefore of the benefits flowing from it) is jeopardized if the laws established in conformity with its just constitution are disobeyed—for, according to Professor Rawls, "Unless one obeys the law enacted under it, the proper equilibrium, or balance, between competing claims defined by the constitution will not be maintained."

Moreover, Professor Rawls also assumes that members of a society that satisfies these conditions have a moral duty, required by the principle of utility (that is, the principle enjoining them to maximize the net sum of advantages) to keep such a just legal order in existence. However, given these various assumptions, the moral basis for the prima facie obligation to obey the law is immediately evident; and I find it hard to understand why Professor Rawls thinks he is faced with a nontrivial problem of justifying this obligation. If the principle requires behavior directed to the maintenance of a just constitution as a moral duty, and if failure to obey the laws enacted under such a constitution imperils to some degree the continued existence of the legal order, it follows that there is also a moral obligation to obey the law. Accordingly, under the supposed circumstances, the principle of utility appears to be the obvious moral foundation for the duty to obey the laws of a just legal order.

However, Professor Rawls believes it is otherwise. He argues, on the one hand, that the duty of obedience is a special case of the principle of fair play; and, on the other hand, he defends the thesis that when the issue arises as to whether one is obligated to obey an unjust law (as, for example, an unjust income tax law), "one is led into no absurdity if one simply throws out the principle of utility altogether (except insofar as it is included in the general principle requiring one to establish the most efficient just institutions)." But how cogent is his argument? It is patent that if the principle of fair play formulates a moral duty that rests on the principle of utility, his argument, even if sound, establishes nothing of consequence. For on this hypothesis his claim that the duty of obedience is a special case of the duty of fair play is not incompatible with the contention he seeks to disprove, namely, that the obligation to obey the law derives from the principle of utility. Let us therefore assume that the duty of fair play is not based on the principle of utility. Even on this assumption, however, it is far from clear that Professor Rawls establishes his point, since the principle of fair play in his statement of it appears to assert nothing germane to the obligation to obey the law that is not already contained in the stipulations concerning the legal order in which alone the obligation has been assumed to exist. For, according to Professor Rawls, there is a duty of fair play only if a number of suppositions are true, one of which is that "there is a mutually beneficial and just scheme of social cooperation, and that the advantages it yields can only be obtained if everyone, or nearly everyone, cooperates." But this supposition seems to me to be identical in content with one of the necessary conditions he has laid down for a legal order, if the obligation to obey the law is to exist in it, namely, the condition (call it C) that the persistence of the legal order and of the advantages accruing from it are imperiled if its laws are disobeyed. However, it is this condition, together with the assumption that there is a moral duty D to maintain a just scheme of cooperation, which we have seen to constitute the moral foundation for the obligation O to obey the law; and though this condition is also stipulated to be a *sine qua non* for the duty F of fair play, Professor Rawls's argument fails to establish that the obligation to obey the law is a specialization of the duty of fair play. Unless I have misunderstood him, his argument, when stated schematically takes the following form, where X and Y are certain conditions that are left unspecified because they are not relevant to the present discussion: O if, and only if, C and D and X; and F if, and only if, C and Y; hence O is a special case of F. But this is a *non sequitur,* so Professor Rawls's introduction of the principle of fair play into his argument seems to me entirely gratuitous.

Nor do I find any more convincing his attempt to show that the principle of utility need never be invoked when considering whether or not an unjust law ought to be obeyed. In the case of an unjust income tax law, for example, he believes that "One would not want to try to justify the tax on the ground that the net gains to certain groups in society is such as to outweigh the injustice. The natural argument to make is to his obligation to a just constitution." More generally, he thinks that in such deliberations one appeals to "the balance of justice" rather than to "the greater net balance of advantages." However, the use of the word "natural" in this context is plainly question begging. In any event, the question cannot be settled either by fiat or in an a priori manner whether considerations of the balance of justice or of the greater net balance of advantages are the controlling ones in establishing one's duty in connection with an unjust law—for the answer to the question depends in general on the gravity of the issues raised by a given unjust law.

By way of an illustration, let me use the headings Professor Rawls suggests for deciding whether one should obey a tax law that is likely to undermine the position of certain minority groups. Suppose that the law had been enacted in accordance with a just constitution, that the law is discriminatory only against a relatively small number of persons (such as those engaged in medical research), that the law had been adopted by a majority in the mistaken belief that it would not be discriminatory, and that there is genuine ground for the hope that the law can eventually be repealed. It is certainly possible that an individual will decide it is his duty to obey the law, despite its injustice, in view of the "balance of justice" in favor of obedience. However, it is equally possible that despite this balance an individual will decide on civil disobedience on the ground (perhaps mistaken, but not inherently ridiculous) that there was no chance of the law being repealed within the next four years, and that the impairment of medical research that would be the immediate consequence of the law will have such adverse effects on the welfare of society as a whole as to outweigh the advantages of compliance with the law. I venture the further conjecture that to this second individual it might seem absurd, Professor Rawls to the contrary notwithstanding, to exclude from his deliberations all considerations of social utility. But however this may be, Professor Rawls certainly does not deny that civil disobedience may sometimes be morally justifiable even in a just legal order. What remains obscure is why he assumes that the grounds for such disobedience can properly be only reasons of fairness or justice and never reasons of utility. Since he obviously believes that considerations of social utility may be relevant in deciding whether a proposed law should be enacted, it is all the more puzzling why he should think that such considerations are no longer relevant in deciding, after the proposal has been enacted, whether the law should be obeyed.

6

The Obligation to Obey the Law
and the Ends of the State

J. ROLAND PENNOCK
Swarthmore College

WHY SHOULD we obey the law? Professor Rawls argues that "the moral obligation to obey the law is a special case of the prima facie duty of fair play." Thus he places the moral obligation to obey law in the same category with many other moral obligations; it is not, he says, "based upon a special principle of its own." Moreover, this obligation does not apply to all laws, but only to those that are derived from a just constitution whose benefits one has accepted and expects to continue accepting. (At the same time, of course, law is often supported by moral obligation that does not spring from the fair-play principle.) In other words, Rawls seeks to justify the obligation to obey law by a theory of obligation that does not apply to all regimes of law and that has many nonlegal applications. I would like to suggest certain difficulties with Rawls's theory, and also to propose a theory of the moral obligation to obey law that is more comprehensive (including some laws not derived from just constitutions) and at the same time more distinctive, that is, designed especially for application to the field of law.

I

Most of my objections to Rawls's theory will appear in the development of my positive argument. First, however, I should like to deal with one general objection, or set of objections, that seems to me to be important and the consideration of

77

which prepares the way for part of my positive argument. Rawls holds that fair play entails an obligation to obey law because we have all benefited by the legal system as a whole and expect to go on doing so. In accepting the benefits of a just constitution, he says, "one becomes bound to it." This theory smacks of contractualism and suggests some of the notorious difficulties with which that doctrine must contend. In stressing the acceptance of benefits, it appears to assume that we have a choice about accepting the benefits of law. If we do not like or approve of the laws of our country we may leave. For many individuals, perhaps for most, this assumption is highly unrealistic—so much so that one may legitimately doubt whether any obligation can be supposed to have been deliberately or freely assumed.

It may be that Rawls intends to place his emphasis upon the receipt of benefits, rather than upon their deliberate acceptance. We are obliged [1] to our parents, we may assume, for what they have done for us, regardless of the fact that we had little or no choice in the matter. Likewise with the laws. But *is* it likewise? We are not obliged or obligated to the laws themselves, even though we may be under obligation to other people, say our fellow citizens, to obey the laws. It is these other people whom we should not harm or whom we should help or support. Specifically, we should do so, following Rawls's line of argument, by doing our part to make it possible for others to enjoy the same kind of benefits that we have enjoyed from the legal system. But suppose I violate the law secretly, so that no injury is done to the general pattern of obedience. Others will continue to enjoy the benefits of the legal system as before. It is difficult to see that I have violated any obligation that flows from the "receipt of benefits" argument.

Rawls speaks, too, of the obligation not to take advantage of the free benefit from the legal system "by not cooperating," that is, by not doing one's share to contribute to the common benefit. The argument requires the assumption that any violation or disregard of the law constitutes "not cooperating." As Professor Brandt points out, some acts of disobedience to the law may be intended to contribute to the improvement of the law and may in fact have that effect, although providing no special benefit for the individual in question.

Finally, Rawls's line of argument for a prima facie moral obligation to obey all laws derived from a just constitution does not seem to be persuasive in a situation in which the violation of law is certain to be punished and the punishment is sufficient to deter most people. Here Holmes's theory that the law presents us with a free choice, to obey it or to take the consequences, seems to cover the situation.

II

It will be noted that I have been stressing the importance of the consequences of disobedience of the law to the legal system. This point sets the stage for my own proposal. Law, in the sense in which the term is used here, is uniquely the instrument of some sort of political system—typically of a state. Without it, the polity could not fulfill its functions; in fact it would be virtually helpless. The ends of the state—of all political organization—require law for their realization. To them, law is the essential means. An obligation to obey and support the state entails an obligation to obey its law, at least in general.

What are the ends of the state? Traditionally they are held to be security, liberty, justice, and welfare. Security includes the protection of life, limb, and property against disorderly elements within or enemy attack from without it. It also includes the protection of the state itself, its institutions and its independence. By extension, security might be made to include men's economic and psychological security, but these human needs and political ends may just as well be grouped under the heading of welfare. Perhaps some persons might question the inclusion of liberty among the ends of the state, although I am confident that an area of agreement would remain after issues of definition and of degree had been clarified. About this core area of significant liberties I suspect that we could even get agreement that failure of a state to protect it would greatly weaken the obligation of its citizens to obey it. But I shall not attempt to support these propositions here. For any who may question them, the other (I believe) universally accepted ends of the state will suffice. To what extent states in fact provide justice in the broadest sense or even how far they may on occasion act unjustly we need not decide. All states provide for the settlement of disputes. They all, at least in some measure, try to do so in accordance with a settled and known law. They all seek to see that those who have suffered injury or loss unjustly are made whole, as nearly as can be. They all lend their support to the enforcement of private contracts within whatever area of free contracting may be allowed.[2] By any definition of justice these matters are fundamental. Finally, we have the catch-all end of welfare. To what extent a state should provide for such essential public services as roads, water supply, sewage, postal service, and schools will depend upon a number of factors, including the means available to it and the extent to which these facilities are or can be made available by private enterprise. But its ultimate responsibility to use its powers to see that these needs are met is today unquestioned.

What I mean to insist upon is, first, that these "ends"—security, liberty, justice, and welfare—are fundamental; and, second, that the state is uniquely essential for their realization. Especially in civilized society, they can not be secured in tolerable measure—let alone maximized—without the inclusive and finally compelling authority of the state. They are fundamental in the sense that they are essential to human well-being indeed to any but the most primitive society.[3]

Thus a state, with its laws as its essential means, rightly commands the obedience of its subjects because, without it, conditions fundamental to human society would be virtually extinguished. Of course, if a state is failing to achieve its ends to any great degree the obligation to obey its laws is accordingly attenuated. If it seems probable that refusal to obey the law, whether by revolt, *coup d'état*, passive resistance, or other means, would result in the establishment of a government that would accomplish its ends more effectively, the kind of obligation we have been discussing would disappear. The problem then would be a matter of estimating the likelihood of peaceful reform, of weighing the costs of resistance, and of calculating the chance of improvement by the means in question. Any obligation to the existing regime would have to be derived from consideration of the pain, loss of life, property, and the like that might be occasioned by the means used to secure the change.

Perhaps one further consideration, not made explicit in the preceding paragraph, should be mentioned. If the legal system is generally obeyed and felt to have some kind of validity, that fact in itself constitutes one reason for not disobeying it under such circumstances that my disobedience will weaken the general support for it. In other words, the consensus represented by a going legal system is a vital basis for a successful polity. For this reason, without reference to the concept of fair play and *regardless of the constitutional nature of the regime,* one should not tamper with it lightly.[4]

III

We have been speaking of the moral obligation to obey the laws of a state considered, so to speak, as a package. What about the obligation to obey a particular law, perhaps one that is rightly felt to be unjust? The first consideration must be the effect of resistance or disobedience upon the whole regime of law. To the extent that disobedience would undermine this regime, the considerations we have just been discussing would be applicable. But frequently, perhaps usually, as I intimated earlier, refusal to obey a particular law (especially if the disobedience to the law is based upon its injustice) has no significant bearing on the effectiveness of other laws. Under such circumstances, in assessing the obligation to obey, we should first look to the effect of the law in question with respect to the ends of the state. It may have little relevance to those ends. It may be an ill-conceived piece of welfare legislation, designed, let us say, to give the state a monopoly of the education of children. Majority decision or no, I can easily conceive of circumstances under which I would feel no moral obligation to abide by such legislation. In fact, I might feel a strong moral obligation to disobey the law—perhaps by evasion, perhaps by overt defiance. In such a situation, following Brandt's analysis, the law might be entitled to a presumptive obligation, but not, on examination, to prima facie obligation.

On the other hand, suppose that the law in question appears to make an important contribution to the security of the state and its citizens, one that can not be equaled by other means, but that at the same time it imposes a special cost upon a minority. For the safety of the state and to protect its citizens from foreign attack, let us assume, it is judged necessary to remove all members of a certain national group from a particular area. To sift the loyal from the disloyal, we may further assume, is impracticable in the time available. All possible measures are taken to assure the comfort and welfare of the group in question. They are given financial compensation wherever that is appropriate, and they are aided in relocation. Yet nothing can wholly compensate for the dispersion of their community, for tearing them up by the roots, and for the countless injuries to feelings and spirit. Should loyal members of the group feel obligated to obey and support the law? How else can one answer this question than by weighing the values involved? Certainly we would not wish to say that security might justify doing injustice, but we might be forced to that conclusion. At least it is hard to say that an increase in the security of a great many might not override a modest amount of injustice to a relatively small number. My way of handling this situation is, of course, not incompatible with Rawls's contention that one has a prima facie obligation to obey the law. However, I believe it is incompatible with his argument that the principle of fair play cannot be overridden by an appeal to anything other than another duty of justice. It is hard for me to see that the appeal to the security of the majority of the people—or, for that matter, to the security of their political and legal institutions—is a matter of justice in Rawls's sense.

If Rawls were to argue, in reply, that no injustice was done to the minority because they would gain more than they lost, the case could be made more difficult by supposing that the law provided for security without taking adequate precautions to minimize hardship. In other words, injustice—unequal treatment and a clear loss of welfare to some—would clearly be involved. Yet, I suggest, it is arguable that the minority would still have a moral obligation to obey the law. Not only, in this case, would injustice be overridden by utility, but the obligation to obey, although it might derive partly from past and prospective benefits, would have to be measured in large part by a calculation of the effects of disobedience on the security, liberty, and welfare of the total population.[5]

Having dealt with cases of the obligation to obey unjust laws, let me turn to a consideration of certain situations in which we may be under no obligation to obey a just law. We have already referred to the case in which punishment is certain. Let us take another, perhaps more realistic, example. Suppose a man with no dependents is driving his car, alone, along a deserted highway. Is he under a moral obligation to observe the speed limit? (We may assume that he can exceed the speed limit while keeping within a reasonable standard of safety to himself.) To hold that he was morally obligated to obey the law would seem to be absurd. On the contrary, if he were arrested by a policeman who had been operating a concealed radar device, and convicted and fined for speeding, would he not have a right to feel morally outraged? Yet I do not see how the fairness principle could be interpreted to achieve the same result, unless, at least, it were interpreted so as to make it virtually equivalent to the kind of test advocated in these pages.

Moreover, assume a slightly different case. Assume that the safety of others *is* involved, but that no one will know of the violation, so no question of encouraging disregard for the

law arises. How in this case does the existence of the law add
to the obligation to attend to the safety of others that would
exist without any law?

In summary, it appears to me that the kind of test I have
been proposing—the test in terms of the state and its ends—
would include all valid cases of obligation to obey law that
could be derived from notions of justness or fairness; and that
it would also have acceptable implications for some (I believe
all) cases where that test is inapplicable or gives the wrong
answer. It is, I suggest, the ends of the state and the institutions
essential for their achievement that provide the most useful
and accurate guide for assessing the moral obligation to obey
law.

NOTES

1. I use the word "obliged" instead of "obligated" to emphasize the fact that the obligation in this instance does not arise from
a promise or other deliberate acceptance of moral responsibility.

2. A qualification would be necessary to make this statement
completely accurate. States frequently recognize a middle ground
of contracts that are legally permissible but not enforceable.

3. Doubtless the suggested ends of the state could all be
subsumed under some such broad term as well-being or welfare,
but the categorization in the text has the advantages of greater
specificity and of concentrating attention on those human needs for
which the state is peculiarly essential. We may also observe at this
point that whether the obligation to seek fulfillment of these human needs is derived from utilitarian, self-realizationist, self-devel-
opmental, or other arguments is not our present concern.

4. It will do no harm to drive home the point here that this
theory of moral obligation to obey law is more comprehensive than
Rawls's theory, in that it is not confined to law derived from a just
constitution.

5. One weakness, it seems to me, of Rawls's theory is that it
seems to suggest, although it is not so stated, that the prima facie

obligation to obey law is a given quantum. Either it is there or it is not. Of course, it may be overridden, but *it* is fixed. Calculation of obligation in terms of effects on ends of the state seems to me to avoid this weakness and to put proper stress on the fact that obligation is a matter of degree.

7

Justice and the Common Good

RICHARD TAYLOR
Columbia University

DO CONSIDERATIONS of justice have an absolute weight with respect to considerations of utility? John Rawls, like many others, believes they do, though he despairs of trying to prove this. I believe, on the contrary, that they have no weight whatsoever with respect to this or anything else.

In these remarks I shall simply note in part I, a bit effusively I fear, that this sort of appeal to principles, so characteristic of philosophers and, of course, judges, is odious to some persons such as myself. It matters not what those principles are, whether they be certain absolute principles of justice, of utility, of racial supremacy, or whatnot. They still, in my view, have no place whatsoever in the thoughtful responses of good men. In part II I shall show that Rawls's view that certain principles of justice are absolute is not, in fact, a philosophical thesis or claim at all, but an exhortation or plea, and one that ought not, in my view, to be heeded. And finally, in part III, I shall show that it would be impossible, anyway, to make the principle of justice that is partially expressed in the dictum that "similar cases should be treated similarly" absolute with respect to certain other things, such as utility or the common good.

Preliminary remarks. Three things need to be made clear at the very outset to avoid the danger of wholly misunderstanding what I am getting at.

The first is that I am not attacking Rawls's conception of justice, which he has worked out with such care and appealing objectivity, and with which I have no fault to find whatsoever. My arguments are directed, not against this or that theory of the nature of justice, but against the claim that justice, however it is conceived, has some absolute priority over other notions. My arguments, accordingly, are directed not against Rawls, but against anyone who assents to this claim, quite regardless of how he chooses to characterize justice.

Secondly, my arguments are not to be construed as any defense of utilitarianism. I shall here set considerations of utility and the public good against considerations of justice only because Rawls has done so. Had he defended the opposite claim—had he, that is, defended the view that considerations of utility are absolute with respect to considerations of justice—then my own arguments would be essentially no different; I would only use different examples. In denying that considerations of justice are absolute with respect to considerations of utility I am not affirming that considerations of utility are absolute with respect to considerations of justice. I want, in fact, to deny that *any* principles are absolute with respect to anything whatever, and my only immediate purpose is to show that considerations of justice are in any case not such.

Finally, it should be noted that part I of my comments to follow, having to do with appeals to principles in general, is purely effusive, intended only to mark out a certain perspective for what follows. It is admittedly devoid of philosophical force, and is not meant to prove anything. These somewhat rhetorical remarks are prompted by what has seemed to me to be a curious fact in philosophical discussions having to do with morality and law: that when anyone is so foolish as to say, or even to come at all close to saying, that something like the will of God should be absolute with respect to certain things, that considerations of racial or cultural superiority should be such, that the needs of the working class, or perhaps the aims and purposes of the wealthy, should have this absolute claim, or anything of this sort, then the response from his audience is apt to be so violent as to preclude any proper hearing for him at all, so eager are they to silence such opinions, all of which have, however, at one time or another been defended by men of the highest intelligence. When, on the other hand, someone enunciates to such a group that *justice* has this absolute priority, then the whole scene takes on a quite different aspect, everyone appearing to vie with his neighbor in being the first to endorse this idea, to uphold it more vigorously than the rest, as if his own goodness depended upon his readiness to affirm it. Indeed, most men only need to let the world "justice" roll from their lips to feel as if they were being borne aloft in a balloon— or at least, so it has seemed to me—and philosophers appear no less susceptible to this than anyone else. I think it is time to protest, and somehow to give some small entry to the notion that human goodness is not to be measured any more by this kind of slogan than by any of the others that have throughout history claimed the verbal allegiance of men.

I

Appeals to Principles. Rawls exhorts us not to uphold unjust laws and practices merely on the ground that there is a greater net sum of advantages in having them. The question is not whether this is true or false, or even plausible or implausible in the usual sense, but rather whether this plea should be hearkened to, whether it would be wise or foolish to heed it. I want to urge that it would be most foolish. Indeed, I feel sure that while there are doubtless worse principles, it is nevertheless principles like this one that, once implanted in the minds of judges, legislators, administrators, and governors and there given some special authority of reason or tradition, are largely responsible for sometimes converting our common social life, which ought to be a blessing to us, into something galling and ugly. It is principles like this that encourage men to ignore our human feelings, great and small, and provide these men even with an excuse for doing so. Let the chips fall where they may, let even the heavens fall, as some say, pay less attention to the feelings of men and their occasional misery—still, if some principle of *justice* is kept quite intact we need never feel very guilty about its consequences in the stream of human life. I believe this is what sooner or later inevitably happens when men stand upon principles of any sort and then declare these to be absolute. What continually astonishes me, however, is how men, and particularly men who think a great deal, seem sometimes unable to decide even the most simple and obvious things, or even to utter a simple yea or nay, without first finding some principle authorizing them to do so. Such principles, however, are of necessity principles that *they* have embraced, provided their decisions are voluntary, so they, the partisans of those principles, are the final authorities for what they say and do after all. By invoking principles, they only create the illusion that they act upon some authority other than themselves, which they suppose would be a presumption. The perniciousness of this, in the lives of those who have suffered at the hands of principled men, is quite plain to the sufferers. They cannot fight back, however, for their foe is no longer a man, but some principle, like the principle of justice, which, they are supposed to feel, it would be wicked to impugn.

II

The Exhortatory Character of Rawls's Remarks. That Rawls's remarks on this point are not assertions or claims in any usual sense, but are instead exhortations or pleas that can, accordingly, be neither confuted nor confirmed in any direct way, is perfectly easy to show. He says that "unjust institutions *cannot* be justified by an appeal to the principle of utility," that "a greater balance of net advantages shared by some *cannot* justify the injustice suffered by others," that "an unjust institution or law *cannot* be justified by an appeal to a greater net sum of advantages," and so on (my italics). Now any claim or assertion to the effect that a certain state of affairs *cannot* occur is absolutely refuted by any true assertion that the state in question *has* in fact sometime occurred. Thus, if anyone were to say that water cannot boil at a temperature other than 100°C. or that no animal can lack a male parent, he would be conclusively refuted by pointing out that water has boiled at other temperatures in the mountains and that male honeybees are always reproduced parthenogenetically. But Rawls's comments are utterly untouched by any true observations to the effect that what he says cannot occur has, in fact, sometimes occurred. We all well know that unjust (but not necessarily bad) institutions, laws, and practices have sometimes been defended, and sensibly defended, by pointing out that they are sometimes necessary for the protection of the common good, that is, by calling attention to the baneful consequences to others of not having them—in short, by appealing to utility. Men have sometimes been forcibly evicted from their property, with compensation, to be sure, but on terms in which they had no say, so that a highway might be built for others to use—that is, so that "a greater net sum of advantages" might be enjoyed by others. During the last war thousands of Japanese in California were forcibly relocated, with no inquiry into their patriotism, on the probably correct ground that there was no time to be just here, that the safety of the nation required fast action. Even in peacetime, when our democratic institutions are flourishing, men who are mentally or emotionally unbalanced, diseased, or who otherwise constitute some threat to the wellbeing of others are often involuntarily deprived of their liberty, under the full authority of the laws, though they have committed no crimes. This *is* justified, and sensibly so, by appealing in one way or another to the principle of utility, to the greater net sum of advantages and smaller net sum of disadvantages to others—precisely what Rawls says cannot ever occur. Numberless other examples are familiar to everyone. Rawls cannot, therefore, have meant that this sort of thing cannot happen, though this is what he said. His remarks were instead exhortations to give greater weight—indeed, he said, *absolute* weight—to considerations of justice, and to resolve *all* conflicts between the requirements of justice and the requirements of utility or the common good in favor of the requirements of justice. But this exhortation is foolish. It is a plea that is at least in practice rejected by all men having any sense of the needs and feelings of men. Principles of justice have themselves their only justification as instruments for fostering the common good, of ensuring, as best we can, the "greater net sum of advantages" to society as a whole and often at the expense of individuals. Usually they work more or less well, but they always work imperfectly, and sometimes not at all. To urge, then, that such principles should have an "absolute weight" even when useless or even pernicious is to convert the instrument into the goal, to subordinate the happiness of men to the very principles that have been worked out to help them achieve that happiness, to convert to an end—indeed, an absolute one—principles that have no significance whatever except as means. It is to "turn human life completely upside down," as Callicles is supposed to have accused Socrates of doing on one occasion when Socrates was, as usual, treating justice as something absolute with respect to various other odds and ends such as pleasure, reputation, and even life itself.[1]

Justice and the Common Good. Here one is apt to get the reply that adherence to a true principle of justice can never really be contrary to the public good, and, conversely, that whatever does truly promote the public good is, *ipso facto*, just. If, for instance, forcibly depriving a man of his property and compensating him so that others may have a nice highway to drive on is really in the interest of the public good, if forcibly isolating certain unbalanced or diseased but innocent persons so that others may go about their affairs in safety, if things like this are really required for the good of the rest of society, then, it is apt to be said, such practices are really just after all and hence constitute no exception to the idea that justice must prevail over considerations of utility.

To fall into this line of thought, however, is absolutely to confuse the whole business. It renders the remark that considerations of utility should always give way to considerations of justice not true and not false, not wise and not foolish, but simply senseless. If adherence to a true principle of justice necessarily promotes the greater good of society as a whole, and if, conversely, the promotion of this is automatically something that is just, then there is no point whatsoever in suggesting that either ought to give way to the other in case of a conflict, for it is then impossible that any real conflict should arise. To uphold the one is to uphold the other. Rawls's remarks, however, to the effect that considerations of utility or the general good ought to give way to considerations of justice in cases of conflict, were *not* pointless. They were enunciated most gravely and earnestly, and they do clearly presuppose the occasional existence of such conflict. One cannot, therefore, explicitly or tacitly characterize either justice or utility in such a way as to yield an automatic harmony between them and still have any point in saying, with Rawls, that one of these ought to be preferred to the other in case they do not harmonize.

Justice as a Positive Ethical Idea. Yet people, and even sophisticated philosophers, do sometimes fall into this confusion and even suppose that they thereby are throwing some light onto something. I have even heard a wise philosopher remark that the evil of an unjust practice is that it weakens men's respect for justice, and thereby diminishes the public good! And the author of that observation supposed himself to believe, with Rawls, that justice has some absolute value with respect to utility.

It is not hard to see, however, why men so easily fall into this trap. Justice, we have all long since been taught to feel, is something good—necessarily so. The common good of mankind, particularly when this conflicts with our own selfish desires, is also something we have been taught to respect as good. Both being good, then, it is hard to see how they could ever conflict or, indeed, how they could really be any different. Having gone that far, it is then very easy to think of an unjust law or practice as really the same thing as a bad or hurtful law or practice.

But there certainly *is* a distinction between what is just and what is beneficial or practically advantageous to men. The concepts themselves are not the same at all. Even if we grant, as is doubtless generally true, that in promoting the one we, as a matter of fact, more often than not promote the other, it is not always true, and conflicts between the two do in fact sometimes arise. We cannot here have our cake and eat it too, and that is why there is a point to Rawls's exhortation always to prefer justice over utility, even though, in my opinion, it is a point that ought not to be heeded.

We all have a fairly clear idea of what is meant by the common good—clear enough, at any rate, so that we can sometimes recognize things that are manifestly contrary to it. We all have also a fairly clear idea of what justice is, clear enough, again, so that we can sometimes recognize certain things as violations of justice. Welfare legislation, for example, is neither just nor unjust as such, though the manner of its administration might be. No issue of justice is involved in the question whether, for instance, public funds should be budgeted for the care of the children of indigent parents or for the construction and maintenance of public parks. These are purely questions of what is available and what is wise in the light of the general need—questions, in short, of utility. But, such funds having been set aside, if it is then suggested that certain children—say, those who are illegitimate or colored—should be excluded from the benefits of such programs, then the question of justice does most surely arise. Illegitimacy or color are not usually considered crimes or wrongs that warrant any different treatment in such matters.

Again, no issue of justice is involved in the question whether a new highway should be built. This is purely a question of utility—the question whether such a highway would be useful and, if so, whether the benefits of it would outweigh the cost. This is no more a question of what justice requires than is the question whether one should buy his wife a new coat or whether the school board should buy new textbooks to replace the battered ones in use. Problems of what justice requires might arise in deciding where and how such a highway is to be built, however—in case, for example, it is suggested that only the houses of the poor, or perhaps only the houses of the rich, should be condemned to make way for it; that it should be paid for by a special tax upon bachelors or Roman Catholics; and so on.

The Volstead Act, similarly, was not in the remotest sense an unjust law, though I have heard it cited as an example of such. The prohibition of the public sale of spiritous beverages is no more unjust than the prohibition of the public sale of drugs. This act violated no constitutional provision whatever, and applied to everyone exactly the same. It was, though perfectly just and fair, simply a bad law: that is, one that was found to do less good than harm.

III

Relevant and Irrelevant Differences. The idea of justice is partially though inadequately expressed in Rawls's dictum that "similar cases are treated similarly." This is, of course, not Rawls's nor anyone else's whole conception of justice, and I am sure that any purported definition of justice, which this is not intended to be, would be inadequate. Nevertheless, this does express an important and essential part of the idea of justice, and it will do for my present purpose.

Here, though, we have to note something that I think Rawls has overlooked, something that is easily overlooked: that some similarities and differences between cases are *relevant* or *significant* and some are not. The class of children, for example, who are under eighteen years of age and the class of those who are eighteen and over differ in one obvious respect. Similarly, the class of children who are colored and the class of those who are not differ in one respect. Yet the first dissimilarity is relevant to the question of what children should according to justice be eligible for public welfare payments, for the use of playground facilities, for driver's licenses, and so on, whereas the latter dissimilarity is relevant to none of these things. Again, the class of those who use automobiles differs in one obvious respect from the class of those who do not, and the class of those who are Protestants differs in one respect from the class of those who are not. Yet this first dissimilarity is at least relevant to the question of how a new highway should be paid for—perhaps by a gasoline tax or by tolls—while the latter is not.

Now we raise this question: What is it that makes some similarities and differences relevant, and others not? It is not enough to say that "similar cases are treated similarly." Any two cases are similar in some respects and dissimilar in others, and we need somehow to determine which of these similarities and differences are relevant and which are not. The legislator who proposes to exclude Negroes as the recipients of welfare payments is adhering to the principle that similar cases are to be treated similarly just exactly as well as the legislator who proposes to exclude children over eighteen years of age. According to the first man's idea, all children who are colored are treated exactly the same: they are excluded. According to the second man all who are over eighteen are likewise treated exactly the same, by being excluded. If, then, one of these men is violating a principle of justice and the other is not, it is *not* because one is adhering to the principle that similar cases ought to be treated similarly and the other is not. It is because one of them has picked out the "wrong" similarities and differences, whereas the other is drawing the line at a difference that is "relevant."

But now we ask: What makes one of these differences relevant to the matter of justice and the other irrelevant? It seems to be just this: That it would *do more harm than good* to apply the first man's distinction, which distinguishes between races, whereas it would *do more good than harm* to apply the second man's distinction, which distinguishes between ages. Each distinction, however, is meant to exclude some class. It would indeed be hard on colored children to be excluded, as such, from the benefits of such public funds—but it is also hard on eighteen-year-olds to be excluded from the same funds for which seventeen-year-olds are eligible. So that is not the difference—that the first man's restriction benefits some persons at the expense of others. They both do that. Both proposals are discriminatory, but one discriminates well and the other ill. The difference is, rather, that the good of society as a whole is diminished by employing the first distinction, whereas the good of society as a whole is enhanced by employing the second. This, however, is a purely utilitarian consideration.

Here it is worth noting, incidentally, that the degree of relevance or significance that most people attach to certain similarities and differences appears to be simply a function of the importance of their consequences: that is, to be determined by considerations of utility. Thus when it comes to building and maintaining highways it is fairly customary, where feasible, to pay the cost from revenues derived from the users of such highways. This is an obvious recognition of the claims of fairness and justice. When it comes to building and maintaining public schools, on the other hand, these same claims of fairness and justice are wholly eclipsed by the more pressing considerations of utility. Everyone is supposed to pay these costs, as he is able, whether he or his children use those schools or not. The idea underlying this is surely that the education of children is of such overwhelming importance in terms of its consequences that certain other considerations are not deserving of serious attention. Those who send their children to private and parochial schools deem this a clear injustice to themselves. They surely do have a point, but it is not a point that counts for much in the minds of those who have a keen sense of the long-range needs of society as a whole. The "greater balance of net advantages shared by some" does, in such cases as this, "justify the injustice suffered by others"—or, at least, so it is quite generally believed, particularly when those who enjoy this greater balance of net advantages happen to be greatly in the majority. These persons are even able to show, with great plausibility to themselves but with none to their opponents, that such a practice is really in keeping with justice after all! All that they actually manage to show, however, is that it is very useful.

It appears, then, that considerations of justice are not absolute with respect to utility after all. Worse than that, it appears that one cannot even *apply* the principles of justice, insofar as these involve the notion that similar cases should be treated similarly, until one has first applied some consideration of utility, or some consideration of what is best for the greatest number—or, if not that, then in any case *some* consideration other than simply justice itself. There is no other way of deciding what similarities and differences shall be deemed relevant or significant for applying considerations of justice. And this, it should be noted, does not result from any performance for utility or anything else, nor from any moral considerations whatever. It is required by the very logic of the matter. No matter how one might try to make absolute some principle of justice and put it, so to speak, into the driver's seat, it must always remain a passenger after all. If it is not borne along by some principle of utility—and there is no reason why it should be—then it must be carried by something other than itself in any case. Some prefer considerations of the common good, the greatest net sum of advantages to the greatest number. Others prefer considerations of the good of their particular race or culture. Still others prefer purely economic or even political considerations. For myself, I prefer considerations of ordinary human feeling, what some of our fathers and mothers once quaintly referred to as Christian charity. This is, of course, no *more* rational than most of the other assorted preferences of men, but it is no *less* so, either. What is clearly irrational is to prefer some bloodless principle of justice as the guiding and absolute consideration.

NOTE

1. Plato, *Gorgias* 481.

8

The Right to Disobey

PAUL WEISS
Yale University

DR. KONVITZ has brought into fine focus the obligations assumed
by those who accept a government by law and yet disagree
with some of the results of its operation. I would like to add a
footnote to his splendid account.

He who accepts the procedures, the ideology, and the
benefits of a legal system is obligated to submit to the enacted
laws, even though he denies their wisdom or even their justice.
The only recourse he has is either to pay the legal penalty for
disobedience or to make use of the procedures that he and the
rest accept in the attempt to modify or to replace the regretted
legislation. The second is the alternative most men most of
the time adopt; it makes possible the continuation of the legal
system while they work for possible changes in the results it
brings about.

There are times, however, when men view with disfavor
not merely the results of a legal system but the very procedures
by which those results are obtained. In place of a majority rule,
for example, they may prefer unanimity, representative government, or even authoritative edicts. If they continue to share in
the ideology and the benefits of that society, they are under
obligation to continue to use the established procedures as well
as to submit to the results of their operation. The only recourse
they have is to pay the penalty for disobedience or to make use
of permitted legal devices, such as education, debates, and voting, with the objective of eventually instituting other procedures. If there are no such devices available, they must find

ways by which those devices can be provided. Failing that, they have a right to disobey, but only insofar as, on behalf of the common ideology, their action serves to bring about another system in which the common benefits are continued or increased. The resistance movement in France during the German occupation was governed by some such outlook. Its quarrel was not so much with the ideology dominating France; it was not predicated on a promise to bring about a state in which greater benefits for all were to be achieved. It was concerned with getting rid of the agencies by means of which the French were being subjugated and humiliated. The intent of the underground fighters was to make possible another state in which the French ideology would be supported and implemented, but they were not concerned with bringing about such a state.

It is possible for one to disagree not only with the results and procedures of a state, but with its ideology—its values, ideals, and aims—as well. If this disagreement is expressed by those who nevertheless continue to accept the traditions of that society, the result is rebellion; if the traditions are rejected as well, we have revolution; if the opposition is on behalf of another set of established traditions, the result is civil war. The justification of these acts lies in an implicit promise to institute a system in which the presumed superior ideology will be implemented so as to benefit all, at least to the degree they had been benefited before. Otherwise a comparative injustice will be replaced by a greater one.

The entire system, with its laws, procedures, ideologies, and even traditions, is justly rejected if these conspire to deny minimal benefits to some of the people. A state is not an absolute good. It is without justification if its structure, design, and operation involve the denial of the basic rights of life, health, education, speech, assembly, and the like. Nazi Germany, the present government of South Africa, and some of our Southern states deny themselves any defense but that which superior strength provides.

In all the above cases men are faced with unjust laws,

corrupt procedures, dangerous attitudes, or vicious policies that they can rightly try to replace with better ones. But a man might take only a minimal interest in a state, regardless of whether it be good or bad. The state may be viewed, even at its best, as not worth much time, energy, or attention. This in root is a position taken by most men, as their practice reveals. They live in the state, they conform to its demands, but they pay little if any attention to how the laws are enacted, what the prevailing values are, or what objectives concern those in power. They are not in revolt; rather, they allow, usually through default, other men to represent them.

Some men, however, turn their backs on the state and its affairs, to concern themselves with a different world of values. No one, of course, can do this entirely, nor all the time. Men live together and must live in consonance with some governing rules, if only for the sake of replacing what now rules them. But scientists and philosophers, religious men and artists, scholars and adventurers conform to what the state demands only in order to be able to live apart from the state. They are concerned with the pursuit of values that can be realized only outside the political arena, whether the state be just or unjust. They can be justified in their withdrawal only if the values they realize are at least equal to those promoted by the state and if what they do contributes to the eventual replacement of what is defective by what is excellent. They in effect appeal to a value shared by states as well as other enterprises. This they maintain and promote in order to make possible the achievement of an ideal civilization. They attend to the task of increasing knowledge, sensitivity, character, and self-mastery eventually for all, and thus, also, for those who ignore these domains to attend to the affairs of state. They are spiritual refugees, men who have moved beyond the reach of politics and law for the sake of a world in which these, too, can have a role. Theirs is the strategy of trying to achieve justice and peace for all by already practicing the arts that truly flourish only when justice and peace prevail everywhere. They not only disobey whatever laws conflict with the practice and attainment of the values of a civilized world, but they avoid as much as possible the area governed by law. The state for them is but one avenue through which men can reach their proper goal; they live in consonance with, though not in terms of, the prevailing system, and then only so far as it does what it ought.

All disobedience to the state is justifiable so far as it is guided by principles and values superior to those now being illustrated or possible. In some cases the primary aim is to get a better functioning state, but one also has a right to disobey bad laws as the last case illustrates because one is concerned with other values at least as comprehensive and vital as those that the state at its best might exhibit and promote.

PART II

Natural Law

A

In Defense of Natural Law

H. A. ROMMEN
Georgetown University

THE TERM "natural law" and the basic rules of ethics and justice for human conduct that it signifies are—as the foundation of ethics and of juridical law—as old as philosophy itself. That what it signifies without a specific reflective and systematic philosophical effort is, as at least one school of anthropology holds, as old as mankind itself, Fritz Kern, in his *Beginn der Weltgeschichte*, based on the so-called Vienna School of the *Kulturkreis* doctrine, explains in a thoughtful chapter called "Lived Natural Law." This "natural law" doctrine as part of a *philosophia perennis* is a philosophy of law that has a long history in the West, a history with ups and downs, so that one may truly speak of an *Ewige Wiederkehr des Naturrechts*. Just because of this long history, the term itself has suffered ambiguities and shifting interpretations and meanings in the development of the human philosophical effort; changing religio-theological beliefs have influenced, criticized, even denied it. So, for some time, one has proposed to give it up and, for instance, substitute for it the term "justice," "fundamental principles of law," or the like. Personally, I prefer to stick with the term, thus being obliged to first make clear what I do not mean by natural law.

First, I do not mean by this term a law that exists or is valid in a prestatal *status naturalis,* to be *in toto* or in part abolished by the positive law of the *status civilis,* as in Hobbes's theory, where to protect the sovereign and the peace and security of the *status civilis,* only the rule *pacta sunt servanda*

survives for just this reason. Nor is natural law just a catalog
of natural rights that, existing in the *status naturalis,* were now
taken over into the *status civilis,* either without a change as in
Locke's theory or by a transformation into civil rights as in
Rousseau's theory. Nor is what I might call the "classical"
natural law an elaborated code of law such as it popularly became in the Age of Rationalism and Enlightenment, when at
every book fair in Leipzig such codes appeared containing
elaborate systems of civil law, including family and inheritance
law, public and criminal law, and even feudal law, logically
more geometrico, derived from first principles that were actually either defenses of the existing positive law or reform-
minded proposals for improvement and thus by no means
minor changes of the law. It would be foolish, on the other
hand, to forget the historical importance of these codes of
natural law on the change from absolutism to constitutionalism
and to the humanization of an older and in part irrational
criminal law and procedure, on the slow realization of civil
equality in private law, on the change from a society and state
with estates of differing degrees of privileges and immunities
(*ständestaat*) to a bourgeois or better civil society as realized
in the Prussian Code of 1794, in the Code Napoleon, and in the
Austrian *Allgemeines Bürgerliches Recht* of 1811. Granted this
meritorious influence, this kind of natural law, often rightly
called an ideological theory for the longings of the *Bürger* and
historically necessary new forms of political and social organization, gave way to the historical school of law. Yet the classical natural law does not propose a whole code of law of
logically derived, more and more concrete and minute legal
rules for all fields of human social life. It claims to be transhistorical but not ahistorical, because it is metaphysical; it is
the foundation of all human positive law and of obedience to
it, and is at the same time, though it "shouts" for positive law,
its critical standard. With Hegel one may say of it that what
matters is to recognize and know the substance that is immanent and the eternal that is present beneath the temporal and
passing which appears.

Second, this natural law is not Roman Catholic in the theological-ecclesiastical sense. One may, of course, say that Catholic theology, with its lapsarian doctrine of the *natura vulnerata non destructa* and its principle that Grace presupposes nature, does not cancel it but perfects it, with the consequences of the *analogia entis* and of a natural theology containing not only no *theologumena* contrary to Natural Law but demanded of it as a preamble of its theology. That is, then, also the reason why natural law has always found, so to speak, a home in Catholic Christian thought, has had in the theology of the church neither an envious competitor nor a ruthless monopolizer, and was considered historically and on its premises a necessary idea.

The great reformers Luther, Calvin, and Zwingli, in spite of their dissenting theology that made the conception of natural law difficult, to say the least, still accepted it, and even Melanchthon furthered it. Grotius, it is true, an Arminian; Althusius the Calvinist, continuer of the natural law school of Salamanca (Vittoria to Suárez), somewhat like Grotius; Pefendorf the Lutheran and his disciple John Wise the Congregationalist—these men had scarcely any difficulty from specific *theologumena* in their theory of natural law. The last (non-Catholic) treatise in Germany on natural right, on the basis of ethics (1867), was by the Lutheran and Aristotelian Adolf von Trendelenburg. Erich Kaufmann, though counted among the neo-Hegelians, is a believing Lutheran and a natural law jurist. So also is my dear friend the Congregationalist theologian Nathanael Micklem; also Hermann Weinkauff, first president of the German Federal Supreme Court, who in an essay professed that his being an Evangelical Christian causes him no difficulty in being a firm and ardent adherent of natural law. Emil Brunner, one-time friend and follower of Karl Barth, and other theologians of the Orders of Creation Theology do not only not deny natural law but are decidedly friendly to it. Brunner speaks of a "*Jus naturale* that precedes positive law, fills its gaps and gives it support" [1] though he contends it is not, strictly speaking, valid law. He says that "the idea of Natural

Law and of unchanging 'Konstanten' in the orders of Creation impose themselves with objective necessity on Christian thinking in the form of these orders, even if one does not wish the word 'Natural Law' [*Naturrecht*]." [2] Yet Brunner accepts also a "natural theology" and, in his political ethic, does come rather near to Catholic political ethics based on natural law, as Richard Hauser affirms.[3] This book is a highly interesting and rather objective comparison of neo-Protestant (Barth, Brunner, Althaus, Gogarten, Wunsch, and others) with Catholic social and political theory based on natural law. It shows also that some writers underestimate the still existing differences between the two ethical doctrines. True, Karl Barth's theology—and that of those who follow him—by his denial of natural theology, his affirmation of the utter sinfulness and perversion of human nature by the Fall, his denial of any *analogia entis*, and his affirmation of the *Deus absconditus* is and must be strictly opposed to natural law. Nevertheless, it seems clear that only in a relative and qualified sense may one speak of "Catholic natural law."

Third, although it is true that the *Weltbild* produced by the natural sciences is very different from the natural *Weltbild* as our unaided senses present it, the common man today has an awe-arousing lack of true understanding of the scientific *Weltbild*. The same cannot be said in the ethicolegal world; here we have not the discrepancy experienced in the natural sciences. The law even presupposes a minimum knowledge of itself, and it deals with generally knowable things: with individual rights and duties, with contracts, property, parents' and children's mutual rights and duties, with group interests and the public interests, with constitutional and administrative (such as tax) law. About the difference between the learned jurist and the common-man, one might say that jurisprudence is the academically trained twin sister of common sense. This was what made Karl Bergbohm, who set out 80 years ago to destroy natural law, complain bitterly in the conclusion of the first volume of his book that all men are born natural law jurists. It should have made him very cautious in the beginning.

Fourth, natural law as *lex naturalis* and as *jus naturale*—*Naturrecht, droit naturel*—though intimately related and the basis of all rules of human conduct, nevertheless are to be distinguished. *Lex naturalis* embraces all the duties concerning the individual person in itself, with other persons, and with God. *Jus naturale*, strictly speaking—like its specific virtue, justice in its three forms, legal, commutative, and distributive —concerns the duties and rights of the person in society, his relation with other persons and toward the human ends and purposes that can only be realized in these various societies up to the *communitas communitatum*, the state, as a self-sufficient juridical order, and finally and *intentionaliter* mankind as the universal community. *Jus naturale*, then, is that part of social ethics that gives to the positive legal order and to the legal authority established by it the power to obligate the consciences of the citizen; at the same time it gives to the conscience of the citizen obligated by authority the enduring critical standards by which to decide (*krinein*—decide) when and under what circumstances authority loses its legitimacy and the obligation thereby ceases. For both authority and subject are bound by the *jus naturale* as a higher law above the positive law. Man is by nature a sociopolitical being as much as he is a rational being, despite the ultimate solitude of what Max Scheler called the intimate sphere which, if not filled by God and transpersonal spiritual values, makes the *horror vacui* of the soul evident in anxiety, in surrender to an unlimited activism, and finally in despair. The *jus naturale*, as directed to the realization of justice in and by the positive legal order, is thus not temporally prior to this order nor, as an unreal (*irreal*) realm of values in Nicolai Hartmann's philosophy, is it wholly transcendent. It is "*in*" the positive order. For the positive legal order has essentially the function to realize, as far as possible, justice *hic et nunc* together with its ordering function and that of securing by the order the rights and

duties of those subject to the legal order. That the legal order
may effectively protect and secure the individual persons and
the families and their many religious, cultural, educational and
economic associations—their forms and number depending on
the general level of civilization and on the communal or individualistic climate of culture—it is necessary that it ultimately enforce conformity to itself. Actually the overwhelming majority conform not out of fear of punishment, but by
the virtue of obedience and by motives of civic friendship and
even of reciprocal utility—the calculus of *do ut des*. Man, with
his *Daseinssorge* and surrounded by danger because of his
being a body-bound person, living into an uncertain future but
gifted by reason, wants to plan his future and secure it and
that of his loved ones. But he can reasonably do this only if he
can expect at least an external conformity of all subjects to
the order *in concreto*. To rely simply on the practice of virtues
by all would presuppose not only that all be virtuous, but also
that all agree about the interpretation of all rules in all possible
circumstances and situations. Man in society and state wants
everyone's conduct to conform to the legal norm, and he se-
cures and guarantees this by going to law—*ire in jus,* as the
old Roman rule said. *Jus* thus could with good reason be called
the "ethical minimum" by Rudolf Stammler. In other words,
not all rules of ethics are open to the juridical form of positive
law: for example, liberality, charity, magnanimity, and personal friendship, though due according to the *lex naturalis,* are
not open to the juridical form. The line that distinguishes the
order of ethics and the *ordo juris* is, of course, shifting from
epoch to epoch and from culture to culture. (It is also possible
that what was once only a rule of ethics is given the juridical
form.) There exists a distinct relationship between the degree
of reliability of the ethical order and the expansion of the
legal order. For instance, the higher the ethical standards of
a profession are, the less will society demand legal, or enforceable, standards. St. Francis of Assisi desired that his followers
be motivated only by love, and he consented only unwillingly
to approve the constitution and rules as the *jus* of the Order

of the Friars Minor. Had he not done so there would be no Ordo Fratrum Minorum today. The juridical form not only gives stability to societies, to the state, and to the community of nations, but it makes them enduring as forms and ends for the succeeding generations of its members.

The *ordo caritatis* and the *ordo justitiae,* of which the order of positive law is *intentionaliter* a proximate realization, are both necessary for the human being with his immortal soul bound in essential union to a mortal body. Thus it is violation of both orders, if one would give out of charity what is already due by justice or demand as a duty of justice what is owed only by charity. But both orders belong to the *lex naturalis.* Christ himself, in Luke 6:32 and Matthew 5:43–48, seems to consider the rule "love thy enemy" a part of the *lex naturalis.* In stressing the order of law as essential, I do not mean to say that the state is restricted to the legal order nor that the state is nothing more than the positive legal order—how eminently and primarily its establishment, conservation, and continuous adaptation to justice is the end of the state. Man does not live only by justice and by positive law, nor does the state. He lives and acts *in* the order of justice, but he lives *by* the many social virtues, by loyalty, by free obedience of free men, by civic friendship, by patriotism, and by the Golden Rule.

The distinction between the *lex naturalis* and the *jus naturale*—not their separation as Thomasius and Kant want it—is of far-reaching importance for the legislator. He should not and often cannot proscribe and punish all violations of the *lex naturalis* and enforce all its rules. Not even every grave sin can or ought to be made a crime. The Canon Law distinguishes sharply the *forum internum* of the confessional for sins and the *forum externum* of violations of the social order and the common good of the Church of Delicts. It is bad positive law, for example, to make fornication between two adults a crime because fornication is not primarily in the social order and the law against it is practically unenforceable. Many German jurists were opposed to paragraph 175 of the criminal code, which made the homosexual acts of males alone a crime. It was called the "extortioner paragraph," since every judge and lawyer knew that to keep these acts under the list of crimes caused more damage to the social order than the forbidden practice itself. The federal prohibition law was also a bad law because it could not be enforced with reasonable effectiveness. To give all rules of *lex naturalis* the juridical form would produce a form of totalitarian state; if not all but too many of these rules were so treated, there would be extreme hypocrisy. Compare such a circumstance with Christ's opposition to the well-intentioned Pharisees, who found successors in Puritanism and Jansenism 1,500 years later.

I shall now try to discuss the following questions: What is natural law? What are its principal and basic rules? What are its premises epistemological, ontological, value philosophical, and the problem of *is* and *ought*? What are its relations to positive law, both as to *lex lata* and *lex feranda*? In considering the latter I shall include a short reference to the jurisdiction of the German Supreme Court in recent years.

The term "natural law" (*jus naturale*) stems from the Greek distinction between *physei dikaion* and *thesei dikaion*. All through the history of legal philosophy, this distinction has significant parallels: *Veritas facit legem, voluntas facit legem;* Reason maketh the Law, Authority maketh the Law; Might makes Right, Right legitimizes Might; mere external enforced conformity makes the law versus the free assent, the obedience of free man makes the law. One should be aware that these oppositions do not exclude each other, but that they form actually preferences and primacies without denying the opposite. Similarly the term *physei* may be used in different meanings. It means, as does the happy translation *natura*, that which remains constant, identical, unchanged despite the process of growth, of development, of change; that enduring identity which also is meant by the term "substance" as opposed to "accident." Since it is taken from the biological life it may mean all living beings, and so it was used by some Sophists and by Ulpianus. But it was mostly understood to mean the *physis*, or nature, of the rational individual substance, the finite person and his *humanitas* common to all human persons, that which entitles us to predicate of a living being that it is man. The origin of the ambiguity is actually that man's being is stratified: he is spiritual being; he is vital, or biological, being; and he is, as body, or as Cartesian *res extensa*, subject to the physical laws, such as Galileo's laws of free fall. As person, as master of his own acts, as *in se* self-determining and thus as a responsible free agent, man—whatever his origin in evolution of biological life—is, as *homo sapiens* and *homo faber*, fundamentally different from mere biological being, from animals. With his intellect and reason he forms a "qualitative jump" in evolution. Between a member of a most primitive tribe and me there is qualitatively a similarity that does not exist between me and a primate. That is why we are able to understand this primitive, but find it so difficult truly to understand literally the most highly developed animal. Despite all the cultural differences between a tribe frozen, as it were, for millenniums in its customs, magic beliefs, or superstitions, and a modern Western man, the former is basically able to accommodate himself to and assimilate Western civilization within his lifespan. This stratified being of man—person, life, and thing—makes it possible (since man is self-determining) that he will surrender to the drives and urges of the vital sphere and act, as we say, like an animal; or he may reverse the order of values and prefer the material values, which are infinitely consumable, at the cost of or sacrifice of the immaterial values: *nec sumptus consumitur.* (Compare an apple and the Jupiter Symphony.) Further, man is a constantly active being, acting from his inner world into the outer world even in the contemplative, the thinking life, so much so that, misunderstanding the old substance-subsistence theory, some modern philosophers speak of man as an "act-center," as mere existing in actualism. Aquinas, on the contrary, understood the human person to be the free master of his own acts, but subsisting by and in himself. It is an aboriginal phenomenon that I always remain this person, with my personal conscience, with my personal, nontransferable responsibility before myself and my fellow men for the acts that issue from me into the social world. Thus, in ceaseless acting, the dynamic element of the term "nature" (as compared to the more static concept of "essence") comes out. The spontaneous self-understanding of myself as a human person shows me that I ought to realize, to actualize myself as a person in my free acts, internal ones and those affecting the world; in this Aristotle, St. Thomas, Kant, and Nikolai Hartmann agree. Being a person means to have the task of becoming ever more perfect than what you already *intentionaliter* are: become by your own acts that which you already are, realize ever more in your life what you, as a free person, are already destined to be. All of this is implicit in the term "*natura humana,*" or "*humanitas.*" This too is meant in the Thomist formulas: theoretical reason becomes practical reason, and the formal cause, or nature, of man ought to become the final cause of his acts. Or the good has to be done, the evil avoided when an act is *in se* good, when it is congruent with human nature, thus conceived, and agrees with it; and evil, if the act is against human nature. Since man is essentially social and grows and perfects himself (not loses himself) in the social world with other persons in many societies, the ends of which are truly human ends and purposes, one is justified in stating as a firm principle: never act against the common good of any of these societies, but help to realize it. This has been for many centuries the root and reason of the now much-stressed term "dignity of man," understandable in view of the experience of National Socialist totalitarianism and of the Communism of today, in which the person and his freedom, self-determination, and creativity are so inhumanly compressed in favor of man as a mere *Gattungswesen* whose labor reproduces itself in its material life process.

These basic principles and what are called the primary and secondary (remote) conclusions drawn from them are not merely purely formal, but by reason of the *natura humana* are dialectically related to metaphysically necessary *bona,* or values, and therefore always to be realized in social life. For without their being realized, social life and its continuous growth

and perfection, the good life and temporal felicity would be
impossible. Also impossible would be secure fulfillment of the
idea of the person in the fruition of the good life protected
by his fundamental rights and the positive legal order.

We consider as primary conclusions the rules of the second table of the Decalogue, the Fourth to the Eighth Com-
mandments (not those of the first table, which are parts of
the *lex naturalis*). They concern the family and life—thou
shalt not murder, that is, kill an innocent person; the prohibition of adultery; the prohibition of theft, which presupposes
the institution of property, both private and communal (public); and the prohibition of perjury, because without such the
legal order is gravely endangered. (The Ninth and Tenth belong again to the *lex naturalis*.) Also to these conclusions belong the personal, or natural, rights derived from the very nature
of the person: life; integrity or inviolability; freedom circumscribed in an expansive or contracting sphere of self-determination, as in the marriage contract, the property and service contracts, and the like; the right of access to an impartial court of
justice; the right of self-defense; the right to personal honor;
but not necessarily the right to participate in the legislative
process, for this would make monarchy contrary to natural
law.

These rights, recognized since antiquity and even by primitive tribes, though not always in their totality, may at certain
times and in certain legal systems not be universally recognized
for all men. The institution of slavery illustrates such lack of
recognition to the greatest degree; the several types of serfdom,
to varying minor degrees. The excuses given by defenders of
slavery, from Aristotle to Calhoun, are that some men cannot,
by their psychosomatic structure, truly determine themselves
by their reason, but are ruled by their passions and ought to
be ruled in the form of ownership by those of nimble mind.
Aristotle seems not to have felt well about this argument; he
freed his slaves by his last will. The classical Roman jurists under the influence of stoic ethics declared that all men are by
nature free. The Sachsenspiegel (1200) said even that slavery

is a sin from the beginning and that only evil men want to make this sin rightful; while Aquinas rather lamely tried to explain it as a consequence of sin, not belonging to what some stoic and some Church Fathers called the primary *lex naturalis* but to a secondary postlapsarian *lex naturalis*—a distinction used by the reformers and even today by some theologians under *heilsgeschichtliche* view. The distinction, not to be confused with the *natura pura* doctrine, was given up by theologians since Vittoria, Molina, and Suárez who refute all the older, doubtful arguments and declare slavery simply to be against the *jus naturale*.

That some of these personal rights are for a time partially or fully taken away in the form of punishment for crimes is no basic problem. Nor is it a problem that the right of property ceases when a person is in danger of death by starvation, but only to prevent this danger. To return the *depositum*, a lent gun, for instance, at the demand of the owner or at the agreed-upon time is a rule of *jus naturale;* however, I am entitled, even obliged, not to return it to the owner who is in a rage against another innocent man and obviously wants to kill him. The rule *pacta sunt servanda* stands before the difficulty that unforeseen fundamental changes of conditions may transform a *summum jus* into a *summa injuria* and lead to the restrictive *clausula rebus sic stantibus,* to the idea of treaties that have become inapplicable (Article 19 of the League's Covenant). A *subtilior consideratio sapientium* then distinguished, as legal history shows, between liability for not keeping the *pactum* by reason of *dolus* or *culpa,* and of nonfulfillment by reason of impossibilty or unforeseeable accidents. The distinction between primary conclusions and secondary, as well as that between primary and secondary *lex naturalis* (until Suárez' critique of the distinction between *jus naturale* and *jus inter gentes* instead of *jus gentium*), was caused by the problem of the unchangeability of the natural law. One reason was exegetical difficulties in the Old Testament, such as Yahweh ordaining the Jews to take along goods and precious vessels borrowed for this purpose from their Egyptian masters (Exodus 3:22).

Another reason was the history-minded thinkers of this period. The rules of the *jus naturale prohibitivum* then became un- changeable, while rules of the *jus naturale permissivum* were qualified in their applicability by the circumstances. These thinkers were also aware of the fact that only the principles and the *jus naturale prohibitivum* are evident and easily recog- nizable by a mixture of intuition and reasoning, since they were, so to speak, deposited in *syneidesis,* from which con- science, God's dowry to mankind, took its judgment of what to do and not to do in concrete situations. The more one de- scends from these principles and primary rules, the more train- ing and discernment (*consideratio sapientium*) is necessary. For practical reason deals with the contingent individual acts of free persons, and logical necessity and certainty recede the greater the difference of the judgment and doctrines of the trained jurists become. It is easy to say that in driving a 100-horsepower automobile one ought to use all possible care for the lives and property of other persons, and that this is a demand of natural law, but reason cannot with logical cer- tainty decide if the rule "drive on the right" or "drive on the left" is a necessary consequence. Pope Leo XIII and those who demanded, by reason of justice and the *jus naturale,* state in- tervention in the form of social legislation were very well aware that not one but several systems of social security were possi- ble and that here as well as in the earlier case, reason and con- science have to weigh (*deliberatio*) the pros and cons of a bill and then make decisions that are determined by positive law as to the general demands of *jus naturale.* An ethics and a *jus naturale more geometrico* is scarcely possible. One speaks of the wisdom of the jurist, not of his mathematical genius. De- duction and induction, theory and experience, are the *meson.* One cannot, as was claimed by the rationalist *jus naturale,* contend that the jury trial and even 12 jurors is a demand of *jus naturale.* One cannot speak of that kind of liberty of con- tract that the majority of the U.S. Supreme Court interpreted to mean that a prohibition of social legislation by the states is a natural right. A contract has, at least in private law, a

good chance to be just only if there exists a modicum of equality of bargaining power. I have the impression that among
other causes it was the doubtful and highly individualistic interpretation of natural rights by the Supreme Court up to
the thirties that is at the root of the disappointment of quite
a few jurists with the idea of the *jus naturale;* this interpretation was actually repudiated by the adherents of the classical *jus naturale*—for instance, John A. Ryan and other pro-
moters of social reform and social justice. A natural law as
developed by Herbert Spencer in the form of a social Darwin-
ism, which started step by step with a change in the meaning
of the term "nature," from Hobbes through Adam Smith and
a mechanist *ordre naturel,* is once and for all very different
from the *jus naturale* of St. Thomas, Suárez, and even John
Locke.

The idea of *jus naturale* has, of course, certain premises.
Epistemologically it presupposes a realist—though not an un-
critical or naïve philosophy—and/or the acknowledgment of
and objective philosophy of graded values. Kant could still
"believe" in a natural law because his practical reason had—
though rather tenuously—access to the metaphysical, or as he
called it, the noumenal, world, while he denied that theoretical
reason had this access; remember his famous (but today oft
forgotten by the neo-Kantians) remark, "I had to push back
science in order to make room for belief." Also the neo-
Hegelians, if and so far as they toned down Hegel's *statolatrie,*
could acknowledge a *jus naturale;* and followers of Max
Scheler's and Nikolai Hartmann's philosophy of value, among
them Helmuth Coing, could establish fundamental legal principles much like the *jus naturale* here represented. Some of
these principles are: granting legal capacity to normal adults;
protection of life and bodily integrity; recognition of the right
to private property; safeguarding the honor and reputation of
the individual; sanctioning a sphere of privacy; permitting freedom of speech, assembly, and religion; granting a right to
education; ensuring fulfillment of contractual obligation; preventing arbitrary treatment of inferiors by their superiors; es-

tablishment of a system of procedures guaranteeing a fair and impartial treatment in all courts by an independent judiciary; no punishment without a *mens rea;* freeing conscientious objectors from military service; outlawing the death penalty; recognizing monogamy as the only legitimate union of man and woman and restricting the freedom of divorce.[4]

Some might say that the classical *jus naturale* does not contain all these rules, for example, that of freedom of religion and conscience. It is true that during the centuries when state and church were intimately fused, not always to their mutual advantage, heresy was also considered a crime by the secular law and punished. But first: all societies get "nervous" when the basic values that form concretely the foundation of their unity and cohesion are aggressively denied. When the Cathari, in the eleventh and twelfth centuries, denied the goodness and validity of the oath and the binding marriage rites in a still-feudal society that was built on a hierarchy of oaths of allegiances and on the family linked with property, dominium, and political rule, society reacted like we react *mutatis mutandis* against the public activity of Communists. Second, it is undeniable that the freedom of conscience and the freedom of religion for Jews and Saracens is recognized by Aquinas as well as by Eike von Repkow. What they could not conceive was that a Christian could become a "stubborn" heretic without a *mens rea*, in sticking to his convictions despite being better informed; this becomes clear by Aquinas' comparing a stubborn heretic to a counterfeiter; we, too, do not assume that a counterfeiter could suffer from an invincible error of conscience and have no *mens rea*. Similes even on wise men— see the present dissent over the insurmountable wall between church and state—have a disturbing influence.

As to the relation of *jus naturale* and positive law, several points may be made. First, the classical *jus naturale* shouts for determination by positive law, which in peaceful times is, after all, much more often an approximation of *jus naturale* and justice than not; and men, though professed positivists, still hunger and thirst for justice, for the steady adaptation of the positive law to some ideals of justice. All too well known are jurists who profess positivism theoretically, but practically sacrifice both time and energy to call for changes in the law in the name of social justice and human dignity; not seldom they put to shame all too self-satisfied natural-law jurists.

Second, although some natural law jurists say that the *jus naturale* is not immediately valid law, most will say the opposite in accordance with the well-known practice of the common-law jurist in England (at least up to the supremacy of Parliament), a practice still found among not a few judges today in the United States. In this respect, decisions of the German courts, especially of the Federal Supreme Court and the Federal Constitutional Court after World War II, are interesting. In various decisions it is said that "the anti-Jewish Nürnberg laws and the law of confiscation, because of their unjust content and their violation of the basic demands of any legal order, are null and void and could never have any legitimate legal effect"; or "that certain laws, despite the fact that Hitler was legally competent to posit valid positive law, were *in se* null and void, if and insofar as in their *content* they violated the commands of natural law (*Naturrecht*), or the universally valid moral laws of Christian Western civilization." As to the inalienable rights, a decision says that these were valid even before the constitution was formally ordained; they were thus juridically valid also during the Nazi rule. Again, when a lower court declared that Gestapo officers, because they thought Hitler's laws had to be obeyed, had no *mens rea,* the Court said "That these accused should have misjudged the obligatory character of these (natural law) rules independent of all positive acknowledgment by authority . . . cannot be taken seriously."

Thus *jus naturale* is the foundation for legitimate authority, limiting it within a frame determined by its prohibitive rules. It is the basis for the obligation of those subject to authority, but it is at the same time the critical norm that empowers them to legitimate resistance against a once legitimate authority that, by grave violations of the common good, has become tyranny, not mere dictatorship. One should not under-estimate what it practically meant when Bodinus or Suárez said that even the sovereign monarch is bound by divine positive law as a Christian and by *lex naturale* and *jus naturale* as human authority; no divine-right theory here. Thus, one of the grave problems of ethics and law, namely, why free men should obey a not-infallible human authority, is brought nearer to solution. Rousseau tried it by an identification: the right will of the citizen as part of the sovereign people is identical with the general will, so that each obeys ultimately only himself.

The *jus naturale* is not a closed system nor a finished code. Renaud, disciple of Hauriou, speaks of a "*jus naturale* with progressive content"; Jacques Leclercq of Louvain speaks of an expanding knowledge of it. See, for instance, the development of the idea of social justice, the necessity to reformulate the doctrine of the just war under our present circumstances, and so on. The natural law is not simply datum—it is also a perpetual task to be realized and refined.

NOTES

1. Emil Brunner, *Das Gebot und die Ordnungen*, p. 657; and *Gerechtigkeit*, pp. 57, 246, *et al.*

2. Brunner, *Gerechtigkeit*, pp. 104, 319 (note 34).

3. Richard Hauser, *Autorität und Macht*, p. 193.

4. *Oberste Rechtsgrundsätze*, pp. 61–112; *Grundzüge der Rechtsphilosophie*, pp. 170–200.

B

The Myth of Natural Law

KAI NIELSEN

New York University

NATURAL MORAL LAW conceptions, grounded as they traditionally have been on metaphysical or theological principles, are
myth-eaten and they ought to be discarded; aseptic, demythologized conceptions of "natural law," like those set forth by
Professor Hart in his *The Concept of Law,* are essentially
sound and are fundamental in displaying the moral foundations of legal systems. Yet we must also come to understand
that assent to the fundamental rules of human conduct that
Hart notes is compatible with an acceptance of a thorough
ethical relativism or conventionalism. I would like here to
back up these controversial claims. In the first sections of this
essay I shall critically examine some defenses, including Professor Rommen's defense, of traditional conceptions of natural
law; and in the last section I shall set forth a qualified defense
of a completely demythologized version of "natural law." (I
shall argue, however, that it should not be called "law.")

I

Professor Rommen rightly points out that, in their long
history, natural law conceptions have undergone "shifting interpretations" and have suffered from ambiguous statement. Yet
he claims that it is possible to state the classical natural law
doctrines in a satisfactory form—a form that will be sufficiently free from conceptual confusion to enable us to accept
them as a necessary foundation for both our moral lives and

our legal systems. It does not seem to me that Professor Rommen or, for that matter, anyone else has succeeded in doing that.

Professor Rommen has indeed, made some tolerably interesting points—points that will enable the natural law theorist to avoid some of the *peripheral* objections to natural law, but he has not faced up to, or perhaps even seen, the crucial conceptual or epistemological difficulties that surround such conceptions. Rommen rightly reminds us that the natural law "is not a closed system nor a finished code." The human animal (within limits, at least) changes, and his social conditions change. With this change the natural law, although remaining in certain fundamental respects unalterable, can change, too, or at least our knowledge of it can change.[1] We should not look at the natural law as a kind of axiomatic system; we cannot derive from the fundamental principles of the natural law the concrete principles of action or develop a legal code that will show us, to use his example, that a jury trial and 12 jurors is a demand of the natural moral law.

This kind of expectation is indeed ingenuous, and where such a defense of natural law is made, such natural law conceptions are no doubt functioning as an ethnocentric defense of the *status quo*. So far I am in agreement with Rommen. Positive laws and moral claims must, on a position like the one Rommen is defending, be in accord with the natural law, but they need not, and often cannot, be derived from it. As Rommen puts it, natural law claims to be "transhistorical"; it "does not propose a whole code of law of logically derived, more and more concrete and minute legal rules for all fields of human social life."

Yet in interpreting natural law in this way so as to make it more nearly compatible with what we have learned about man from the study of cultural anthropology and with what we have learned about the nature of moral reasoning, we lose what for many is the deepest appeal of the natural law. Any man who is reasonably thoughtful and tolerably nonevasive about himself and others will find that thinking about specific

moral problems and problems of social policy is a very difficult
and often a very messy thing. Quite apart from the stock philosophical difficulties, there are often—and I would say typically
—deep perplexities about how we are to act. We thirst, no
doubt immaturely, for some sure guide, some certain set of
rational principles, that anywhere and at any time will lift
this anxiety-arousing perplexity from our shoulders and give
us, at least in certain essentials, a sure guide as to how we
ought to live and die and how we ought to order our society.
Natural law seemed to give us such a guide; it seemed to provide us with a rational foundation for such a certitude on
fundamental moral matters. But there is a fly in the ointment.
To give natural moral law conceptions a ghost of a chance
of being intellectually respectable, we must relativize them
along the lines Rommen indicates. Yet when this is done the
natural law loses much of its allure and loses its apparent advantage over, say, a pragmatic moral theory such as John
Dewey's. If a *"jus naturale more geometrico* is scarcely possible" and if we must rely on the judgment and wisdom of the
jurist and moral agent, we will lose that certainty, that abso-
luteness that natural moral law conceptions seemed to provide.

   To this it might be replied: "But in essentials we still have
a sure guide. The basic principles of the natural moral law are
self-evident in themselves and will provide a certain limit—a
limit free from the vicissitudes of time—to what can man justly
do to man and to what can legitimately be said to be law."
But can it? Let us see. For Aquinas and the classical natural law
tradition the primary natural law, from which all others are to
be derived, is 'good to be done and evil to be avoided' (*bonum
est faciendum, malum vitandum*). But this is a tautology, an
analytic statement, and from an analytic statement or set of
analytic statements no substantive moral conclusions can possibly follow. If, as Father Victor White avers, "Nature, or rather
the rational creature's consciousness of his nature" tells him
good is to be done and evil is to be avoided, it still does not tell
him what to do.[2] Such a vacuous first principle could not possibly be the foundation for any morality or any legal system. It

cannot tell us *what* is good or *what* we ought to do or *what* is bad and wrong. All we are justified in concluding from this "capstone of the natural law" is that if we call something "good" then we must also say that, everything else being equal, it is to be done or sought. But this bit of information about our linguistic behavior can hardly function as a basis for an objective ethic, when man, with his pervasive *Daseinssorge*, seeks to discover a foundation for his moral life and a basis for a moral criticism of law. The most brutal and depraved Nazi could wholeheartedlly and honestly assent to such a "principle." It is compatible with any and every moral code. We indeed get certainty here at the very base of the natural moral law, but only at the price of utter vacuity. There is also an emptiness about the principle Rommen states as "Never act against the common good of any of these societies, but help to realize it." Until we know *what* is good we do not know what to do or to refrain from doing. Perhaps shoving Jews in gas chambers was for the common good of Germany? Similarly, if we say, as Father White has, that "I can see . . . by the very fact that I am endowed with reason, that I ought to act reasonably," we have *not* made a moral discovery. "I ought to act reasonably" is another vacuous utterance. We make what Wittgenstein called "a grammatical remark" when we say that a moral agent should do what, in the circumstances in question, is the reasonable thing to do; for we cannot say that it is the reasonable thing to do if we are not also willing to grant that it is the thing to do in the circumstances in question. "I grant that this is through and through the reasonable thing to do, but what should I do?" is a logical oddity.

With what are incorrectly called the "primary conclusions" of such "basic moral principles" we do, however, get *some* content, some substantive moral claims. (I say they are incorrectly called 'primary conclusions,' for substantive moral conclusions cannot be derived from nonsubstantive premises.) Some of them— 'Life ought to be preserved,' 'One's integrity and property ought to be protected,' and 'Man ought to propagate his kind in a nonincestuous way'—are, as Mead and Linton have pointed out, accepted as moral norms in all known societies.[3] In all known societies sexual unions between mother-son, father-daughter, and brother-sister are forbidden. In those few societies where there are, for certain very definite purposes, sanctioned but carefully limited exceptions, they are, as Miss Mead points out, clearly treated as exceptions.[4] Similarly, she points out, in every known society there is some institution of private property, some condemnation of unjustified killing, and some regulation of sexual relations between spouses.

These ways of regulating behavior are panhuman (though this does not by itself definitively establish they are good) but, as Mead also realizes, such an overall cross-cultural agreement is compatible with radically different and conflicting specific practices. For some justified killing (morally approved killing) includes killing unwanted infants and the aged; for some it includes killing one's political enemies and races or ethnic groups that are disapproved of; for others it includes the killing of members of other tribes to collect their skulls and make a fine roast; but for others all such killing is plainly murder. For some, fidelity to one's wife entails sleeping with her and her alone; for others, it permits and sometimes even involves sleeping with various other people, male and female. The man in a moral quandary about conventionalism in morals wants to know something more specific than 'Sexual behavior should be regulated in some way,' 'Some kinds of killing ought to be prohibited,' and the like. He wants to know, for example, whether his society's code about these matters would be better if it were more like the Swedes and less like the Irish or if killing of deformed babies is justified. The old, if you will, ethnocentric conceptions of natural law seemed to provide reasonably unequivocal answers to these things—answers that presumably gave a rational underpinning to Christian and sometimes specifically Catholic moral beliefs.[5] In relativizing the theory so as to make it at all adequate to meet what was genuine in the conventionalist's challenge, the natural moral law has been so watered down that it can no longer serve as a support for such beliefs. It avoids the Charybdis of ethno-centrism, only to fall into the Scylla of ethical relativism. A good Nazi or a Communist could, with a minimal amount of dialectic ingenuity, show that his moral code was compatible with such nonethnocentric primary and secondary precepts of the natural moral law.

If to this it is replied, 'This only shows that a knowledge of the natural law is buried in the hearts of all normal people' (presumably some Nazis were in some sense normal), then I will reply that it also clearly demonstrates that such concep-tions cannot provide a basis for a moral criticism of the law or an objective and rational foundation for morality.

II

The above criticisms, concessive as they are to traditional natural law conceptions, do not really get to the root of the difficulties. There are deeper underlying difficulties that, I believe, show the classical doctrine of natural law to be a thor-oughly confused conception. In his defense of natural law Rommen claims to be setting forth the epistemological and metaphysical foundations of natural law, but I can find no clear statement of them in his essay, let alone a defense or justification of them, that in any way attempts to meet the epistemological and conceptual difficulties that at least appear to be endemic to this position.

Rommen rightly enough tells us that natural law is not just a catalog of natural rights that, existing in a state of nature, were taken over into society, nor is natural law something that is temporally before the positive legal order. Rather, natural law is thought to be "in" the positive legal order when-ever the latter has any genuine claim to validity. It claims "to be transhistorical, but not ahistorical because it is metaphysi-cal." It is "the higher law above the positive law" and it is "directed to the realization of justice in and by the positive legal order." It is that part of "social ethics that gives to the positive legal order and to legal authority established by it the power to obligate the consciences of the citizen; at the same time it gives to the conscience of the citizen obligated by authority the enduring critical standards by which to decide . . . when and under what circumstances authority loses its legitimacy and the obligation thereby ceases."

Such a description does little to help the man perplexed about natural law. We do not know what Rommen intends by 'metaphysical.' What is a "metaphysical reality," and are there any such realities, and how could a law of the sort that prescribes a certain kind of human conduct possibly be a metaphysical reality? We need to be told exactly what this "reality" is and, since it is not part of the legal system, we need an explanation of how it could be a law, let alone a law that is the foundation of all law. And what is intended by a "higher law" or an "unwritten law"? In what sense could such principles be laws? Why not simply claim that they are fundamental moral rules or principles to which all law ought to conform? These and a host of questions like them come immediately to mind, but they are left completely untouched by Rommen.

At one point he talks of a "metaphysically necessary *bona*, or values" dialectically related to human nature. One need not be a positivist or even an antimetaphysician to complain about vagueness here. Yet it is just by the use of such an undefined, completely unexplicated phrase that Rommen seeks to show that the basic principles of the natural law are not vacuous formulas. But we can do nothing at all with this until he explicates for us what 'a metaphysically necessary *bona*' is. How does it differ from an ordinary *bona* or from a logically necessary bona? And what, by the way, is a logically necessary good?— or even a necessary good? And how do we know that there are any?—or *do* we know that there are? Again a host of questions of this sort spring to mind—questions that Rommen seems completely oblivious of—but until we make some start on questions like these and until we make some start on the questions I asked at the end of the paragraph before this one, no defense of such classical natural law theories has even been seriously attempted, much less justified.

III

In Aquinas we have what, at a certain level, at least, is an admirably straightforward statement of natural law. Let us briefly look into the case he and some of his most astute contemporary defenders have made for the classical doctrine of the natural moral law. At the outset it is important to keep steadfastly in mind that Aquinas' theory here is, in Father Kossell's phrase, "deeply rooted in metaphysics and theology." [6] It makes sense only on the assumption that the universe is purposive and that there is a divinely providential government of creatures. If there is no God or if we have only the God of the Deist, the classical natural law theory is absurd, for there will then be no providential governing of creation, no plan for man of which the natural law is a part. For Aquinas, the natural law is that part of the eternal law that man can apprehend with his unaided reason. Men do not create this law; it is not a rule or principle or fiat they have proclaimed. Human beings are not the measure of the natural law, they simply apprehend what emanates from God's reason. But still it must be an ordinance, a directive principle, and this implies that someone must issue it. It could not just be there in the nature of things. And this fits very well with Aquinas' thinking, for a law, where we are talking about the laws regulating human conduct and not "laws of nature," is for Aquinas "an ordinance of reason for the common good, promulgated and emanating from him who has care of the community." [7] The eternal law (*lex aeterna*) is the sum of God's ordinances. It is an expression of Divine Reason directing all God's creatures. The natural law is the rational creature's apprehension of this law; that is, it is his grasp of the mind of God. We, of course, now see as through a glass darkly, but we still supposedly have some natural knowledge of how we ought to govern our lives, and this knowledge is an apprehension of God's plans for us. The rest of God's ordinances, the so-called divine law, can only be known through revelation.

Here we have the natural law in its full theological re-

galia—a regalia that Copelston, Maritain, and (if I understand
him correctly) Fuller regard as essential for the viability of
natural law.[8] But there we have some very questionable and,
to put it mildly, excessively vague notions. We must remember
in this context that Aquinas, unlike Scotus and Ockham,
thought that God's intellect is logically prior to His will. This
is supposed to entail that goodness is not *simply* an expression
of divine fiat, is not simply an expression of God's will (a kind
of theological noncognitivism), but is somehow an attribute
of God's very reason and, as a "transcendental attribute" of
that necessary being that is God, a kind of necessary reality.
God cannot be a logically necessary being, for a logically
necessary being is a self-contradiction, but could anything that
is properly called 'God' be merely a physical necessity either?
And again, if we say God is "metaphysically necessary," what
have we said? This is not, of course, the place to go into natural theology, but such classical accounts of natural law are
fully dependent not only on the intelligibility of natural theology and "God talk" in general, but on the truth of the central claims of such a natural theology. For such a natural law
theory to be justified, God, in fact, must exist; and it must
be a further fact that God's nature is essentially what Aquinas
says it is. But the claims, first, that such natural theology is in-
telligible, let alone true, and, second, that God exists is a fact
are, to put it very, very conservatively, debatable claims. Yet
traditional concepts of natural moral law are completely dependent for their viability on the soundness of such claims.
Surely this is a very shaky foundation on which to rest such
claims. There is a serious question as to whether 'God exists'
or 'God's intellect is logically prior to His will' have truth conditions—that is to say, their very *factual* intelligibility, not to
mention their truth or even their probability, is seriously in
question.

  Before any sustained defense of such traditional conceptions of natural law can be made, we must give some account
of such conceptions and some account of such expressions as
'Divine Subsisting Reason.' After all, to put it quite bluntly,

do we understand, and can we at all show, what it would be like for it to be true or false or even probably true or false for there to be an ordinance of God's reason promulgated by God for the common good? What, logically speaking, would count as a verification or even a confirmation or disconfirmation of such a statement? Sometimes verificationist arguments are out of place, but here they seem to me quite apposite; and if it is claimed they are not apposite, we, at the very least, need to be told exactly why they are not apposite. Presumably it is a fact that there is a God and that He promulgated natural laws. Well, if it is, we very much need to know what *counts* as evidence for such an assertion. But what evidence have we been given for this and what evidence could be given for this? What would evidence look like here? Before such natural law conceptions can be successfully defended, we need unequivocal answers to such stock questions.

IV

Someone might reply that if we take sufficient note of the purposive behavior of the human animal, we will find sufficient evidence for the natural law. To discover purpose, to see what the end of human living is, is just another way of apprehending something of the mind of God, and to do that is to have a grasp of the natural law (God's ordinances of reason that may be grasped by man's unaided intellect). The natural law, as Father White puts it, "is the rational creature's own knowledge of his purpose as manifested in his nature and in the exigencies of his nature, and of the manner in which that end of his nature is to be attained by the means at its disposal." [9]

It is plain enough that there is an "end directedness" in the activities of men. Men have aims and goals and purposes; they act to achieve certain ends. If our lives were devoid of purpose, if man did not have a purpose, then it would be false that there is a natural law; but we can see that human life is purposive, so we have good grounds for accepting natural law. As Professor Bourke has remarked, in the course of taking me to task for an earlier criticism I made of the Thomistic doctrine of the natural law, modern anthropology supports "the Thomistic notion of a purposive human nature." Anthropologists see man "as a very distinctive human nature." [10] Man is the only culture-producing animal.

There are multiple confusions here, and when they are untangled a bit, we will see that such considerations do not constitute evidence for the natural moral law. It may well be true that men have a certain nature—that is to say, that there is a property or some set of properties that all men and only men—or at least all and only adult normal men—in fact possess. A language and a culture may be just such properties. But this does not entail that man, like an artifact, has some essential nature, some function that he was cut out or made to achieve. The word 'man' is not so circumscribed that there is some function or role a being must achieve in order to be properly denominated a man.[11] If some creature with a body exactly like ours lived in isolation in the woods and behaved in other respects like we do but belonged to no tribe, we would not be justified in refusing to call such a creature a man; and if beings lived together and did many of the characteristic things that we do but did not speak, we still would not be justified in refusing to call them men.[12] We can say what pencils or screwdrivers are for; we can say what waiters and bookies are for; but we cannot in some plain and uncontroversial fashion say what man *qua* man is for. (To say man exists to worship God is to beg the very question at issue.)

Human beings have purposes; they often act for an end in the sense that they have certain goals and aims. But what evidence do we have that man has a *function* or some *final cause* that, like a robot, he was programed to achieve? That there are certain properties that men and only men have does nothing to show that men were made to achieve or realize these properties or any other state; that men form goals and have aims does nothing to show that men were cut out for a purpose.

In fact, as Kurt Baier has shown in his inaugural lecture "The Meaning of Life," there is a semantic confusion about 'purpose' lurking here.[13] When we show the purpose of a stapler or a refrigerator, we show what it was designed to do; when we show the purpose of a liver or a toenail in the bodily economy, we show its functions in the smooth running of the body; when we show the purpose or purposes of having postmen or lawyers we exhibit their role or roles in human society. In all those cases 'purpose' does roughly the same job. To indicate the purpose is to exhibit the function or role of the thing or person in question. But when a student says 'My purpose in taking this course is to learn more about modern physics' or when a woman says 'My purpose in coming here is to see about a job,' 'purpose' has a very different use. Here it marks the aim or intention of the person in question. It is not at all used to exhibit the role or function of people. My thesis is simply this: the purposive behavior and the purpose that is evident in human living is of this latter sort. Men have desires and they form intentions; they seek out certain things; their behavior is goal directed. In that sense there most certainly is purposive behavior. But this purposive behavior does not at all show that men have the kind of 'nature' that natural law theorists talk about or that men have a function or a final end in virtue of which they might, as Rommen puts it, realize or actualize themselves.[14] That there are purposes *in* life does not at all show or even suggest that there is a purpose *to* life or a puprose *of* life or that man was made *for* a certain purpose. But it is this last sort of purpose that we need in order to show that there are natural moral laws. But as far as I can see there is not a shred of evidence that man has a purpose in this last metaphysical or theological sense. In short, the kind of purposive behavior that is evident in human living can exist in a Godless world. 'There is purpose in human living' does not imply, contextually or otherwise, that there is a God, Logos, or a natural law. The other, puzzling, "conception" of purpose might involve such a metaphysico-theological commitment, but it is not at all evident that there is such purpose and the

factual *intelligibility* of such a conception is itself in serious
question. Since we do not know what would count as evidence
for such purpose, we can hardly cite it as possible evidence for
the natural law.

V

Let us, however, concede for the purposes of this discussion that God's in His heaven and that He has made pronouncements of the kind the classical natural law theorist says
he has; let us also concede that somehow we can discover or
intuit that man was constructed for a certain purpose. This
by itself would still not enable man to simply discover or apprehend that he ought to act in a certain way, for such "discoveries" would still simply be *facts* about man and about
"what there is," and we still face Hume's hurdle: we cannot
derive an ought from an is; from purely factual premises no
normative conclusions can be validly deduced. So even if there
are natural laws of the kind the Thomist and classical natural
law theorist talks about, it still does not follow that they have
provided us with an adequate foundation for a rational ethic.
In short, the natural law theorist has committed something
very much akin to what Moore called the "naturalistic fallacy."
Suppose to avoid this difficulty it is argued that to ascribe
some purpose to man or to things is to give one to understand
that whatever such an ascription is made about *ought* to function in a certain way; that is to say, suppose it is denied that to
ascribe *purposes* to people or things is to *merely* make a factual
statement. But if such an argument is made, the natural law
theorist will be saddled with still another difficulty; if this is
the case about ascriptions of 'purpose,' then it cannot be the
case that we can discover what we ought to do simply from
apprehending what is the case, for in making an ascription of
purpose we have already made a moral judgment in which we
have of necessity brought into play our own conception of
what ought to be or what ought to be done. We cannot discover or apprehend what we ought to do from observing the

behavior of men, from observing what the universe is like, or from hearing what God commands.[15]

To the general claim that natural law theories have not gone over Hume's hurdle, it can be justly replied that one can rightly go around it, for not all moral reasoning is deductive; any non-prejudiced account of the logic of moral reasoning will make it apparent, as Stuart Hampshire and others have shown, that factual statements are characteristically held to be relevant reasons for certain moral claims.[16] A tells B that B ought to help his wife more around the house. B asks why and A reminds B that his wife is pregnant and that in that state women get fatigued very easily. J claims we ought to send military aid to India. S asks why and J replies that China will eventually overrun India if we do not. Characteristically we support our moral claims with factual statements, though, as Hume has shown, the factual statements by themselves never *entail* the moral claim. The discoveries we make of God's ordinances do not enable us to deduce what we ought to do, but they do constitute our ultimate good reasons for acting as we do.

The above attack on the deductionist model seems to me well taken, but it will not help out the defender of the natural moral law. When we judge that a certain factual statement or a set of factual statements F is a good reason for a certain moral conclusion E, we always use certain canons of relevance, in virtue of which F is judged to be a good reason for E. But when these canons of relevance are themselves explicitly stated, they will be found to invoke substantive normative principles, and in the nature of the case, there will be some substantive normative principles used in our judgments of relevance that will *not* be derived from, or even made in accordance with, other higher-order substantive normative principles. There will be at least one substantive normative principle that will not be derived from another substantive normative principle, and this principle cannot be derived from factual statements or analytic statements. Thus in making moral judgments, such judgments cannot be obtained merely from the apprehension of natural laws. In the nature of the case, man must, in part at least, be "the measure of all things moral." For any fact —metaphysical or otherwise—to be a good reason for a moral judgment, we must have at least one underived substantive normative principle in virtue of which our factual or "factual-metaphysical statement" becomes a good reason for the moral conclusion in question.[17]

The classical natural law theorist wants to give us an objective foundation for an appraisal of legal systems and ways of life that will be grounded in the nature of man and God— a set of principles that man can discover simply from knowing his own nature and from his knowledge of God. I have argued that such a theory is unsound because (1) there is no evidence that there is such a God or that man was made for a purpose; (2) such natural law conceptions are compatible with a thoroughgoing ethical relativism and thus will not provide the foundation for law and morals it purports to provide; and (3) that even if there is such a God and man was made for such a purpose, no moral conclusions could be derived or grounded on such "metaphysical facts." It is for reasons of this sort and other reasons that I have not had space to develop here that I have contended that the classical conceptions of the natural moral law are myth eaten.

VI

Yet it would be very odd indeed if a conception that has played such a central role in human thought should be a sheer confusion. Like Hart, I believe that there is a common-sense core to natural law conceptions. If we demythologize them in the way Hart does, if we strip them of their metaphysical and theological plumage, this perfectly sound common-sense core can be revealed.

What are the elementary truths, important for an understanding of both morality and law, that are embedded in such natural law conceptions? If we start with the simple fact that most men most of the time wish to survive, we can come to appreciate the point of having at least some of these "natural laws." Given survival as an aim, morality and law, as a matter of fact, must have a certain content. Without such a content law and morality "could not forward the minimum purpose of survival." We can see, given the *fact* of human vulnerability to attack, that any social arrangement that is to be viable must have some prohibitions against indiscriminate killing and the infliction of bodily harm. Furthermore, given the fact of a rough equality of strength, agility, and intellectual capacity among men, some mutual forbearances and compromises are also plainly a necessity of social living; and given the fact of limited resources among human beings, where some things are won by human struggle, some minimal concept of property and some concept of respect for property is indispensable in any society that is to be viable. "If crops are to grow, land must be secure from indiscriminate entry, and food must, in the intervals between its growth or capture and consumption, be secure from being taken by others. At all times and places life itself depends on these minimal forbearances." [18] Furthermore, the universal recognition of the necessity of keeping promises has its rationale in the need for such public self-binding performances "in order to create a minimum form of confidence in the future behaviour of others." [19] Without such confidence social living, plainly crucial to human survival, would hardly be possible.

Here we can see a quite secular, quite mundane rationale for certain of those rules and social arrangements that have been called, mistakenly, I believe, "natural laws." No society could ignore them and remain viable; no system of law or morals could in any thorough way subvert them and still serve the universally desired aim of survival. In stressing the importance of these truisms the natural law tradition has, in Hart's words, shown "a core of good sense." If to defend natural law is to defend such a claim, then natural law is indeed defendable. To remain viable any society must give allegiance to such practices. It is worthwhile to learn from Mead, Linton, and Redfield that all known societies do in fact give allegiance to such conceptions, and it is even more important to see, as Hart, Toulmin, and Baier have been at pains to show, that such practices are not simply the thing done but have a rationale.[20] We must not forget, however, that cross-cultural acceptance of such general practices is perfectly compatible with the existence of sharply conflicting moral principles.[21] After all, even under Communism there are certain kinds of property rights.

I would, however, like to enter a caveat concerning this limited defense of natural law. It is a mistake to call these principles of conduct "laws." These fundamental moral principles and practices—practices that any social organization must acknowledge if it is to be viable—may, as they are in our Constitution, be *made* a part of the law. But to *be law* they must be so incorporated into a legal system. Indeed, morally good or just laws must acknowledge such moral principles, but this does not make them laws; and that a society that persistently flouts such principles cannot long survive does not make them laws either. This last consideration only shows that a society that did not live in accordance with such practices could not survive, and thus, as a trivial point of logic, its legal system could not survive either; it would not at all show that its legal system was not a legal system.

It is plain enough—look at Rome, Germany, South Africa—that there have been countries with legal systems that did not even extend all those minimal protections and benefits afforded by the principles of conduct we have called "natural laws," to *all* peoples within their jurisdiction. From the moral point of view we must criticize such systems, and by political action we must seek to put an end to such systems. But, as Hart has well said, this "should not obscure the fact that municipal legal systems, with their characteristic structure of primary and secondary rules, have long endured though they have flouted these principles of justice." [22]

Legal obligations and moral obligations are plainly not identical. A man might be convinced that he has no moral obligation at all to pay his taxes, since tax money is being spent on the construction of nuclear weapons, and yet he can openly acknowledge that he is legally bound to do so. His moral position may be a hopelessly confused one, but he is not saying something unintelligible. There is no contradiction or logical oddity, there is not even a deviation from a linguistic regularity, in saying 'This law is too iniquitous to be obeyed, but all the same it is the law.' Austin was surely right when he said "the existence of a law is one thing, its merit or demerit another." The whole tradition of natural law, secular or theological, tends to obscure these things. It seems to me that in concluding I can do no better than to quote Hart, from whom I have so shamelessly peculated in this section:

> So long as human beings can gain sufficient co-operation from some to enable them to dominate others, they will use the forms of law as one of their instruments. Wicked men will enact wicked rules which others will enforce. What surely is most needed in order to make men clear sighted in confronting the official abuse of power, is that they should preserve the sense that the certification of something as legally valid is not conclusive of the question of obedience, and that, however great the aura of majesty or authority which the official system may have, its demands must in the end be submitted to a moral scrutiny.[23]

Instead of saying with Augustine, *"Lex inuista non est lex,"* we should say that there will be times when the law of some brutalitarianism is such that all moral men should resist it, should refuse to obey it. These fundamental moral principles that support a just legal system *need* not be laws at all, and above all they *cannot* be the ordinances of Big Daddy's reason promulgated for the common good, for such a conception is thoroughly mythical.

NOTES

1. This point has been even more forcefully stressed by other knights of the natural moral law. See Jacques Leclercq, "Natural

Law and the Unknown," *Natural Law Forum*, VII (1962), 1–15; Charles Fay, "Natural Moral Law in the Light of Cultural Relativism and Evolutionism," *Anthropological Quarterly*, XXXIV (October, 1961), 177–91, and "Toward A Thomistic Anthropological View of the Evolution or Obligation," *Natural Law Forum*, VII (1962), 38–53. It is, however, a mistake to say, as Leclercq does, that although the actual content of the natural law remains invariable, our *knowledge* of the content of the natural law must always remain variable. If we cannot know a natural law without a changing, variable content, then we cannot, to put the point conservatively, have any grounds or justification at all for asserting that the content of the natural law actually is invariable. We can, however, make an even stronger point against Leclercq. Given his argument, we have excellent grounds for claiming that his contention is factually meaningless, for it involves what *purports* to be a factual statement—for example, 'The content of the natural law is permanent'—that, on Leclercq's own showing, is completely devoid of truth conditions. But where 'The content of the natural law is permanent' is devoid of truth conditions, it is factually meaningless.

2. Victor White, "Word of God and Natural Law," *Writers on Ethics*, ed. Joseph Katz *et al.*, (Princeton: Princeton University Press, 1962), p. 481.

3. Margaret Mead, "Some Anthropological Considerations Concerning Natural Law," *Natural Law Forum*, VI (1961), 51–64, and Ralph Linton, "The Problem of Universal Values," *Method and Perspective in Anthropology*, edited by R. F. Spence.

4. Margaret Mead, *op. cit.*, p. 52.

5. Not all Catholic thinkers are as hesitant as Rommen and Leclercq are in "drawing conclusions" from the natural law that support specifically Catholic doctrines. For one recent example of such an ethnocentric use of natural law conceptions, see C. B. Daly, "A Criminal Lawyer on the Sanctity of Life," *Irish Theological Quarterly*, (October, 1958) pp. 330–66; (January, 1959) pp. 23–55; (July, 1959) pp. 231–72.

6. Clifford G. Kossel, "The Moral View of Thomas Aquinas, *Encyclopedia of Morals*, ed. Vergilius Ferm (New York: Philosophical Library, 1956), p. 12.

7. Thomas Aquinas, *Summa Theologica* I–II, Qq, 90, article IV.

8. Fuller makes it plain enough that he is not an adherent of

the Catholic faith, but certain of his remarks in his dispute with Hart would most naturally be interpreted as supporting the claim that a viable theory of natural law needs such a theological backing. See Lon L. Fuller, "Positivism and Fidelity to Law," *Society, Law and Morality,* F. A. Olafson ed., (New York: 1961), pp. 494–5.

9. Victor White, *op. cit.,* p. 481.

10. Vernon J. Bourke, "Natural Law, Thomism and Professor Nielsen," *Natural Law Forum,* V (1960), 116.

11. Stuart Hampshire, "Can There Be a General Science of Man?", *Commentary,* XXIV (1957), 164–67. Sometimes the words 'man,' 'human,' and the like have a distinctively moral or normative use, as in 'Hitler was scarcely human,' 'No human being could bring himself to act as he did,' 'Be a man!' or 'He's a real *Mensch.*' Here creatures who in a biological sense are clearly human beings are said not to be human. Where 'man' or 'being human' or 'being scarcely human' function in this moralistic way, we cannot build our moral knowledge on our purely factual knowledge of man and man's relation to God and the world, for used in this way, the very word 'man' presupposes a prior and independent knowledge of good and evil.

12. This is not, however, as simple as it may seem. As a matter of brute fact, many of the characteristic things human beings do involve speech; take this away and there would be little distinctively human behavior left. Yet there could be enough for it to be true that if creatures really acted in this way and still did not speak, we would still be justified in saying they were human.

13. Kurt Baier, "The Meaning of Life," (Canberra, Australia, 1957). In the above contexts, see also my "On Human Nature and Morality," *Social Research,* XXIX (Summer, 1962), 170–76, and "Conventionalism in Morals and The Appeal to Human Nature," *Philosophy and Phenomenological Research,* XXIII (December, 1962), 217–31.

14. Furthermore, such an appeal to self-realization runs afoul all the standard difficulties inherent in self-realizationist theories. John Hospers gives a clear statement of them in his *Human Conduct,* (New York: Harcourt Brace and Co., 1961), pp. 79–81. Rommen appears to be completely unaware of such elementary difficulties in such an appeal.

15. I have argued for this in some detail in my "Some Remarks on the Independence of Morality from Religion," *Mind,* LXX

(April, 1961), 175–86, and "Morality and God," *Philosophical Quarterly*, XII (April, 1962), 129–37. Note also, in this context, A. C. Ewing's, "The Autonomy of Ethics," *Prospect for Metaphysics*, ed. I. T. Ramsey, (London: Philosophical Library, 1961), pp. 33–49.

16. Stuart Hampshire, "Fallacies in Moral Philosophy," *Problems of Ethics*, ed. R. E. Dewey, *et al.* (New York: Macmillan, 1961), pp. 435–50; and Stanley French, "Hume's Hurdle," *Dialogue*, I. (March, 1963), 390–99.

17. I have developed this side of my critique of classical natural law conceptions in sections VIII and IX of my "An Examination of the Thomistic Theory of Natural Moral Law," *Natural Law Forum*, IV (1959), 63–71. Bourke has criticized my arguments here, but his criticisms seem to me to be vitiated by confusions and misunderstandings. Those who argue that we cannot "derive an ought from an is" (to put it in slogan form) need not be committed, as I certainly am not, to a Humean "atomism of sense-data." One can accept, which seems to me plain enough, that there are real interconnections between events without committing oneself to the belief that *moral* statements can be derived from purely *factual* statements. 'That Fathers tend to like their daughters more than their sons' is a complex factual statement capable of confirmation or disconfirmation but 'That sons owe something to their fathers that they do not owe to other men' is not a factual statement capable of confirmation or disconfirmation, but a moral statement. There are no facts corresponding to such moral statements, and Bourke is mistaken in thinking that moral terms "name complex relations." What does 'ought' or 'good' name? In 'A is under B,' 'under' does not stand for an individual, but 'A is under B' is verifiable enough—but what would verify 'A ought to help B'? 'Under' does not stand for a sense constituent, but what it stands for is clearly ostensively teachable. But what does 'ought' stand for? What relation does it name? For any relation mentioned, could we not ask if X ought to have that relation? Since this always remains an open question, does this not indicate that 'ought' is not a name for that relation? For Bourke's arguments, see Vernon J. Bourke, *op. cit.*, pp. 118–19, and "Metaethics and Thomism," *An Étienne Gilson Tribute*, (Milwaukee, Wisconsin: Marquette University Press 1960), pp. 26–27.

18. H. L. A. Hart, *The Concept of Law*, (Oxford: Oxford University Press, 1961), p. 192. See also, in this context, Marcus

Singer, "Hart's Concept of Law," *The Journal of Philosophy*, LX (April 11, 1963), 217–19.

19. Hart, *op. cit.*, p. 193.

20. Hart, *op. cit.;* Stephen Toulmin, *An Examination of the Place of Reason in Ethics*, (Cambridge: Cambridge University Press, 1948); and Kurt Baier, *The Moral Point of View*, (Ithaca: Cornell University Press, 1958). I have tried to do something of this sort in my "Appraising Doing the Thing Done," *The Journal of Philosophy*, LVII (November 24, 1960), 749–60.

21. Paul W. Taylor, "Social Science and Ethical Relativism," *The Journal of Philosophy*, LV (1958), 32–44.

22. Hart, *op. cit.*, p. 201.

23. *Ibid.*, pp. 205–6.

C

An Analysis of
"In Defense of Natural Law"

WOLFGANG FRIEDMANN
Columbia University Law School

PROFESSOR ROMMEN's concept of natural law is indeed a catholic one. He quotes with apparently equal approval Brunner's formulation that "The ideas of natural law . . . in the orders of creation impose themselves with objective necessity on Christian thinking in the form of these orders," postwar German judicial utterances that "certain laws, despite the fact that Hitler was legally competent to posit valid positive law, were *in se* null and void, if and insofar as in their content they violated the commands of natural law, or the universally valid moral laws of Christian Western civilization," or the essentially Thomistic formulation that "*Jus naturale* is that part of social ethics that gives to the positive legal order and to the legal authority established by it the power to obligate the consciences of the citizen; at the same time it gives to the conscience of the citizen obligated by authority the enduring critical standards by which to decide . . . when and under what circumstances authority loses its legitimacy and the obligation thereby ceases." In an adaptation of Hegel's formulation, natural law is "the substance which is immanent and the eternal which is present beneath the temporal and passing which appears."

Both the biological conception of natural order (*physis*), as used by the Sophists and by Ulpian [1] and the normative-rational concept of natural law, as an order imposed upon human beings as endowed with reason and the capacity to distinguish between good and evil, is accommodated within pro-

144

fessor Rommen's broad concept. But it seems that he also accepts Stammler's "Natural Law with a changing content," for he is clearly and emphatically opposed to a static concept of natural law. He praises and accepts the need "for the steady adaptation of the positive law to some ideal of justice." He approves of those who, whether they accept or reject natural law, "call for changes in the law in the name of social justice and human dignity."

The present commentator has not found it too easy to decide where Professor Rommen stands with regard to the determination of basic human rights by natural law. While he says, at the beginning of his paper, that natural law is not just a catalog of natural rights, he later enumerates a scale of human rights—based on the second table of the Decalogue—that corresponds rather closely to the usual enumeration of bills of rights: sanctity of the family and of life, prohibition of adultery and of theft—which means recognition of private and public property—integrity of person, both physical and intellectual (presumably this is what is meant by "freedom circumscribed in an expansive or contracting sphere of self-determination"): impartial justice, self-defense, personal honor, and so forth.

Those who know Professor Rommen's admirable *Natural Law* will interpret his exposition as an acceptance of a basic immutable order, derived from divine creation and the nature of man, as a being endowed with reason and a moral sense, in short, "human dignity," but permitting the greatest latitude in the adaptation of law to changing social needs. In this approach, Professor Rommen is not far removed from the philosophy of the late Pope John XXIII's great encyclical *Mater et Magistra.*

But Professor Rommen's catholicity goes even further than this. The most significant—and in a sense the most startling— of all of his contentions is surely his integration of existentialism into the ideology of natural law. "Thus, in ceaseless acting, the dynamic element of the term 'nature' (as compared to the more static concept of 'essence') comes out. The spontaneous self-understanding of myself as a human person shows me that I ought to realize, to actualize myself as a person in my free acts, internal ones and those affecting the world; in this, Aristotle, St. Thomas, Kant, and Nikolai Hartmann agree." Or again: "Become by your own acts that which you already are, realize evermore in your life what you as a free person are already destined to be; all these are implicit in the term *'natura humana,'* or *'humanitas'* ". For Professor Rommen this existentialist conception of man, as one who must realize in his life what as a free person he is destined to be, is compatible not only with the theology of St. Thomas, but apparently also with the philosophy of values of Max Scheler and Nikolai Hartmann. And why not include Heidegger, Jaspers, and, indeed, Sartre, the central theme of whose writings is certainly the realization of an individual's destiny by the freedom to choose?

But surely there are basic and absolutely decisive differences between the "existentialism" of a Thomas Aquinas, for whom the choice given to man between good and evil is firmly grounded in an objective order, as laid down partly in Scripture and partly in universal reason (as interpreted by the Church as the authoritative exponent of at least part of God's wisdom); the *Wert philosophie* of Scheler and Hartmann, which, building on Aristotle, has indeed recognized a scale of values but not—and here I strongly disagree with Professor Rommen—an absolute *content* of good and evil; and modern existentialism. For the existentialist, the human being is lonely, thrown into existence, with nothing to guide him but his freedom of choice, the yearning to develop himself, to unfold his destiny, to become what he is, unguided by God or an objective and compelling order.

Professor Rommen does not go quite so far as to include Hegel himself among the proponents of natural law, but he does include the neo-Hegelians who, while rejecting some of the master's more fantastic deductions from his philosophy of state and law (such as the demonstration that the hereditary and reactionary Prussian monarchy of his time was the dialectically necessary fulfillment of the absolute world spirit) accepted his main method and approach: the dialectic overcoming of opposites—both logically and historically—in a synthesis; this spurious elimination of the conflict of values, between authority and liberty, between state power and world order, between freedom and slavery—all this by the ingenious device (so clearly exposed by Benedetto Croce) of confusing logical opposites and historical and political contrasts. The results of this approach were demonstrated by modern fascism and National Socialism.

Professor Rommen's deeply humanitarian philosophy is indeed far removed from these perversions. But there is, I submit, a great danger in the attempt to eliminate the deep and abiding conflicts of values, by an all-too-elastic and all-embracing concept of *jus naturale.* That mankind yearns for absolute standards, especially in times of trouble and the undermining of accepted values, we will all accept. But we cannot escape the dilemma: that either the concept of natural law becomes so all-embracing that it seeks to comprise the most opposed and incompatible philosophies of life; or that, under the name and invocation of "nature," whether based on God, reason, the spirit of history, or whatever the beholder may select, it postulates one particular philosophy, one specific set of values that it seeks to adorn with the halo of universality.

Is there anything in the concept of "nature" that we may accept as truly basic and necessary to human life? In this commentator's view there is only one—and this is a philosophy shared by Aristotle and Bentham, by St. Thomas and Sartre, by Kant and Hegel: that man is a creature endowed with the capacity of reasoning as well as of choosing between alternative courses of action, rejecting those that by some standard he regards as "bad" and accepting those that by the same standards he accepts as "good." Perhaps we can deduce from this one practical consequence: that man cannot be a mere object of law, a chattel to be disposed of like an inanimate thing.[2] Hence, we may perhaps say that to treat human beings as things, without legal capacity, without legal powers and rights, or to dispose of them as raw material for fertilizers, is a denial

of human "nature." As we will see later, this does not necessarily solve the problem of natural law as a yardstick by which
Nazi crimes could be judged.

But even if we do accept this minimum of "nature," the
definition of man as a being endowed with reason and a sense
of values, we are left with conflicts between alternative values,
equally compatible with "nature," conflicts that are either
disguised or distorted by the invocation of natural law.

The remainder of this paper will be devoted to a brief
discussion of the application of "natural law" to some of the
vital problems of our time. That the theory of natural law must
stand the test of application to these hard problems of law is
surely in accord with Professor Rommen's approach to the
whole philosophy of natural law. It is also an elementary application of the appraisal of law as "practical," not "pure,"
reason. Law is the authoritative order of human behavior in
society. If natural law cannot give valid and compelling direc-
tives to such behavior, it is worthless.

OBEDIENCE TO STATE LAW AND THE
COMMANDS OF A HIGHER "NATURAL" LAW

Professor Rommen clearly supports—although he hardly
discusses—the various decisions, both of the inter-Allied war
crimes tribunals and of postwar German courts, holding that
certain Nazi laws, such as the anti-Jewish Nuremberg laws, the
confiscation of Jewish property, or—as we must infer from a
reference to these decisions—the participation in measures
ordered by the state and directed to the extermination of
masses of Jews or other enemies of the Nazi regime, are null
and void as being contrary to a higher moral order, a "natural"
law.

We may accept that orders, legitimate under the positive
law of the Nazi regime, to exterminate or degrade in the most
barbaric fashion millions of human beings in gas ovens and
concentration camps, are an elementary offense against human
dignity. But two questions immediately arise: First, where is

the line to be drawn between laws so offensive to elementary human values as to be null and void and the vast number of other laws objectionable to Western Christian or any enlightened human civilization but less conspicuously barbarous or less widely accepted among different nations? The equivalent of the Nuremberg racial laws is still found in a number of state laws of the United States, and most conspicuously in the Republic of South Africa. The confiscation of the property of "enemies of the state" is a deplorable but widespread practice in our times, applied by states such as Burma, Cuba, Egypt, and Indonesia. It might be argued by some that the confiscation of private enemy (now former enemy) property by the victorious Allies after World Wars I and II is against natural law, since it extends the war between states to vindictive measures against the property of individuals. Or could it perhaps be said that the amendment to the Indian constitution that took away from the law courts the right to fix the proper amount of compensation payable to those whose property had been nationalized is against natural law? Is it null and void in the light of a higher order? Here we come to the basic weakness of natural law—that, once you open the gates, almost anything can be declared as contrary to natural law and order, according to the philosophy of the beholder. Not surprisingly, therefore, the defenders of capitalism and socialism, of nationalism and world order, of the right to revolution and the right to suppress revolution in the name of the established order, all can and do invoke natural law in their favor.

The second—and related—question is who decides whether natural law has been violated. The Nuremberg and Tokyo judgments, the many judgments given under the same rules in occupied Germany, and the postwar German judgments do not solve the questions: indeed, they illustrate the dilemma. The Nuremberg judgments, despite some rather vague references to natural law, essentially rely on the positive law binding them, that is, the power of government assumed by the Allied powers by virtue of the unconditional surrender of the German state. The Nuremberg judgments speak in the name of positivism applying a new and different law. That law responded infinitely more to the moral ideas of the great majority of mankind than the Nazi law that it had overthrown; it was, nevertheless, in the name of a new positive order that the tribunals could solve with relative ease the problem that law should have prevailed for those who had to make the choice between obedience and resistance. It is, of course, quite easy to say, under the shelter of the new order and backed by the authority of arms, military government, or a new constitution, that the accused should have acted in a certain manner. And whether such condemnation is justified in the name of some basic moral order or by the retroactivity of the new positive laws—a matter debated in the well-known controversy between Professors Fuller and Hart some years ago [3]—the real dilemma is not solved thereby. At what point did it become a legal—as distinct from a moral—duty for officials to refuse, at the risk of their jobs or perhaps of their liberty, to work in the drafting of annihilation statutes or of racially condemnable legislation? At what point did it become the duty of soldiers to risk being shot by their superiors rather than to execute barbarous orders leading to the extermination of civilians? Perhaps, nearly 20 years after the Nuremberg judgments, we would be a little more confident about these matters if the doctrine that state laws, contrary to elemental moral principles must be disobeyed—such as the launching of aggressive war, the killing of innocent civilians, legal measures depriving an individual of the ordinary rights and decencies common among civilized people—if the doctrine that such laws are null and void had been universally accepted by mankind. Such an assertion would be absurd. Only a few months ago the Chief Justice of England asserted, in a trial against newspaper reporters who had refused to disclose certain confidential information, that the duty toward the state was the highest duty of every citizen. What government, American, British, French, let alone Soviet, would accept the right of resistance against a "first strike" preventive nuclear attack on a potential enemy country? The conviction of the large majority of the German and Japanese war criminals can be justified as a response of the—fortunately victorious—powers to cruelty and devastation on an unprecedented scale. The elaborate procedures could be justified not as a genuine judicial process, but as the best means to disclose and bring to public attention the evidence of deeds that might otherwise have been left unrecorded. But to justify these convictions in the name of a universal natural law is an act of self-deception.

Personally I can see only one guideline to distinguish acts that must be condoned in the nexus of the still overwhelming legal authority of the state over the individual, and acts that deserve punishment. However, it is an obvious precondition that the objectionable order must have been overthrown and replaced by a new order that embodies the new values: this is the element of free moral choice. Here I agree with Rommen's existentialist approach, the emphasis on man as a being capable of deciding: applying this test, I do not find it possible to condemn in the name of natural or any other law the hundreds of thousands or millions of individuals who participated in the processes of aggression or maltreatment, by joining some organization of the state, by fighting or continuing with their ministerial duties. They may be ethically condemnable as cowards or knaves, and it may be perfectly proper to disqualify them from office under an alternative legal order. But if the law were used to hold all these people to be criminals, it would lose its essential function—that of being the regulator of general standards of behavior. And Professor Hannah Arendt's recent book on the Eichmann trial should have shown clearly enough to all how elusive a concept guilt is.

By contrast I see no juristic difficulty in the condemnation of the very leaders of the Nazi regime. They are like the top executives of corporations, who in modern juristic theory are regarded as the alter-ego of the corporation rather than merely as its servants, and who therefore have in recent American and English decisions been held guilty of crimes committed by the corporation. Men like Hitler, Göring, Goebbels, and Himmler were not servants of the Nazi regime obeying orders: they

were its very essence. Nor do I see any difficulty in the conviction of the wives who, to rid themselves of their husbands
and carry on with their lovers, used a wartime Nazi statute to
denounce the husbands who, on home leave from the front,
had privately made derogatory remarks against the Nazi
regime. These women had a choice. They chose to have their
husbands killed or imprisoned under the cover of obedience
to the state, with the real motive of having liberty in their love
affairs. The standard to be applied is simply whether elementary loyalties between husband and wife should take precedence over what was in effect a free option to carry out the
frenzied order of a totalitarian state. The applicable scale of
values was that of the post-Nazi legal order, but insofar as these
women had made a free choice between alternative values, the
moral issue is clear. In none of these cases does anything seem
to be gained by the use of the terminology of natural law.

The issue of disobedience to unjust laws has recently come
much nearer home. In his moving "Letter from Birmingham
City Jail" of April 16, 1963, Martin Luther King justified the
advocacy of resistance to Southern segregation laws in the
following words:

> There are *just* laws and there are *unjust* laws. I would be
> the first to advocate obeying just laws. One has not only a legal
> but moral responsibility to obey just laws. Conversely, one has
> a moral responsibility to disobey unjust laws. I would agree
> with Saint Augustine that "An unjust law is no law at all."
>
> Now what is the difference between the two? How does
> one determine when a law is just or unjust? A just law is a
> man-made code that squares with the moral law or the law of
> God. An unjust law is a code that is out of harmony with the
> moral law. To put it in the terms of Saint Thomas Aquinas, an
> unjust law is a human law that is not rooted in eternal and
> natural law. Any law that uplifts human personality is just. Any
> law that degrades human personality is unjust. All segregation
> statutes are unjust because segregation distorts the soul and
> damages the personality. . . .
>
> Let us turn to a more concrete example of just and unjust
> laws. An unjust law is a code that a majority inflicts on a

minority that is not binding on itself. This is difference made legal. On the other hand a just law is a code that a majority compels a minority to follow that it is willing to follow itself. This is *sameness* made legal.

Let me give another explanation. An unjust law is a code inflicted upon a minority which that minority had no part in enacting or creating because they did not have the unhampered right to vote.[4]

The claim to disobedience in the name of natural law is here put on two different grounds: one is that the segregation laws are unjust because "segregation distorts the soul and damages the personality," and such law is contrary to eternal and natural law. The second reason is that laws that differentiate between different groups of people and impose handicaps on one group without its consent are unjust and therefore invalid.

The present writer is in strongest sympathy with the moral stand taken by King and his supporters. Resistance to the segregation laws can, moreover, be justified legally on the simple ground that the U.S. Constitution is the highest law of the country and that the state of Alabama, like some other states, has defied the highest positive law of the country, as authoritatively interpreted by the Supreme Court of the United States.

But the argument of natural law reveals typical weaknesses of natural law philosophy. Southern lawyers and legislators have justified their racial stand by appeal to a natural order of creation that has made blacks and whites different. The same philosophy is, of course, advocated by the Black Muslim movement. Apartheid is ruthlessly applied by the South African government. The same philosophy underlies the caste differentiation in India—officially repudiated but still dominating the social life of the country. However repulsive these doctrines may be to most of us, the principle of inequality of human beings and races is not only practised in many different countries and civilizations, but it is a principle actively debated by anthropologists and biologists. Here, as in so many other issues, the question of what nature ordains depends on your point of view. And, as so often, an ideological concept of nature is fused with the biological aspects.

King's second argument is a paraphrase of the famous Aristotelian principle that equals should be treated equally, but Aristotle distinguished between "distributive" and "corrective" justice. It is for positive law, based on certain given ethical and political principles, to say who is equal before the law. "Corrective justice is justice between equals. It presupposes an act of distributive justice which has granted . . . equal status to the parties" (Radbruch).

If King's contention were to be taken seriously, such laws as in the Swiss constitution denying the right to vote of women, or the withholding of certain public rights (such as the right to strike) from public servants or people of military status, might well be held void as contrary to natural law. Certainly the women of Switzerland have not been given the chance to consent to their votelessness.

Negroes who are deprived of the right to vote and of participation in legislation and administration have every reason to feel a burning sense of injustice. They can, however, appeal to the highest *positive* law of the country, the U.S. Constitution, for support—and where a lower law conflicts with a higher law, disobedience to the lower law is not a revolt against positive law in the name of natural law. It is a vindication of the existing law.

THE RIGHT TO LIFE AND THE LEGITIMACY OF BIRTH CONTROL

The legitimacy of birth control is today not only one of the questions most vital to human survival and dignity but also one of the theoretically most contested. The Catholic Church continues to condemn any form of birth control other than the rhythm method as contrary to natural law, since it is an interference with the natural God-given processes of reproduction. The Church equally prohibits, in the case of an unavoidable choice between the life of a mother and the life of the child to be born, the killing of the embryo.

Professor Rommen has not specifically commented on this matter, but surely birth control would be a most vital application of the need, acknowledged by him, to adapt law to new social conditions and needs. Contrary to the whole course of history until a few decades ago, the balance between life and death has been drastically altered, since man has been able to hold down famine and disease to relatively insignificant proportions and to increase immensely the chances of survival of new-born children by improved hygiene. The ability to do so is the result of conscious interference of man with the workings of nature, as with floods, diseases, the failure of monsoons, and other causes of famine. The refusal to adjust legal doctrine to these new realities does not mean a stoic acceptance of the courses of nature: the Catholic Church accepts the results of modern science and technology and of medicine that interferes with the natural diseases of the human body. It simply refuses to redress the balance, at the expense of human dignity that the Church, like all defenders of natural law, regards as a basic human value. Even at this time millions of human beings, for example in the big cities of India or Latin America, lead a life somewhere between man and animal, bereft of the elementary human dignities. All the tremendous efforts of the Indian government and foreign aid have not sufficed to mitigate the effects of this population increase. In these circumstances to forbid birth control as contrary to natural law means to accept interference with nature on one side of the scale but not on the other and consequently to sacrifice human dignity to a doctrine developed in the entirely different conditions of previous centuries. Many modern Catholics are becoming increasingly doubtful about the theoretical and moral foundations of this doctrine. The case against interference with nature was already given away when the Church sanctioned birth control by the rhythm method. It seems extreme sophistry to assert that the deliberate use of the calendar in the regulation of sexual intercourse is compatible with the order of nature, whereas the use of manufactured contraceptives is not. In either case the human will interposes itself between instinct—carrying out the divine purpose of procreation—and action. The use of contraceptives may be more effective than that of the rhythm method. This is a technical, not a moral, issue.

In another matter affecting the creation of life, the Catholic Church, which officially opposes artificial insemination even as between husband and wife, seems to have confused the biological meaning of nature, and its normative meaning. When Pope Pius XII, in a speech to the midwives of Italy, condemned artificial insemination as a "laboratory" method, he used the biological concept of nature under which the procreation of children presumably must be the result of normal intercourse. Unwittingly he seems to have put this biological interpretation of nature above the ethical normative interpretation of marriage as a union that in the eyes of the Church has the principal purpose of procreating children. It may indeed be asserted that if a married couple, faced with the inability to produce children in the ordinary way, decides to use the only method that permits them to have children, they fulfill the higher ethical purpose of marriage despite the absence of the normal satisfaction of sexual intercourse.

Wittingly or unwittingly, the various commands of "natural law" in this field constitute a choice between different values. Mankind abandoned the pure obedience to nature from the moment that it sought to improve the conditions of wild nature by husbandry, by the use of the plow and of the steam engine, by medical surgery and a thousand other means. Whether birth control, artificial insemination, or abortion are legitimate is a decision to be made not only by weighing the competing values and interests against each other, but by reassessing the effects of any particular course of legal action in the light of social conditions, which have drastically changed in our time as compared with previous centuries.

THE SANCTITY OF PRIVATE PROPERTY AND
THE LEGITIMACY OF PUBLIC ENTERPRISE

The majority of natural law philosophers, from Locke to Cathrein, and the successive encyclicals of the Church since *Rerum novarum* have asserted the essential integrity and necessity of private property as part of the natural order. Here, as in other respects, the encyclical *Mater et Magistra* of Pope John XXIII begins to break new ground by emphasizing more strongly than any predecessor not only the social obligations of property but the legitimacy of public and communal property for the welfare of the community.

Anthropologists, legal historians, and legal philosophers have debated the primacy of private property or communal property. On the whole it seems that communally held property has prevailed among primitive agricultural communities, and that the division of cultivated land into privately held properties is a later development. On the other hand, some form of private property in some things must have prevailed from the earliest times of organized social life. If it is merely asserted that some protection of some private property is essential to a legal order, there is very little to argue about. Certainly the Soviet as well as the American legal system—and the vast majority of legal systems from the Soviet system to mixed economies and essentially capitalist legal orders—can agree on the existence and protection of private property in some form. The controversy begins as to the extent and significance of private property in the social system, and here Professor Rommen has rightly asserted in his "natural law" that natural law does not demand any particular economic system.[5] The great majority of modern legal systems condemn the confiscation of property without compensation as against the universally acknowledged right to expropriate property for compensation for public purposes. But where, for example, colonial entrepreneurs have exploited the natural resources and labor of a country under the protection of military, political, and economic force, is a subsequent confiscation of such property against natural law? Whether and to what extent the expropriation of property is justifiable must be decided in the light of infinitely various circumstances and conditions. The modern literature, both of municipal and of international law, shows the immense range of circumstances as well as of doctrines in this respect. Again, natural law is little more than a means of special pleading, a way to lend emphasis and appeal to the view that happens to be held by its advocate. Those who plead for the expropriated foreign interests in newly emancipated countries will invoke natural law for the duty of full compensation. Those who represent the more radical views of ex-colonial nations will plead for the right of expropriation without, or with very little, compensation as being the only way to restore the "natural" rights of the people after centuries of exploitation. Whether the one or the other view is exaggerated is irrelevant here. Like the solution of every other issue discussed here, this solution must be sought in a complex and painful adjustment of competing values, in which ethical, political, and social beliefs, as much as sheer questions of force and power, produce a solution.

Nor can we find refuge in the *oberste Rechtsgrundsätze*, as formulated by Professor Coing and specifically commended by Professor Rommen. We may indeed recognize, with Coing or Radbruch, that there are essential properties to institutions, the *Natur der Sache*, we may accept that there are certain inherent characteristics of the institution of contract or of marriage. Contract implies some kind of agreement of wills, as expressed between two or several parties, on a common objective. But what more can we say? Is there any compelling order, whether from outside or from within the nature of the institution, telling us that there should be damages for breach of contract only in the case of fault or in any situation of default by one party? Can natural law tell us whether and under what circumstances a supervening change of circumstances should permit the discharge of contractual obligations? Can it tell us whether a contract concluded between parties of grossly unequal economic power should be valid, voidable, or totally void? All these are questions answered differently by different systems and in changing circumstances, in the light of both changing social philosophies and economic facts. But all these various solutions and situations are part of mankind's existence, of its "nature." Again, marriage is a union of a man and a woman of some permanency. But whether the union must be monogamous or not is a question on which various religious and social philosophies differ sharply. It would therefore have to be implied that Christianity is the only order of law compatible with "nature" if one were to assert that Moslem law, the older Hindu law, or the customs of the African tribes are contrary to natural law. The assertion that the beliefs of a large proportion of mankind are contrary to nature, is characteristic of earlier periods of Christianity but hardly accepted in the modern, more tolerant, attitude of the leaders of the churches of various denominations. Does natural law compel the discrimination between legitimate and illegitimate children? Such was indeed the consequence of the stricter Christian theory that to some extent still prevails in the interpretation of wills and in the official status of illegitimate children. But surely it can be asserted with equal justification that any child put into the world, presumably by the will of the Creator, inside or outside a union, should have the same opportunities of "becoming what it is," of developing its potentialities, of unfolding as a human being; and that discrimination between new-born children according to the legitimacy of their descent is a relapse into a barbarism that might well be condemned in the name of natural law.

The categories and examples could be multiplied. I believe that Professor Rommen would agree with many of the actual analyses and answers to specific legal problems attempted here. Yet he maintains the defense of natural law, a natural law that —as stated at the beginning of this comment—is so comprehensive as to embrace the orthodox doctrines of various shades, neo-Hegelianism and modern existentialism. It may be said that this is merely a matter of taste and of terminology. I do not agree. The case against natural law is not that there is not a yearning for absolute and compelling standards. There certainly is. It is not that natural law—as expounded by Professor Rommen and others—leaves room for adaptation and variety, since only the most rigid of natural law doctrines deny such adaptability. The case against natural law is that its method of approach and its terminology disguise the need to decide between alternative values. It gives the illusion of certainty and of guidance where there is none. It is one way of shielding man from the loneliness of decision, as legislator, as judge, as statesman, or as ordinary citizen. But we cannot evade the choice. We must articulate our system of values whether instinctively or as an elaborate system of philosophy. If we do so, we will find that there are the competing demands of justice, security, and utility—as classically formulated by Gustav Radbruch—and that there are ultimate choices for the sake of which you may fight your enemy but which you cannot scientifically demonstrate—as has been shown by Max Weber and, in very different language, by Oliver Wendell Holmes. "To decide oneself is to live"—as was once said by Radbruch. Let us accept this choice, humbly but resolutely!

NOTES

1. *"Jus naturale est quod natura omnia animalia docuit."*
2. The borderlines between animate and inanimate things are somewhat fluid, in biology as in theology. In some religions, animals, or at least certain animals, are equated with men or even gods. To Buddhism all life is sacred. But at least we may accept as a universally held *minimum* that man is a creature who, endowed with reason and feeling, cannot be treated as a mere object.
3. 71, Harv L. R. 593 (1958).
4. *The New Leader,* June 24, 1963.
5. Yet this has been more or less asserted by a prominent modern advocate of natural law, Jacques Maritain, who, in his "Man and the State," regards the conduct of industrial enterprises by the state as contrary to natural law.

1

Unnatural Law

RAZIEL ABELSON
New York University

THE CONCEPT of natural law is as flagrant a contradiction in terms as one could hope to find in the wonderland of metaphysical jargon. It is one of those magical formulas that reunites verbally what logic has divided, like "ontological necessity," "intellectual vision," "timeless existence," "substantial form," and other verbal devices for eating one's conceptual cake and having it too. The cake one wants to eat in this case is the human conventions that support law, while retaining the law itself. Nature urges and laws coerce, so why not have the best of both worlds even if they are logically incompatible? Where logic draws back, terminology can still rush in.

Those who like to square circles and read sermons in stones will never be persuaded to desist. But just for the fun of it, let's unpack the meaning of "natural law" and see how mixed up it is. However else they disagree, experts on natural law all agree in confusing laws with rules.[1] A contemporary legalist, Hans Kelsen, explains the role of this concept in legal thought as follows:

> Rules of law, if valid, are norms . . . stipulating sanctions. A norm is a command. . . . A command is the expression in an imperative form of the will that somebody shall behave in a certain manner. . . . Positive law is essentially an order or coercion. Unlike the rules of natural law its rules are derived from the arbitrary will of human authority.[2]

Here we have a fine specimen of the confusion that infects philosophy of law. Rules are equated with laws, laws with norms, and norms with commands. We may disregard "norms" (Kelsen's technical term and thus his own affair) and merely note, in passing, the transparently false assumption that all acts of will are arbitrary. I want to concentrate on the central blunder in Kelsen's account, namely, the equation between rules, laws, and commands. To appreciate the incoherence of this equation, we must do a bit of what J. L. Austin called "linguistic phenomenology."

Laws, regulations, and commands and principles, rules, and instructions belong to a single family in that they are all expressible in the imperative mood, as Kant was the first to notice. But there are differences among these siblings that Kelsen ignores, in common with most writers on natural law. The most obvious difference is that between laws, regulations, and commands on the one hand, and principles, rules, and instructions on the other. The first group sound more forceful than the second; they convey a note of authority and obligation. We *obey* laws, regulations, and commands, whereas we choose to *follow* principles, rules, and instructions. Should we disobey the former, we can expect punishment, whereas if we disregard the latter we may be sorry later, and then again we may not. The first group are enforced, whereas the second are, at best, sound advice whose rejection is likely to bring unpleasant consequences. One is easily tempted to bridge the categorial gap with a metaphor, as Hobbes and Bentham did, in describing the unpleasant consequences of folly as "nature's sanctions," or as experimental psychologists do, in referring to pain or deprivation as "punishment." By means of this terminological alchemy, principles and rules of conduct are transmuted into natural laws. But the trouble with such metaphors is that they obscure an essential difference between the terms they compare, namely, that laws and regulations are backed up by coercive power, while principles and rules are, to use Kant's felicitous term, *autonomous*. To follow a rule or principle means to choose to act in a certain way. If one is coerced into acting in that way, one is not following a rule, but obeying a command or a law. We need laws and regulations just because the consequences of disregarding wise rules are insufficiently certain or frightening, so that governments must resort to punitive measures to ensure adherence. We may then characterize laws, regulations, and commands as "coercive imperatives," and principles, rules, and instructions as "advisory imperatives."

Let us briefly glance at the differences within each of these two categories of imperatives. Laws, like principles, are very general in scope—in their ideal form, to which we can only approximate, they are, like laws of science, unrestrictedly universal. Commands, like instructions, are "single-shot": they apply only to the situation in which they are uttered and to the agents to whom they are addressed. Regulations and rules belong in a vague middle ground between universality and uniqueness of reference. An officer gives a command to a soldier, "Smith, assemble that machine gun"; regulations require specific groups (as privates) to perform specific tasks (cleaning their rifles); whereas laws require everyone to perform or to refrain from some general type of action, such as burglary, reckless driving, or bribing a public official. Similarly, instructions guide us in performing an individual task (such as assembling some piece of equipment); rules guide us in performing fairly specific but almost infinitely variable types of activity (such as playing chess, entertaining guests, writing plays, and negotiating treaties); whereas principles guide us in the universal "art of living" by advising us to be truthful, charitable, impartial, and the like.

Returning to the comparison between the two general categories of imperatives, there are two crucial differences to be noted. We have already touched on the more conspicuous one, namely, the difference in obligatory force. This difference is partly, but not entirely (as Kant saw and Hobbes failed to see), explainable by the threat of punishment that backs up coercive imperatives. Kant recognized that coercive imperatives are *intended* as unconditional, whereas advisory imperatives (rules of skill and counsels of prudence) apply only on the condition that the agent to whom they are addressed is *interested* in our advice. In Kant's language, the former are categorical, the latter, hypothetical. A second and equally important difference (that Kant refused to recognize when he classified moral principles as laws) is that coercive imperatives leave no room for individual judgment, whereas advisory imperatives presuppose the ability of the agent to direct his own affairs and to decide whether or not an exception may be made to a generally sound procedure. These two differences are not unrelated. The second is the pragmatic ground of the first. We enforce imperatives precisely in order to prevent people from using their own judgment.

In directing the behavior of animals other than man, we use only coercive imperatives, and of these, only the most specific kind: commands. We cannot direct animals by means of regulations and laws, because animals are not rational enough to understand general imperatives and apply them to specific cases. It is equally pointless to offer one's dog instructions, rules, or principles, because dogs are not rational enough to appreciate good advice and to regulate their own behavior accordingly. Clearly, there are two kinds of rationality that animals lack: the ability to classify particular cases under general classes, and the ability to appreciate good advice. Aristotle called the first kind of ability "theoretical reason" and the second kind "practical reason." We may refer to them more simply as "intelligence" and "wisdom."

We can now see more clearly what is the point of each type of imperative. We need *coercive* imperatives wherever we cannot rely on either the prudence or the moral character (both of which are essential to wisdom) of those whose conduct we want to direct. We need *specific* imperatives, whether coercive or advisory, where we cannot rely on the intelligence of the agent. In directing a dog, we employ only the most specific of coercive imperatives: commands. Where human beings are the agents, we consider two factors in deciding which type and which level of imperatives is appropriate. If we do not trust people's intelligence, we employ commands and instructions rather than laws or principles. If we do not trust their

wisdom, we resort to coercive rather than advisory imperatives. A completely authoritarian society, regulated solely by
a hierarchical chain of direct command, is one in which each
person treats his fellow of lower rank as a man treats his
dog.

It is a serious conceptual error, then, on the order of a
"category mistake," to confuse coercive imperatives with advisory imperatives. Nevertheless, there are two considerations
that may help explain why many philosophers and jurists have
committed this very mistake in supporting doctrines of natural
law. In two kinds of contexts, rules resemble regulations and
principles resemble laws. One such context is that of a game;
another is that of moral judgment.

First, the game: The rules of a game are more binding
than the rules for entertaining guests, writing a play, or negotiating a treaty. Rules of a game define the activity they govern. (I am not referring here to rules of strategy *in* a game,
which guide us in playing it skillfully, but only to the rules *of*
the game). If a person insists on moving his knight in a straight
line, he is not making a move of chess, either because he does
not know how or because he does not care to "play the game."
To play a game means, in part, to follow its rules. In this logical sense, one must follow the rules to perform the intended
activity. One can entertain guests, write an *avant-garde* play,
or cleverly negotiate a treaty while disregarding accepted
rules, and frequently such departures distinguish the skillful
and creative performer from the dull mediocrity. But the rules
of a game permit no such exceptions, and, in this respect, resemble coercive imperatives. The latter are *intended* to be
obeyed in all cases, although—and this remains a crucial difference—they do not logically guarantee obedience. We cannot
say, because a man has broken the law, that he is not doing
what he set out to do (that is, does not know what he is doing), which we can say of someone who makes an illicit move
while playing chess. The coercive necessity of laws and regulations is not logical but physical and psychological.

Incidentally, the peculiar logical necessity of following

rules of a game renders the Wittgensteinian notion of "language games" somewhat more misleading than illuminating. To decide philosophical issues by appeal to the rules of language alone is to assume that one cannot tamper with the rules. Yet there would be no poetry, no witty conversation, no delicious slang, and no exciting stylistic innovations if language were, in this respect, like a game. One plays a game for its own sake; one follows the rules that define a game because one wants to follow them rather than because the rules guide one toward achieving something else. (One might, of course, play golf in order to make business contacts, but in such case he is only going through the motions of golf, he is not really playing —unless, that is, he becomes absorbed in the game and temporarily forgets about his ulterior objective). Yet language is not used just for its own sake, unless we are doing crossword puzzles or playing scrabble. Only then are we playing language *games*.

Second, moral judgment: Principles of life resemble laws in a more important way than do rules of the game, and it is this fact that lends plausibility to the Kantian idea of moral laws and to the Thomistic doctrine of natural law. Human beings usually cherish the skills most distinctive of their species—thus, in particular, the ability to be rational. We tend to rate general knowledge higher than knowledge of particular facts, principles of science above specialized information, and ethical rules of conduct above detailed instructions. The broader the scope of a rule, the more painful we find departures from it, even in exceptional circumstances, such as lying to an incurably ill patient. Consequently, we are strongly tempted to transform such principles into virtual laws by ordaining punishment for transgressions, in an effort to ensure universal compliance. Now an easy way to make a rule a law is to *call* it a law, and so those who prefer the easy way to the effective way bemuse themselves with *natural law à la Aquinas* or with *moral law à la Kant*.

Now it seems to me as unwise to speak of moral laws as of natural laws. Although laws may tend to impede or encourage natural morality, neither laws nor the actions they govern are, in themselves, moral or immoral, natural or unnatural. The adjective "moral" is the highest term of commendation in our vocabulary; only persons (not rules or laws) can deserve such praise, and surely not as a result of a single action. The best of men may act wrongly, in violation of a law or of a socially beneficial rule, and the worst of men may, on occasion, do what is right. Morality has to do primarily with those persistent and hard-earned traits that make up a person's character. Moral character is related to rules of action only by a psychological route. The moral man, as Kant observed (although he did not stick consistently to this insight) respects principles, that is, tries to follow rules of general scope that apply as well to others as to himself, and accordingly he refrains from making exceptions in his own favor. A strong conscience or sense of principle is thus one criterion of morality. Benevolent feeling, as Hume insisted, is another, since it is our feeling for our fellowmen that guides us toward socially beneficial principles. And so morality is indeed a fulfillment of man's rational nature, but it is also a fulfillment of the emotional nature he shares with other animal species, particularly with dogs, who are usually very affectionate creatures.

Our psychological tendency to respect principles makes them take on the superficial appearance of coercive laws, but this should not blind us to the essential difference that the former are advisory and autonomous, whereas the latter are coercive and thus heteronomous. Glossing over the difference in the name of natural law leads us to forget the main point of laws as against rules—namely, that we need laws when we can not trust people's practical wisdom. The attempt to produce or extend morality by legislation (which is what the proponents of natural law are really up to) rather than merely protect society from undesirable actions is therefore self-defeating. Coercive imperatives can produce careful men, but not good men. A morally good man, as Kant saw, respects his own principles more than any punitive threat, and thus more than any law. The doctrine of natural law maintains that just laws coincide with the natural promptings of man's conscience. Yet, if this were true, laws would be unnecessary. Perhaps, in an ideally organized society, wherein every citizen's natural capacities are developed in socially useful directions, laws would become unnecessary and the coercive apparatus that Marx identified with the state would "wither away." But this ideal of the complete fulfillment of man's rational nature presupposes and therefore cannot cancel the difference between coercive and advisory imperatives. It is self-contradictory to claim simultaneously that we can trust human nature and that man needs laws. A philosopher who believes in natural law is like a man who professes faith in the fidelity of his wife but has her followed by a private detective.

The concept of natural right, although often conflated with that of natural law, is a somewhat different story. Although it has serious defects, it contains a large element of truth, and it is worth noting that liberal social philosophers of the eighteenth and nineteenth centuries generally appealed to natural rights rather than to natural laws.

Rights are permissive, whereas laws are coercive. Rights consist of what one *may* do; laws specify what one *must* do. Natural rights, if there were such things, would serve as limitations on what may be compelled by law and would provide a useful standard for rejecting some laws as unjustly restrictive. This eighteenth century doctrine has appealing features, but it suffers from a logical defect similar to that of natural law. Rights don't grow on trees. It is wishful inconsistency to claim the right to do something that is prohibited by law. One can, of course, claim that we *ought* to have a certain right, and that the law which denies it to us is unjust, but to say that we ought to have a right is not the same as to say that we have it.

When writers defend the concepts of natural law and natural right they frequently argue that there must be some objective standard for evaluating social institutions and practices, on pain of moral anarchy.[3] This argument blithely assumes that human nature is the only candidate for election as an "objective standard" of ethical judgment. Of course, if a

writer defines natural right or law as any standard of judgment other than arbitrary decree (as Kelsen does in the passage quoted earlier), then the doctrine is true only because it
is perfectly vacuous. In any case, a standard is one thing; a
right, law, or principle is quite another. A standard for evaluating rights, laws, and rules is not itself a right, law, or rule. It
does not inform us what we may or must do; it is not an imperative of any kind. Now human nature is indeed a reasonable
standard of justice, but why and how it serves as a standard is
seldom clearly understood.

It is a postulate of ethical judgment that "ought" implies
"can" or, in simpler language, that one has a duty to do something only if it is possible for him to do it. Now whatever is
contrary to human nature, whatever frustrates the most urgent
needs or tendencies of man cannot, on this postulate, be justly
required of any person. Laws that forbid women to have children or require people to take their own lives are manifestly
unjust because they are contrary to natural tendencies. But nature is not the only standard of justice, and consequently it is
an essentially negative standard. It is a necessary, but not a
sufficient, condition for a law to be just that it be in conformity
with human nature. Our understanding of human nature en-
ables us to denounce a law as bad, but not to commend it as
good.

Catholics and Anglicans tend to interpret nature as a positive or sufficient standard of good laws. They seem to reason
from the converse and the contrapositive of our postulate,
that is, from the assumptions that "can" implies "ought," and
"cannot" implies "ought not." For them, natural capacities and
needs *sufficiently* determine moral and legal obligations. But
this position, once clearly stated, is clearly wrong. It is reasonable to argue against a law prohibiting women from bearing
children or one requiring people to take their own lives on the
grounds that procreation and self-preservation are such strong
natural tendencies that most people cannot obey such laws.
But to argue in the same way in favor of laws requiring women
to bear children (by prohibiting birth control) or requiring

people to endure endless torment (by prohibiting suicide) is to commit the fallacies of illicit conversion and illicit contraposition. It is to reason that, because "ought" implies "can," "can" also implies "ought" and "cannot" implies "ought not." (Thus, if one *can* bear children one *ought* to; if most people *cannot* take their own lives, everyone *ought not* do so.) One might as well argue that, since no one can live forever, immortality should be forbidden by law and that, since most people can swim, everyone ought to jump in the lake.

We can now see why the doctrine of natural rights, muddled though it be, is both more liberal and closer to moral truth then the doctrine of natural law. The idea of a right is essentially permissive; it is a limitation of coercion rather than a ground of coercion. We have seen that the demands of human nature may reasonably be cited as a standard for rejecting laws, but not as a source of laws nor as a sufficient standard for commending laws. Considerations of basic human needs may be sufficient for deciding what ought to be permitted, but not what ought to be enjoined or prohibited.[4] One may, if one insists, call such considerations "natural rights," but it would be more conducive to clarity to call them necessary conditions of justice.

NOTES

1. The term "natural law and also the basic rules of ethics and justice . . . that it signifies, are . . . as old as philosophy itself." H. A. Rommen, in this volume.

"Whatever the practical reason naturally apprehends as man's good belongs to the precepts of the natural law." St. Thomas Aquinas, *Summa Theologica*, II, 1, Q. 94.

"Natural law, that is, a rule of reason . . .", Francisco Suárez, *Selections from Three Works*, ed. J. B. Scott (Oxford: Clarendon Press, 1944), vol. II, p. 335.

"By natural law I mean . . . a universal pattern of action . . . required by nature itself for completion." John Wild, *Plato's Modern Enemies* (Chicago: University of Chicago Press, 1953), p. 64.

2. Hans Kelsen, *General Theory of Law and State* (Cambridge: Harvard University Press, 1945), pp. 30–31, 392.

3. For example: "The most basic thesis involved in this theory is that value and existence are closely intertwined." Wild, *op. cit.*, p. 65.

"Laws are just to the extent that they are conducive to the common good. . . . The nature of things *and not convention* determines in each case what is just" [my italics]. Leo Strauss, *Natural Right and History* (Chicago: University of Chicago Press, 1953), p. 102.

4. The present struggle for civil rights legislation would seem (for sympathizers like myself) to disconfirm my claim that human needs are a reasonable standard only for limiting laws and not a sufficient condition for passing them. Is not the proposed civil rights legislation sufficiently justified by the natural right of the Negro for equality of status and opportunity? I think not. There are no natural rights to eat in restaurants or to vote in primaries. No one in his right mind would claim the right to eat in a restaurant when he cannot pay the bill. Why then, may a restaurant owner discriminate according to the color of his customer's money but not according to the color of his skin? The answer is that the first kind of discrimination is essential to the functioning of our economic system, whereas the second kind is damaging to social health and harmony. Again, no one would argue that vagrants or criminals have a natural right to vote. The sufficient ground for protecting the Negro's right as granted by the Fourteenth Amendment is that proportional representation of all class and group interests is essential to the proper functioning of democratic government. Thus the grounds of such positive laws are concrete and pragmatic rather than abstract and metaphysical.

2

Natural Right Valid in Itself and Allegedly Relativistic Eudaemonism

DAVID BAUMGARDT ‡ (1963)

Ord. Prof. em. Berlin University

> *You will be like God knowing good and evil*
>
> —*Genesis* 3:5

OF THE countless champions of natural law, Professor Rommen is certainly one of the most circumspect, wise, and conciliatory. Evidently he is fully aware that nothing is achieved by such a sweeping condemnation of all opponents of classical natural right as has been carried through such works as Professor Strauss' *Natural Right and History*.[1] In Strauss' earlier writings the criterion of moral decay, from at least the days of Thomas Hobbes down to Max Weber, was the disbelief in a personal God. Now, as with many other ethicists and jurists, it is the repudiation of natural law coupled or not coupled with theism.

Professor Rommen does not advocate such widespread dogmatic prejudices. He does not insist on a strict rigidity of natural law, but freely grants that the *jus naturale* has a "progressive content" and that there is "an expanding knowledge of it." And yet it seems to me that he has gone only half the way that man, the thoroughly finite being, has to go in the realms of secular knowledge, not only in science but in the humanities as well.

Professor Rommen illuminatingly compares the "constant, identical, unchanged *jus naturale*"[2] with the "enduring identity that . . . is meant by the term 'substance' as opposed to 'accident'" in the traditional theories of nature. True enough that the two substances in Descartes's metaphysics and even the one in Spinoza's system represent a strictly unchangeable "being" in contrast to the ever-changing world of the empirical phenomena of nature. But how much insight into reality could be conveyed by referring to the allegedly unchanging world of the substance? Practically none.

Only after Galileo abandoned the adherence to a knowledge of an absolutely stable substance of nature could science gain an increasingly deeper knowledge in physics. The concept of stable substances was and had to be replaced by the discovery of stable relations, an unchanging context of functional relations between observable phenomena. A similar *"Revolution der Denkungsart,"* as Kant called it, seems to me unavoidable, long overdue, and most wholesome in ethics and the philosophy of law as well. For only thus can we be saved both from a morally nihilistic relativism and from arbitrary positive law.

Even Kant's categorical imperative, one of the epistemologically most refined expressions of natural law, has proved incapable of answering concrete controversial questions in ethics or, for that matter, even some noncontroversial ones. Love of one's enemy, for instance, generally practiced as a moral maxim in the sense demanded by Kant, would lead to its own nullification. Therefore, it would have to be considered markedly immoral according to Kant's own presuppositions. But Kant himself had to admit that love of one's enemy is, in fact, a principle of the highest moral value.[3]

Augustine and Thomas Aquinas base ethical judgment, along with divine law, on natural law or, as Augustine calls it in his *Civitas Dei, "justitia vera"* in contrast to *"ius, quod ei, qui plus potest, utile est."* [4] And yet the eternally valid natural law explicitly sanctions, according to Thomas, positive laws and actions that today are rightly thought not only unlawful but even criminal, such as the whipping of a slave by his master [5] and the mutilation of limbs by state authorities in times of peace.[6] But if thus from natural law in Kant it has to be inferred that highly moral laws are immoral and from Thomas that criminal laws are ethically justifiable, how much trustworthy guidance in morals and jurisprudence can then be attributed to the allegedly supreme and eternally valid natural law?

Is, then, only a "progressive content," an "expanding

knowledge" revealed in this development of moral ideas since Thomas?—or rather, the fact that on the basis of natural law what is morally right cannot be properly distinguished from what is utter wrong, that the concept of natural right is too empty a concept to permit in many cases any valid inferences to be drawn from it? As Professor Werner Friedmann emphasized, the real trouble with natural law is that it unwittingly can serve as a cloak to hide from us the difficulty of the decisions we have to make, especially in the numerous cases of conflict between specific duties and concrete rights.

In the theory of natural right, the burning thirst for a clear and simple criterion of right and wrong has led us to maintain falsely that the mere thirst proves the existence of water or even wine. There is no doubt that all men who abhor the cruelty of arbitrary positive law, let alone the whims of dictators and mobs, pine for just, moral laws outlawing man's inhumanity to man. But must not this superior principle of truly moral and just law be sought in another way than by the presupposition of an abstract, allegedly self-evident truth that pays no regard to the detailed, concrete evaluation of human happiness and misery?

To summarize the argument against Christian, Jewish, or pagan defenders of natural law, I should, perhaps, best make use of my interpretation of the biblical Paradise story. In the state of innocence, man was not at all in need of a knowledge of good and evil, right and wrong. On the contrary, he was forbidden to eat the fruit of the tree of absolute moral and legal insight. Since the Fall, however, we must remain fully aware that we no longer have the intuitive certainty to distinguish between absolute right and absolute wrong.

As in science, in psychology, in historiography, and in all other fields of secular knowledge, in law, too, we have to limit ourselves to a search for objectively valid truth "in the sweat of" our "brow" (Genesis 3:17) and within the confines of a carefully worked-out theory of relativity that, to the finite mind, is the only alternative to relativism and nihilism. If we still try to rely on the possession of simple, absolute knowledge in morals, we only deceive ourselves with the vain boast of being "like God" in absolute ethical judgment.

In short, what alone is left to us as finite beings is to find out which line of action, in every concrete case, gives to all concerned the profoundest and most lasting happiness. Only such action can be called the "right" one, but not an action dictated by a seemingly ready-made principle handed over to us by the knowledge of a vague and unspecific natural right. Even Hegel, certainly not a Benthamite, vigorously protested against the all-too-proud pronouncement *"fiat justitia, pereat mundus."* He insisted, *"Ein schlechtes Recht ist es, wobei die Welt zu Grunde geht."* [7]

Great leaders of mankind have always realized this, and in cases of great conflicts between two demanding rights they have chosen and had to choose only that one that, to the very best of their critically examined knowledge, promised the greatest foreseeable happiness to all men affected by their choice. But if this is the case, it has frankly to be brought to the foreground and not only tacitly be admitted in passing. Moreover, not only in statesmanship but in ethics, too, far greater efforts have to be made to concentrate on a full exploration of what constitutes human happiness and human suffering in all concrete cases at issue. The only alternative to the fata morgana of an absolutely constant or progressively but unqualifiedly expanding knowledge of natural right is, in my opinion, therefore, a consistently and subtly thought-out eudaemonism or hedonism (despite the ill repute generally and unjustifiably attached to the term)—a theory I have tried to develop in detail in my principal systematic work soon to appear.

NOTES

1. Leo Strauss, *Natural Right and History* (Chicago: University of Chicago Press, 1953).

2. See also Heinrich Rommen, "Natural Law in Decisions of

the Federal Supreme Court and of the Constitutional Courts in Germany," *Natural Law Forum*, IV, No. 1 (1959), 12, 20; and Rommen's work on *Naturrecht*, 1936.

3. Immanuel Kant, *Grundlegung zur Metaphysik der Sitten* ed. T. Fritzsch, 1904, Erster Abschnitt, p. 28.

4. Augustinus, *Civitas Dei*, ed. B. Dombart (1877), II, 389f., liber 19, caput 21; Thomas Aquinas, *Summa Theologica*, secundae partis pars prima, quaestio 94, articulus 2c.

5. See *Sancti Thomae Aquinatis . . . opera omnia*, ed. Petrus Fiaccadorus (New York, 1948), III, "Summa theologica, secundae partis pars secunda," quaestio 65, articulus 2, 245b: *"Quia filius subditur potestati patris, et servus potestati domini, licite potest verberare pater filium, et dominus servum causa correptionis et disciplinae."*

6. *Ibid.*, "secunda secundae," p. 245b: *"Sicut autem civitas est perfecta communitas, ita princeps civitatis habet perfectam potestatem coercendi; et ideo potest infligere poenas irreparabiles, scilicet occisionis vel mutilationis."*

7. This Hegelian formula is to be found in the especially valuable lecture notes taken by Heinrich Gustav Hotho, the editor of Hegel's lectures on aesthetics in the first edition of Hegel's works (1832ff.) who attended Hegel's lecture on *"Grundlinien der Philosophie des Rechts"* in the winter of 1822–23. The manuscript of these lecture notes was in the possession of my late friend Dr. Heinrich Levy, Woodbrooke College, Birmingham, England, and has not been published hitherto.

But also Hegel's formula in *Werke*, VIII (1833), ed. Eduard Gans, ¶136 and ¶130 is rather graphic: *"Man kann von der Pflicht und dem Recht sehr erhaben sprechen, und dieses Reden macht 'das Herz weit'; aber das Recht . . . ist . . . nicht das Gute ohne das Wohl ('fiat justitia' soll nicht 'pereat mundus' zur Folge haben)."*

3

Huntsmen, What Quarry?

STUART M. BROWN, JR.
Cornell University

PROFESSOR ROMMEN suggests that his strong commitment to the theory of natural law may be connected with a basically humanist outlook, whereas the view of his two main critics in the present discussion, Professor Nielsen and Professor Friedmann, may be connected with a basically scientific outlook. In making this suggestion, Rommen referred explicitly to C. P. Snow's thesis about the modern Western world as divided into two cultures, the one humanistic and the other scientific, the members of one culture being increasingly unable to communicate effectively with the members of the other. Rommen's suggestion implied, therefore, a failure of communication between himself and his critics, and an explanation of this failure in terms of the difference between humanist and scientific outlooks. The first implication is true: there clearly was no communication between Rommen and his critics. In particular, Nielsen and Friedmann appear to have misunderstood both natural law theory and Rommen's defense of it. But the second implication is false: the difference between humanism and science provides no explanation of the misunderstanding. Both the humanist and the scientific outlook were conspicuously absent from the entire debate, and Snow's thesis almost certainly lacks explanatory power in any case.

Certainly Rommen's exposition and defense of natural law theory is not in any sense humanist. What he gives us are the dead bones of the theory, and an appropriate label, in Latin or German, for each bone. But from this we can no more understand the living theory, its implications for human life and practice, and its plausibility than we can understand a living man from an anatomically accurate description of the human skeleton. Skeletons, after all, are at best ludicrous and implausible surrogates of living organisms; at worst, they are repulsive remains, evidence of death. But then natural law theory must be something very different from the skeleton Rommen describes. For there is a sense in which the theory, even if it were false, could not be ludicrous, implausible, or dead. Belief in natural law has persisted over long periods of time. Large numbers of men, many of them possessing extraordinary intellectual powers, have subscribed to this theory in the past and do now subscribe to it; many do so and have done so quite independently of any sectarian religious belief. Some of these men—Cicero is an example—have expressed the theory simply and eloquently, without employing any technical terminology whatsoever. The task of the humanist, even of the humanist who does not himself believe in natural law, is to explain these facts by displaying the theory as in some important sense serious, credible, and alive. The task is to reveal the theory as a living thing, as a constitutive part of at least one way in which men achieve some understanding of themselves, their world, their actions, and their ideals. Rommen, forgetting that skeletons are at best kept in closets, did not accomplish this and appears, in fact, to have been confused about it. Consequently, he provided no defense of natural law theory.

But Rommen's failure to defend the theory in the manner required does not excuse Nielsen's and Friedmann's failure to understand it. In particular, it does not excuse their failure to consider seriously the first two of Rommen's main contentions about natural law: (1) that natural law is not a code and (2) that natural law is not a Roman Catholic invention. Both of these contentions are true. Yet both Nielsen and Friedmann argue—"declaim" would perhaps be a more accurate term—on the assumption that natural law is somehow distinctively Roman Catholic and either is a code or entails one. Consequently, they misunderstood the theory they are attacking, and their criticisms are without weight. This is not because they have a basically scientific outlook on life.

The explanation, I think, is that the real target of Neilsen's and Friedmann's criticisms is the Roman Catholic version of natural law rather than natural law theory as such. Natural law has a special setting in Roman Catholic theory and practice. It is used by the church to support rulings on matters of morals, like the strictures against divorce and birth control, and these rulings have the status of items in a legal code that are binding upon all Catholics by virtue of their faith. Only on the assumption that Catholicism is Friedmann's real target can one explain Friedmann's references to divorce and birth control. Only on this assumption can one explain his strange suggestion that existentialism is the alternative to natural law, for only in the context of contemporary theological discussion is it plausible at all to suppose that there are but these two alternatives. And only on the assumption that Catholicism is Neilsen's real target can one explain his extraordinary contention that belief in natural law implies or logically requires belief in the existence of God. There is, of course, a good reason for making natural law theory, in its Catholic reason, the main target. The reason is that most if not all of the contemporary interest in natural law theory is due to the church's espousal and use of it. Natural law theory is a live and controversial issue in large measure because the church uses it to support controversial rulings on moral questions. To attack the theory in the setting of Catholic theory and practice is, therefore, to attack the most interesting and viable version of it. But to have a chance of success, any attack of this kind must be launched at clearly identified objectives, at critical areas in the foundations of church doctrine, clearly understood and expounded. Unfortunately, neither Neilsen nor Friedmann attack in this way. In consequence, their shots are wild and miss. The following two considerations show just how far they miss.

First, there is a clear sense in which natural law cannot be Catholic as distinct from Protestant, Jewish, or pagan. It can be given, and has as a matter of historical fact been given, a number of very different theological settings. It can be put, and has in fact been put, to very different uses, including its use by lawyers and judges in secular courts of law. Furthermore, any given principle of natural law may be applied in different ways depending upon differences in circumstances and upon differences in human understanding of what the circumstances are. But despite all of these ways in which it is proper to speak about different versions, uses, and applications of natural law, there is a sense in which natural law cannot logically be different or admit of different versions. That cruelty is wrong and that killing or denying life to another human is wrong are, let us suppose, examples of natural law. But it would be nonsense to suppose that cruelty and killing are wrong and that there are Catholic and pagan versions of this fact. At most, one might suppose that the difference between Catholic and pagan either implies or is somehow connected with a difference in the ways certain facts are regarded and that this difference may be reflected in somewhat different applications of natural law principles. Cicero stated it as follows:

> There is in fact a true law—namely, right reason—which is in accordance with nature, applies to all men, and is unchangeable and eternal. By its commands, this law summons men to the performance of their duties; by its prohibitions it restrains them from doing wrong. Its commands and prohibitions always influence good men, but are without effect upon the bad. To invalidate this law by human legislation is never morally right, nor is it permissible ever to restrict its operation, and to annul it wholly is impossible. Neither the senate nor the people can absolve us from our obligation to obey this law, and it requires no Sextus Aelius to expound and interpret it. It will not lay down one rule at Rome and another at Athens nor will it be one rule today and another tomorrow. But there will be one law, eternal and unchangeable, binding at all times upon all peoples; and there will be, as it were, one common master and ruler of men, namely God, who is the author of this law, its interpreter, and its sponsor. The man who will not obey it will abandon his better self, and, in denying the true nature, will thereby suffer the severest of penalties,

though he has escaped all of the other consequences which men call punishment.[1]

Now any instances of this law must be universal moral truths, known independently of special religious revelation, and determinative *of* our beliefs about God rather than determined *by* our beliefs concerning Him. If the fact that cruelty is wrong is an instance of this law, then it is self-contradictory to suppose that in certain times and places, different from our own, cruelty might be all right; and to be ignorant of the fact that cruelty is wrong exhibits a defect in human understanding rather than any defect in religious insight or religious knowledge. It is impossible even for God to make cruelty all right. A good God could not both create a world in which we can be cruel to one another and also condone our being cruel. And an evil God could not by fiat make evil good or oblige us to perpetrate evil by being cruel. God, we may believe, was free to create any world He wished. But being a good God and having created a world in which cruelty is possible, He cannot but forbid it.[2] This moral truth about cruelty, then, determines what we do and can believe about God and the moral relationship in which as a person He stands to us. It is not itself determined by our beliefs in Him. Cruelty is not wrong because God forbids it; He forbids it because it is wrong. Whether or not there is God to forbid it, cruelty is wrong. It is in this sense that there are and can be no versions of natural law corresponding to its different theological settings.

The supposition that belief in God's existence is an implication or necessary condition of belief in natural laws is self-contradictory. It contradicts the notion of natural law, the notion of a kind of truth accessible to all normal human beings quite apart from special religious revelations and beliefs. Whatever makes it plausible to believe that God created a world in which there are natural laws must make it plausible to suppose that there are such laws whether or not God exists. That God created a world in which as a matter of natural law cruelty is wrong is plausible just because cruelty cannot but be wrong and because God himself could not have made cruelty all right.

One might, of course, accept on the basis of faith alone the doctrine that there are natural laws and also accept on the basis of faith alone certain moral statements as cases of natural law. But in order for this to be possible, one must assume that the natural laws that are in fact accepted on the basis of faith alone can in principle be known independently of faith. If we thought that there were genuine cases of natural law that we ourselves could not know independently of faith, we would have to conceive of ourselves as suffering from some radical defect of intelligence and understanding.

In view of all this, why does Nielsen argue on the assumption that belief in the existence of God is a necessary condition of belief in natural law? There appear to be but three possible answers to this question. First, Nielsen may just misunderstand natural law theory on this point. He may have misinterpreted the references to God in passages like the one quoted from Cicero.[3] But Cicero, as a careful rereading will show, makes exactly the right point; namely, that with respect to what men are obliged to do by reason of the one true law, it is as if men were subject to one God who has proclaimed one law for all. Second, Nielsen may understand natural law theory but may suppose that only an ill-founded faith in God leads men to believe in the truth of the theory. He may suppose, that is, that there are no natural laws, no universal moral truth of the required sort, and that only religion dupes men into holding the false beliefs that there are. But Nielsen does not say this. Moreover, this must be established by argument and not assumed. Otherwise, all the basic questions will be begged. Third, Nielsen may believe that Catholics accept the Church's strictures on birth control and abortion, say, because of their faith rather than by reason of natural law or their own knowledge of how the law applies to these cases. This belief is certainly true. Of course, Catholics do and must submit to the authority of their Church on matters of this kind. But this fact has no bearing at all upon the contention that belief in the existence of God is a necessary condition of belief in natural law. There are, of course, two important questions here. The one is concerned with the nature of the difference between those institutions that do and those institutions that do not undertake to justify their rulings on matters of morals by appeal to universal moral truths. The other question is concerned with how, in detail, an institution brings universal moral truths to bear upon problems like birth control and abortion. How do we ascertain these truths, what are the truths with application to these matters, and how do they apply to the specific circumstances that obtain? Both Friedmann and Neilsen discuss matters that assume answers to these questions, though they never ask or argue them directly. They leave the hard core of natural law theory, even the Catholic Church's very special use of it, quite undamaged.

The second of my two considerations concerns the relations that, according to natural law theory, obtain between certain general facts about the world and those universal moral truths that are natural laws. According to the theory, this relationship between facts about the world and morality is logical: the universal moral truths, which are natural laws, are thought to be logically dependent upon the world's having certain general features. Nielsen denies this relationship, and Friedmann's remarks about existentialism imply its denial. Again, neither offers arguments in support of this important contention. They affirm or assume it as if it were a self-evident philosophical proposition or perhaps a basic dogma of modern philosophical faith.

Whether or not such a relationship obtains, it is extremely important to emphasize two features connected with it. First, it is by virtue of this relationship that the notion of natural law is connected with the notion of truth. If cruelty is prohibited as a matter of natural law, it is prohibitd by virtue of certain facts about human beings, that human beings can and do suffer, for example. By virtue of facts like these, "cruelty is wrong" is true, though the implications of this truth for human action may differ depending on differences in the circumstances under which suffering does or may occur. This explains why, as Rommen rightly insists, natural law is not like a code. The items in a code of law need have no such logical connection with truth. The items in a code are enacted, proclaimed, or customary; they may be restricted in application to a given time and place; and they may exhibit the interests and plans of any person or group of persons, of God or man or social class, in a position to proclaim law or enact it or to influence its enactment and preservation. As none of this properly characterizes natural law, natural law is not a code and cannot properly be conceived as such. Second, it is by virtue of this relationship between natural law and certain general facts about the world that natural law theory is but one of several theories of ethical cognitivism. I stress this here because of the frequent assumption and argument that natural law theory is the only form of cognitivism. Friedmann's remarks about existentialism as the sole alternative to natural law theory imply this. But there are other possible forms of cognitivism. It has been held, for example, that there is moral knowledge about what we ought to do, but that all cases of this knowledge are concerned with what we ought to do in particular circumstances that may or may not be repeated.

But clearly there are logical relationships between cases of natural law and certain general facts about the world. It is a general fact about human beings that they can and do suffer. They suffer physical pains, intense disappointments, and mental anguish. We may even go so far as to say that suffering is a characteristic feature of human nature, for any group of beings who looked like us but knew not pain or sorrow and did not suffer deprivation would be other than human. It is also a fact about our world that almost all men are in a position both to cause and prevent other persons' suffering. Finally, we cannot understand what suffering is and conceive of it as other than an evil. We may choose to endure it to achieve a good or to avert an even greater evil; and the ability to endure it, whether or not we choose it, is one of the noblest of human traits. But we could not understand this if we thought suffering was other than an evil in itself. We could not understand it as something to be endured, something that impairs our physical and intellectual powers and numbs our responsiveness. By reason of these facts, cruelty is wrong: it can never be right for anyone—out of carelessness, callousness, hate, or self-gratification—to cause another's suffering. So cruelty, which is a somewhat more restricted case of this, can never be right.

The connection between the moral truth and the general facts can be made more evident by imagining a somewhat different world. We can imagine a world in which there would be no suffering, or in which people were not in a position to cause suffering, or in which suffering caused by other persons could not be avoided or occurred only infrequently and unpredictably. Now in worlds such as these there could be no cruelty. The descriptions of these worlds entail that cruelty, as we understand it, does not occur. This is, therefore, a logical feature of these worlds. But this being so, it is a logical feature of our world that the occurrence of cruelty depends upon the fact that human beings can and do suffer and regularly do cause suffering in predictable and avoidable ways.

I am not claiming that this kind of relationship between moral truths and facts about the world is sufficient for a full-blown natural law theory. I do not suppose that in two paragraphs I have been able to say all that ought to be said about it. I am frankly uncertain about whether natural law theory, in full-blown form, is true. But I am quite certain that there is much more to it than Nielsen's and Friedmann's comments allow. I am quite certain that their criticisms do not touch it. Rommen did not defend the theory. But against criticisms like Nielsen's and Friedmann's, the theory needs no defense.

NOTES

1. Cicero, *De re publica*, 3.23.
2. This is a partial paraphrase of an argument by Nathanael Culverwel in *An Elegant and Learned Discourse of the Light of*

Nature, Oxford, 1669. See Compagnac, *The Cambridge Platonists*, Oxford, 1901, pp. 253–255.

3. Perhaps the most frequently misinterpreted reference of this sort is in The Declaration of Independence: "We hold these truths to be self-evident, that all men are created equal, that they are endowed by their Creator with certain unalienable rights," etc. It is frequently argued that belief in God as endowing men with rights is a necessary condition of belief in man's having natural rights to life, liberty, and the pursuit of happiness. Nothing could be further from the truth. What is self-evident is that men have these rights, whether or not God exists. God's existence is not self evident: belief in God is a matter of faith or inference.

4

Human Nature and Natural Law

Columbia University

> Can humanity be something re-
> mote? If I decide to be human, be-
> hold! Humanity is here.
> —*Confucius*
> There are good reasons, in fact, for
> supposing that all the gods could
> learn from us men in several re-
> spects. We men are more—hu-
> mane.
> —*Nietzsche*

I

It must be an embarrassment to the Thomistic defenders of
natural law that their dictum "there cannot be an unjust law"
might as easily sloganize the main thesis of legal positivism,
which defines justice as what the law requires. It is embarrass-
ing on a second count as well, for it is a standing objection to
the natural law doctrine that its formulations are so accom-
modatingly open as to allow any interpretation, in this case
one that exactly characterizes a theory of law precisely antithet-
ical to the natural law doctrine itself. The dictum, in fact,
is analytical on either interpretation, as a consequence of
contrary stipulations, namely, "If it is unjust, it is not a law"
(Thomism) and, contrapositively, "If it is a law, it is just"
(positivism). It would, however, be more consonant with their
intention, as well as more accordant with usage, were Thomists
to allow logical room for the expression "unjust law." For
correct application of this expression very nearly presupposes a
position outside any system of positive law from which the
latter may be appraised and, in the extreme instance, justifiably

187

resisted. That there should be an extralegal position is, after all, a thesis of natural law, and it should be a comfort to its defenders that such a position is nearly presupposed by an expression most of us would like to feel has a correct application. And surely what most of us feel can scarcely be disregarded by the theorists of natural law.

Were every law a natural law, then indeed there would be no unjust laws. But we cannot pretend to so much, and not even every just law could consistently be regarded as part of natural law. Compatibility with natural law, if it is to be just, is the most we can demand of a given positive law not otherwise part of natural law—which of course gives us a criterion for an *unjust* law: "Whatever has been recognized by usage, or laid down in writing, if it contradicts natural law, must be considered null and void." This criterion, however, leaves it an open possibility that there should be a pair of positive laws, *L-1* and *L-2*, each compatible with natural law though incompatible with one another. In such a case, appeal to natural law would help not at all in deciding which of them to follow, and some criterion other than coherence with natural law would have to be invoked, whatever it might be. Certainly it will not do to say that any law incompatible with a positive law that itself is compatible with natural law is an unjust law. This would be analogous to arguing that if we have three propositions, *P*, *Q*, and *R*, such that *P* is compatible with *Q* and incompatible with *R*, then *Q* is incompatible with *R*. For this argument yields counterintuitive results: "*A* is a bank clerk" is compatible with "*A* is married," and the latter incompatible with "*A* is a bachelor," but it could hardly be contended that "*A* is a bank clerk" is incompatible with "*A* is a bachelor." Not only that, but such an argument would yield an easy proof that every non-Euclidian geometry *is* consistent if Euclidian geometry is consistent. We generate a non-Euclidian geometry by replacing a Euclidian postulate *P* with one of its contraries, say *Q*. By hypothesis, *P* is compatible with the remaining Euclidian postulates, which then must be inconsistent with *Q*, so that every non-Euclidian geometry is contaminated at the source. But in fact there is a well-known proof of Klein's that every non-Euclidian geometry *is* consistent if Euclidian geometry is. So this argument violates common sense and human reason in its traditionally most exalted employment, mathematics; and since natural law has appealed both to common sense and human reason in support of itself, it cannot consistently wish to be inconsistent with *them*. And, finally, one good reason why every law cannot be a natural law is this: there exist pairs of inconsistent laws, or at least contrary laws such that neither of the laws can seriously be considered unjust, as, to take the trite example, traffic laws in England and France. But if *both* sets of laws were natural laws, natural law would be inconsistent, and every actual or proposed law would be consistent with it. So we must regard natural law as consistent with many actual and proposed laws inconsistent with one another, and in any piece of legislative deliberation there is, accordingly, room for appeal to criteria other than coherence with natural law, which by itself cannot determine which of these laws to enact. The fact that considerable agonizing may be involved in such procedures does not, however, as some persons seem to feel, invalidate the claims of natural law. But these claims must now be interpreted in terms of an essentially negative criterion: inconsistency with natural law does (at best) determine which laws are unjust. But natural law would fail in even this function if it ruled in advance that there can be no such laws.

II

"The recognition that the ultimate test of the validity of law lies *beyond* law itself," writes Professor d'Entreves in drawing our attention to what he regards as the Achilles' heel of Positivism, "is nothing but a natural law position." This is too abrupt. Perhaps any moral position lies beyond the law itself and pronounces upon its validity. Indeed, we have seen that consistency with natural law is not a sufficient criterion and that others must be appealed to in cases of deliberation. But some of these might be moral positions (possibly, for example, fair play). It is always possible that occupants of differing extralegal moral positions should render different and even incompatible appraisals of existing or proposed laws. Or they might give the same appraisal for different and perhaps incompatible reasons. A law that forbids divorce save in cases of demonstrable adultery would be regarded unjust by group A, which regards divorce under any circumstances as incompatible with the sanctity of the marriage bond, and by group B, which regards any limitations on divorce as incompatible with an absolute right to the pursuit of happiness, understood as compassing sexual or emotional felicity. So there are a good many positions outside the law, and even if one were to demonstrate, via some sort of transcendental deduction, that there *must* be such a position, it would remain to be shown that the natural law position is it.

I think that the theorists of natural law would probably urge that natural law lies beyond moral as well as legal systems and pronounces upon the validity of both. Even so, it would provide once more nothing better than a negative criterion, for there are perhaps moral systems incompatible one with another, though each compatible with natural law. On the other hand, there is a compensating strength in this weakening of the natural law position: it cannot be urged in objection against natural law that there are, in fact, competing moral codes. For moral, no less than legal, diversity would be consistent with the existence of some uniform and invariant natural code. So natural law might after all be ultimate in a way in which other moral systems are not: it allows second-order validations, appraisals of appraisals.

The ultimacy of natural law is allegedly guaranteed by the two facts that it is analytically related to the nature of man, and that men are everywhere and always the same, however diversely they may moralize, and however diverse the legal systems they be regulated by. Indeed, I suspect that the word "natural" (or its Latin equivalent) must originally have been used to point a contrast with observed diversities in morals and laws: as though such diversity was not "natural," but arbitrary and local. The argument would perhaps have been this: Men are no more naturally Romans than Sabines or Carthaginians. They are naturally social, however, and to live in any society, men must follow some set of rules. So living in a society and following rules are natural to man. Yet some rules must be of a kind that, unless they were followed, societies, and hence men, would perish. These rules, too, are in the nature of man, and natural law comprises them. The fact that societies have survived proves that these natural laws are followed, whether they have been codified and conventionally enforced or not.

Whether this was the argument or not, I think, little matters, though some elements in it have been the ones singled out for attack on the natural law doctrine itself. Thus the distinction between nature and convention collapses before a thoroughgoing conventionalism. But even if one is not a conventionalist, one might seriously question whether there is such a thing as human nature, invariant from society to society or time to time within the same society. Moreover, even if some rules must be followed if societies are to survive, it does not follow that even these rules are the same and invariant from, for example, society to society. And even if they were, there would be a logical question as to whether they could be deduced from a description of human nature: for the latter, characterized descriptively, cannot logically entail any prescriptions at all. And, finally, instances of such purportedly universal laws, as "Seek good and avoid evil," are charged with being so general as to admit of any interpretation whatsoever. Finally, many societies that have survived for rather a long time have lived, at least in part, in accordance with laws we might be disinclined to regard as just. So some laws that are perhaps incompatible with natural law are compatible, nevertheless, with survival.

These arguments impress me as having a certain force, and I cannot say whether they can in fact be met in such a way that the doctrine of natural law, as I have just characterized it, can be salvaged. Perhaps it cannot and ought not to be. Perhaps, indeed, the general laws that must be (if the argument is correct) necessary conditions for living in society at all are so marginal that they could, even if articulated to the satisfaction of all, hardly serve as truly useful negative criteria of unjust laws. For as limiting conditions of social existence, they could never be socially abrogated, even though every society that satisfied them (and the claim is that every society must satisfy them) was governed by positive laws we would want, perhaps, to characterize as unjust. And *these* laws would be quite out of reach so far as their impugnment in the name of natural law would be concerned.

Still, the idea that there should be some extralegal criterion of injustice, and this in some manner connected with our concept of humanity, is attractive and possibly plausible. For there is, I think, a sense in which prescriptive or normative notions are built into our concept of what it is to be human, so that one might say that natural law has a basis in our conceptual structure. There need be nothing sacrosanct about this conceptual structure, but it *is* ours, and to the extent that we employ it we are rather more committed to something like natural law than critics of this doctrine have been prepared to recognize. If we are, then that doctrine is in some measure correct in saying that we are, and in some measure correct in saying what we are committed to. Preempting a perhaps over-used catchword of contemporary philosophy, this language game is played. In the remainder of this paper, I want to suggest, with some considerable tentativeness, a weak defense of natural law along these lines.

III

To begin with, I think there is no predicate in our language that does not have, in addition to a descriptive use, a prescriptive or normic use as well (though there may be predicates with an exclusively normic use). In case there should be predicates of which this is not the case then, if F is such a predicate, we may say this about F: the instances to which F correctly applies are absolutely uniform in quality, so that no differences among these instances can constitute grounds for preferring one over another. This, incidentally, takes care of predicates with null extensions: their instances are trivially uniform in quality, there being no instances. In case, finally, there are variations among the instances of F and "F" lacks a standard normic use, then no generally accepted criteria exist in the ethicolinguistic community in whose language F is a standard predicate, for invidiously distinguishing among the instances of F. The fact that predicates have a normic, in addition to a descriptive, use is due, then, to the facts that (1) there are qualitative variations among their instances and (2) some variations are, for whatever reason, preferred over others. There is, of course, always room for idiosyncratic normic uses when there is no generally accepted normic use for F: a connoisseur of $(\hat{x})Fx$ may have become sensitive to variations among these and begin to use F normically: and we can learn, and perhaps ourselves adopt this normic use providing only he instructs us in his criteria. We, too, then become good judges of $(\hat{x})Fx$.

Normic usage is commonly plain from context. We employ normic auxiliaries like "real" ("a real boy") or "true" ("a true friend"), or we say things like "That's what I call an orange" (not implying that my use is deviant, but that this orange stands out in its kind) or "I don't call *that* an orange" (not implying botanical unauthenticity, but lowness on the scale of orangehood). Normic uses do not always imply that the thing so designated stands high on the speaker's preference scale—for example, "real trouble" and "proper messes" are what we would prefer to avoid.

The normic use of any F is closely connected with its descriptive use. Thus no original error in ascription of gender is being rectified when we say of someone that he is not a real man; but it would be normically inappropriate to say this of A if it were descriptively false that A is a man. We take the wind out of his sails who exclaims "I don't call *that* an orange" when we point out that *that* is a lemon: by failing to be an orange altogether, it cannot be considered a failure *as* an orange. In general, A being F descriptively is a necessary condition for A being F or not-F normically. Again, consider a certain fruit, orangelike in every respect except taste. There are obviously qualitative variations in the tastes of oranges— which is part of what makes for a normic use of "orange"—but there are tastes that plainly lie outside the range of variability, such as the taste of normal bananas. So imagine a fruit orange-like in every respect except that it tastes like a normal banana. This would be a new species of fruit, hence not an orange de-scriptively, hence, since a necessary condition is lacking, not an orange normically. So in general it is normically wrong to apply F to A when A has a property incompatible with the commonly accepted necessary and sufficient conditions for anything to be descriptively F. Our reason for calling some-thing an orange can never be that it has a special property outside the accepted range of variability: it is only on the basis of variations in that range that something qualifies for the normic use. Finally, it seems to me that criteria for normic usage are no more and no less conventional and arbitrary than are criteria for descriptive use (certainly the opponents of natural law are in no position to cite a doctrine of natural kinds on their own behalf). The difference lies in the fact that there is a possibility of agreeing over descriptive criteria while disagreeing over normic ones, although it seems to be a viola-tion of some necessary condition to suppose they can agree over normic usage while disagreeing over descriptive usage: they would then not be talking about the same thing.

Our concept of F comprehends the descriptive as well as the normic criteria for F-ness. Divergences are always possible at the borderline, to be sure, and there is an abstract possibility that some men may regard something as inferior in the scale of F-ness that others discount as F at all. The chief thing to emphasize, however, is that there is sufficient uniformity in normic usage to allow us to infer, when someone says of a particularly shriveled and bitter orange that it is a normic orange (as "What an orange!"), that either he is voicing a bit of irony (and normic usage is what makes irony possible) or violating a rule no less fixed than the one he would be violating were he to say, of this same fruit, that it was a lemon. It little matters for our purposes whether, in making a normic use of *F*, we are doing something over and above describing it, like commending or discommending it. The important thing is that we are at least describing it, as we must be if there are any criteria at all for normic application of the term. So our normic use may be true or false (which is our criterion for descriptiveness). And of course there are criteria, even though disagreement might arise as to what they are or whether something in fact satisfies them in a given instance. A normic use is therefore not *deduced* from a descriptive use: it is a specially restricted description already. It says that certain determinate variations in the determinable characteristics of *F*-ness are, in fact, present. It may, of course, also say more than that.

Now it seems to me incontestable that the predicate "is human" shares these features, with some added complications, some of which I shall comment upon here.

1. Being human descriptively is, of course, a necessary condition for being human normically, but in case an individual is subhuman though biologically human, this fact is often regarded as rendering inappropriate the normic ascription of not being human. For instance, this is so when the individual is mentally defective—is not a "person." With our predilection for seeking psychological excusing conditions, we are likely to search for subhuman traits in individuals who behave in consistently nonhuman or, as we say, inhuman ways. Perhaps we are wrong in doing this. A recent and much mooted discussion of Eichmann, for example, makes the point that Eichmann was a "normal" human being in every respect, though far, indeed, from a normic human, which means that we must look for a social rather than a psychological explanation of his behavior. And it is perhaps true that the biological "is human" is not obviously inapplicable to individuals who are obviously

normically inhuman. Indeed, less dramatic instances can be found than erstwhile top Nazis: man's inhumanity to man is not uniquely instantiated in the modern totalitarian state, nor is man's humanity to man uniquely instantiated outside such states. So someone who explains Eichmann's inhumanity with sole reference to social circumstance will have a problem of accounting for instances of human behavior under just those circumstances. But here I am concerned only with logical features of the predicate.

2. When we apply the predicate "is human" normically to a human being, we do not do so on the basis of some special peculiar gift that makes him stand apart from his fellows. A normic human being may be otherwise undistinguished, nor is normic humanity a distinction in the order, say, of a certain remarkable musical gift—though being normically human is sometimes a distinction among the class of specially gifted individuals. For with the highly gifted, we tend, rightly or wrongly, to be surprised when they remain or behave humanly, "just like you and me," in spite of having the gift. The point in saying this is that being normically human is something we in fact expect of otherwise normal human beings, though superhumanity, like subhumanity, is sometimes considered an excusing condition of sorts when someone fails to behave humanly, or with "human decency."

3. One further feature of the predicate "is human" is this: we sometimes tend to regard being just normally human, in contrast with subnormally or supernormally, as an excusing condition of sorts. I have in mind the sense in which we say 'tis human to err, or in which, when someone succumbs to temptation, that he or she was only human, or that it is too much to expect a mere human to have done otherwise. I mention this only to emphasize, however, that reference to someone's normal humanness is never an excusing condition for doing something that is incompatible with normic humanity. Human weakness is not considered incompatible with being normically human, and normic humanity is something we feel justified in expecting *mere* humans to exhibit, not just saints

and moral heroes. There are limits to what we can expect of human beings, and if we expect them to be normically human, that cannot be a terribly difficult thing for them to be.

Now what I wish very tentatively to suggest is this. Natural law might be interpreted not as something *deduced* from our concept of normic humanity, but as exactly a characterization of this concept. That is to say, there are certain kinds of actions, attitudes, and dispositions that normic humans exhibit as a matter of fact: and natural law is only a description of that sort of behavior. That it should also be prescriptive is due to the fact that not every human being in fact always acts that way. But it is a way we may expect them to act, not merely in the sense in which England expects each man to do his duty, but also in the sense in which we expect birds to come forth from eggs: it is an inductive, and not merely a moral, expectation.

Who except a normal human being is to say what normic humanity consists in? Whether we ourselves are that in every instance, it is we who apply the term, it is we who apply it to some actions and individuals and not to others; and the rules for applying it are more or less fixed. They are sufficiently fixed so that, in the extreme case, were someone to be saying that Hitler was normically human, he would be violating these rules: Hitler is very nearly a paradigm case of someone to whom the predicate does *not* apply. Some Nazi sympathizer might say that Hitler was a good man just because he was not human (normically). But this is to acquiesce in at least our use of "human," if hardly in our use of "good." For although the analysis of "good" remains cloudy, so that it is perhaps not as clear as one might wish what is entailed by calling someone good, it seems to me plain that some predicates, when applied to individuals, entail that those individuals are, insofar, good. The normic predicate "is human" seems to be one of these. And, indeed, when we say that someone is a good man, we almost always mean that he exhibits the traits of normic humanity that, I am suggesting, natural law might be regarded as describing.

What, then, is this concept? The moment we do seek to describe it, we run into certain difficulties, not because we have any great doubts concerning where and when to apply it, but because there is a special and perhaps inexpungeable openness in the class of cases to which it applies. Let us just concern ourselves with human acts, supposing that we can define a normic human being as one who acts humanly, and who, whatever be his dispositions, never acts inhumanly. I think having inhuman dispositions is compatible with someone being normically human: perhaps I should underscore my ascription of normic humanity to an individual whom I discovered to have sadistic and brutal dispositions upon which he never acted. So let me ask someone to consider the class of actions that fall under the description "the human thing to do." For one thing, I do not think we could specify this without first requesting a description of the cases it applies to. For the human thing to do depends very much upon variations, to which whoever wants to do the human thing must be sensitive, trying to adapt his action to circumstance always in a way that is compatible with the principles of normic humanity. Amongst the circumstances are the feelings of the individuals involved, and part at least of being human consists in being sensitive to these feelings, to acknowledge that one is dealing here with mere human beings. So there is no one single thing we could cite. To be able to do the human thing is to be able to act spontaneously human in a novel case. And we who apply the term are no less spontaneously able to recognize its correct applicability in a novel case where it is exhibited. There are, in brief, no recipes.

Perhaps it might be said that every action of this sort exhibits a quality of kindness. In a measure this is correct, and kindness *is* one of the components of our concept of normic humanity. Still, I do not think this helps very much, because exactly the same sorts of features are to be found with our concept of kindness as with our concept of "the human thing to do." There is no one set of things the doing of which qualifies someone as a kind man. We cannot, in brief, "unpack" the predicate "is kind" into a closed conjunction of conditional sentences, the antecedent of which describes the circumstance and the consequent of which prescribes the appropriate action. On such an account of kindness, humaneness, and the like, it impresses me that naturalists and intuitionists in ethics might join forces: there is a sense in which these terms are never fully analyzable, though where they are analyzable, they are so with reference to "natural facts."

For the present this is as far as I should wish to go. It would suggest, perhaps, why natural law would itself have to be considered a nonstatic code, varying in a way as circumstances vary, consonantly only with the requirement of humanness. The question then remains of showing the connection between natural law, so considered, and this legal system or that. It is a very weak connection, amounting to little more than that positive law should not be incompatible with normic human behavior. This does not mean that acting in the name of the law need always be doing the human thing, but only that it should not be incompatible with that. The only thing really incompatible with that is acting inhumanly, and whoever so acts in the name of the law or whatever law requires men so to act might be regarded as unjust by natural law criteria. The negative stipulation that the law should not license inhuman action tells us, of course, very little about what the law should positively be. On the other hand, it is perhaps quite enough that there should be a limit beyond which it would be intolerable for the law and for its executors to go, and that this limit should be internally related to our concept of what it is to be human. Natural law requires only that we act, in law and elsewhere, in ways compatible with normic humanity, with what the Chinese would term the *tao* of humanity. Taoists refused to go beyond that: according to them one should govern men "the way one fries small fish." That, of course, is not enough. But to say what more should be done requires more than natural law can provide us with. It cannot pretend to say what more must be done. I have only tried to say what it might pretend to.

5

On Defining and Defending Natural Law

WILLIAM K. FRANKENA
University of Michigan

NATURAL LAW is far too often attacked or defended, destroyed or revived, without its being made clear just what is being talked about. In these reflections I shall try to do something toward showing what is or ought to be debated in such discussions, though I cannot be either as exhaustive or as rigorous as I should be.

We may note at once that it is not a law that is being attacked or defended. One can attack or defend laws, of course, but this is not what is being done in debates about natural law. When one criticizes or supports a law, one presupposes that there is a law to be criticized or supported; but when one discusses natural law one is raising precisely the question as to whether there is a law of a certain sort, namely, a law that is natural. One is discussing, not a law, but a thesis about law; not a legal question, but a metalegal one.

This suggests the first move to be made in settling the dispute. The statement "there is a law that is natural" is a contradiction in terms, an opponent may say. A law by definition involves an act of legislative will or perhaps a custom; it cannot be something natural. Much depends here on the meaning of "natural," and we shall come to this, but for the moment let us focus on the meaning of "law." There are then at least three lines of reply that a proponent of natural law may make at this point. (1) He may say, quite correctly, (a) that we do use the term "law" in such a way that there are, in fact, laws

200

that are natural, such as those in the physical sciences. He may even go on to contend (b) that it is just such factual, or scientific, laws or generalizations that are in question in debates about natural law. Indeed, this is exactly what at least some ethical naturalists, as they have been called since 1903, hold. They maintain that ethical terms can be translated into natural or scientific ones and, hence, that ethical principles and general value judgments simply are generalizations about what goes on in nature. R. B. Perry and S. C. Pepper are the best recent examples, but it may even be that the Thomists, who are not intuitionists or noncognitivists, are also holding that their natural laws are laws in this sense. At any rate, the ethical naturalists (or at least some of them) are subscribing to a kind of natural law theory, and one who asserts both contentions (1a) and (1b) is equating the debate about natural law with the debate between the ethical naturalists and their opponents (intuitionists and noncognitivists) that has dominated so much of this century. If he asserts only (1a), of course, as he may do, he is only claiming that he has some right to use "law" in a sense not recognized by his opponent.

As for his other lines of reply: (2) He may, then, deny (1b) and insist that his natural laws are not natural laws in the scientific sense (or that ethical principles cannot be reduced to empirical generalizations), and still hold that there are general norms of conduct that are properly called laws, though not in a scientific sense. Or (3) he may allow that the word "law" is inappropriate in the case of ethical and political principles and say that he is concerned only to maintain that there are general standards of conduct that are "natural." If he takes this third line, he must explain just what he means by "natural" and show that there are standards of conduct (normative generalizations) that are natural in his sense. And, of course, he must show that his sense of "natural" has some connection with the natural law tradition. If he takes the second line, he must do this, too, but he must also show that his standards may properly be called "laws."

In other words, there are two claims that the proponent of natural law may make (so far, that is, for we shall find still others):

A. There are rules or principles about our rights and duties that are *natural* (in some sense of this term connected with the natural law tradition).

B. These rules and principles are *laws* in some proper sense, not just valid principles about rights and duties.

Further, he may assert and defend A alone or both A and B. Just what form of natural law theory he holds will depend on what he means by "natural" and "law." Either way he can be an ethical naturalist, an intuitionist, or even, as we shall see, a noncognitivist—or perhaps some fourth kind of an "ist."

Let us consider line (2), which involves asserting both A and B in the face of the opponent's move. Let us also, for the time being, suppose that the proponent has established A, that is, he has established as natural some principles of the form:

M. We ought to love our fellowmen.

N. All men ought to be treated equally.

O. Everyone has the right to life, liberty, and security of person.

If he is no quibbler about terms, he might then be willing to call M, N, and O laws or moral laws. But then he is in effect taking line (3), for all he means by a moral law is an ethical principle, or, perhaps, a valid ethical principle. Strictly speaking, line (2) involves more. It involves saying that some "natural" principles like M, N, and O are "laws" and not just valid ethical principles, but not meaning by this merely that they are embodied in, or enforced by, human law. This is a possible position that is taken by some theologians, for it may be that what is called for in M, N, and O is also commanded by God. Then one could quite well call them laws, and if one thought that what is enjoined in them is not right because it is commanded by God, but is commanded by God because it is right, then one could also regard them as enjoining what is naturally right, in short, as natural laws.

However, the opponent of natural law might then retort as follows: "You can, indeed, claim that MNO are natural and valid principles of conduct and also that they are law, assuming that you know that God commands them. MNO are natural, you have shown, and they are law, but they are not natural *qua* law, or law *qua* natural, and you really have no right to talk as if they are just naturally laws. Their being both natural and legal is due to an act of God's will." The retort has its justice, but the complexities and resources of the natural law theory are not yet exhausted. Its proponent can readily find a good sense in which MNO are natural in addition to being laws and are laws because they are natural. For, in one important sense, "natural law" means "law that is known to be law, not by revelation, but by our natural faculties (unregenerated)." Hence the proponent may argue, first, that, God being righteous, we can be certain that He will command and enforce what is right; second, that we can know this by our natural faculties, and also that MNO state what is right; third, that we can therefore know by our natural faculties that MNO are law; and hence, finally, that MNO are natural law in a perfectly good sense. What they call for is naturally known both to be naturally right and to be law. Such a view was, in fact, common among natural law theorists of the seventeenth and eighteenth centuries such as Hobbes and Berkeley, Cumberland and Clarke, and probably Locke. To attack it one must show that nothing can be naturally right, commanded by God on this ground, and naturally known to be so. One cannot merely contend that the phrase "natural law" is a contradiction in terms when it does not mean "scientific law."

I have, however, been talking here as if one who takes line (2) must be a cognitivist in his views about MNO. But this is not true. Verily, the ways of the natural law tradition are many and past all finding out! It is clearly possible for a theologian to hold that MNO are simply divine commands or imperatives, justified perhaps, but not true or false. Then they are laws and he is a noncognitivist. But he can still maintain that we can know that God commands MNO, not by revelation, but by our natural faculties, and thus claim that MNO represent laws that are natural in the sense of being naturally known to be divine ordinances. It is all a question of what he thinks can be established by natural theology.

Consider another possibility, one more palatable to contemporary taste. Suppose a philosopher subscribes to MNO and holds (x) that they are expressions of attitude, not true or false statements; (y) that they and the attitudes expressed in them are nevertheless justifiable by reference to naturally known facts about man and the world; and (z) that they provide a basis for evaluating all human codes, institutions, laws, and the like. Is he a natural law theorist or not? He is certainly asserting some theses in the natural law tradition, namely (y) and (z). And is it so clear that (x) is incompatible with the tradition?

Incidentally, a theologian may believe that MNO are revealed and still be either a cognitivist or a noncognitivist. For he may hold either that they are true but not known to us unless revealed by God or that they are commands and that the very act of revelation is the act of commanding us to obey them. And, if he is a cognitivist, he may even contend that they are natural laws—not, of course, in the sense that they can be known by our natural faculties, but in the sense of being true by virtue of the nature of things (in any of the several senses in which this may be the case). He may also be an ethical naturalist in Moore's sense.

Most of what I have been saying so far has borne on the question whether anything natural can properly be called law or not. But the main thesis at issue in the debate about natural law is surely not B but A, at least if we expand A to read:

A': *there are* valid *principles about duties and rights that are* natural. All except those persons who quibble about the use of the term "law" will agree that there are natural laws if they are convinced of A. The key words, of course, are "valid" and "natural." Now "valid" may mean "true" as against false, in the sense of these terms in which noncognitivists say, or used to say, that ethical judgments are neither true nor false, whatever that is. But noncognitivists (or nondescriptivists or whatever those thinkers should be called who hold that ethical judgments do not function like "roses are red") have mostly come around to saying that ethical judgments may at least sometimes be justified or rationally acceptable (and even "true"), even though they do not ascribe properties to things or assert relations between them. So let us say that there are two senses of "valid"—"true" and "justified." Now surely a philosopher who holds that principles like MNO are natural and valid in the first sense falls squarely within the natural law tradition. But what if he says that they are natural and valid only in the second sense? Is this not enough to bring him into the fold? Would traditional natural law theorists have distinguished the two positions? Some people have certainly attacked natural law theory even though they themselves held that there are principles like MNO, which ascribe rights and duties to men as men and are justified by facts about the world that are knowable by our natural faculties. But were they, then, differing with it in any very essential respect?

My main point, however, is that the term "natural" in A' has many senses even within the natural law tradition, or, alternatively, that A' has a number of senses:

1. There are valid principles like MNO that ascribe rights and duties to men simply by virtue of their being human or of their nature as men. This thesis will itself have two senses, corresponding to the two meanings of "valid" just distinguished. We may call them (1a) and (1b). People who hold (1) in either sense would be said to believe in natural rights. Why not in natural law?

2. There are principles of this sort the validity of which can be established by our natural faculties. This thesis too will have two senses. (2a) will say that they are true and their truth can be known or shown by our natural faculties, (2b) that they are justified on the basis of what we can know by such faculties. (2a) entails (2b) as (1a) entails (1b), but not vice versa. (2) entails (1) but not vice versa. It is usual to think of reason as the faculty involved, but one may doubt

that rationalism, even in a broad sense, is essential to the natural law theory, for some intuitionists or ethical realists have held that emotion is cognitive and is the organ of our basic ethical insights—for example, Max Scheler and Nicolai Hartmann. Yet they deserve a place in the tradition as much as any other intuitionists.

3. There are principles of the kind in question that are true because our having the rights and duties involved follows logically from facts about human nature as such or about the world, all of this being known through our natural faculties. This thesis implies that the "Ought" can be deduced logically from the "Is," and is often thought to be identical with or entailed by, the natural law theory. E. W. Hall rejects the natural law thesis on the ground that it involves this thesis. But he himself insists that "there is value," that there are objectively valid and naturally known (he holds they are emotionally known) "Ought structures" that parallel factual ones but are different in character from them—so that ethical judgments are not "true" but "legitimate." Hence he seems to affirm at least as much natural law doctrine as he denies. Is it essential to natural law doctrine to fuse the Is and the Ought or to regard the latter as deducible from the former? What about Aristotle's distinction between theoretical and practical wisdom? What about Kant? What about Samuel Clarke, Richard Price, and the intuitionists? (3) would, however, be accepted by naturalists and ontologists. It entails (2) but is not entailed by (2).

There are other theses in the natural law tradition that are related to these and to one another:

4. Our rights and duties do not depend wholly on the offices we hold, the agreements we have made, the commands addressed to us, or the laws (human) that prevail. This follows alike from (1), (2), or (3).

5. There are valid principles in the light of which we may evaluate all human institutions, laws, codes, actions, and so forth. This, too, follows from (1), (2), or (3) alike.

6. There are ethical principles that hold even in a state of

nature. This also follows from (1), (2), or (3). It is essentially equivalent to (4) and (5). In theology there has been a related but different concept. It has been held, for example, that slavery is contrary to natural law, but was made valid by man's fall.

Well, one could go on. But this list of theses shows, along with the previous discussion, that there are a number of doctrines in the natural law tradition, not a single theory, and that an attacker or defender must be clear just which ones he is and is not for or against. (3) is the strongest claim, but as far as I can see it is not essential. A case can be made for saying that one believes in natural law if one believes in any of the theses listed in any of their senses. I think it will also be clear that a number of metaethical theories are compatible with holding most of the theses in at least one of their senses. Intuitionism, noncognitivism, and some other theories are excluded by (3). Intuitionism, naturalism, and other forms of cognitivism are excluded by (1a) and (2a). But that is all.

It is also important to note that although the theses stated have been put in a metaethical cast, there are also theses that are purely normative and that are nevertheless such that, if one subscribes to them, one is saying something that belongs in the natural law tradition. The ethical principles M, N, and O are themselves such theses. As soon as we begin formulating theories about their natures and validity, as we do in the above theses, we are embarked on metaethics, but while we are merely asserting or denying them and giving our reasons we are, or should be, doing normative ethics. The natural law tradition includes both metaethics and normative ethics, and, while there are problems about distinguishing the two, one must try to be clear what one is doing when.

I may perhaps illustrate this remark as follows. One way of denying that there are natural rights and duties is to deny (4), that is, to deny that a human being has any rights or duties as such. They are all created by the offices or roles he enters into, the promises he makes, or the commands and laws addressed to him. Here one who is inclined to object may ask if man as man has no obligation or right to assume any offices, to fulfill the duties of those he assumes, to keep the agreements he makes, or to obey the commands and laws addressed to him. If so, then there is, after all, a sense in which there are natural rights and duties. Against this, however, the opponent of such rights and duties often contends that these underlying obligations and rights rest on human convention or on divine ordinance and are not valid in the nature of things. But to say this is to say that there are human conventions that confer certain rights and duties upon all men as such, that is, that they "endow" us with "certain inalienable rights" and duties, or that there is a divine ordinance that does so (as our Declaration of Independence implies, even though it also holds "these truths to be self-evident"). However, even if one accepts this metaethics, which seems to make rights and duties matters of *nomos* instead of nature, one may still, when one is doing normative ethics (enunciating ethical principles oneself), subscribe to such principles as M, N, or O. And then one is, after all, asserting in a sense that there are natural rights and duties. Perhaps this is why the sophist Antiphon can stand near the source of the natural law tradition.

One more point remains to be made. Talk about natural law in ethics and politics seems to imply that the basis of thought in these fields consists of certain general norms. Hence an opponent of natural law might argue that this is not the case. The basic judgments of right and wrong or good and bad, he might claim, are particular, like "This experience is good," "This is the right thing to do in this situation," and general principles of the sort we have been talking about are either not available at all or are derivative from particular ones and not very helpful. Henry Sidgwick's "perceptual intuitionists" argue along this line, and so do the existentialists and situationalists, religious or antireligious. Yet there is a sense in which even such a particularist may admit that there are such things as natural morality, natural rights, and natural duties (if not natural *laws*). For he may still hold that his basic particular judgments are knowable by our natural faculties or justifiable on natural grounds and do not depend on revelation, will, decision, or the like. In fact, he will hold this if he is a perceptual intuitionist, though not if he is an existentialist. And, if he does, he is at least admitting that there is a natural body of moral insight, and to that extent he falls within the natural law tradition after all.

H. L. A. Hart has recently suggested a "minimal content for natural law." As a somewhat less minimal suggestion, I am inclined to propose that we should put down as a natural law man anyone who does at least the following: (1) He subscribes to ethical principles such as MNO. (2) He holds (a) that we are justified in accepting them, directly or indirectly, by truths known by our natural faculties (though not necessarily by logical deduction); (b) that they justifiably ascribe rights and obligations to all men as such, independently of their offices, agreements, laws, or whatever; and (c) that they may therefore serve as a standard by which to measure all human institutions, rules, and actions. These propositions are compatible with a variety of metaethics, whether metaphysical, theological, or empirical, rationalist or non-rationalist, cognitivist or noncognitivist. It seems to me, however, that they are the important doctrines in the natural law tradition to be for or against. I do not say that the other propositions that may be or have been conjoined with them are not interesting or significant, but I do suggest that they are not essential to natural law theory or at least should no longer be regarded as essential to it.

6

Elements of Natural Law Philosophy

JEROME HALL
University of Indiana Law School

THE TITLE of this symposium implies that there is a particular philosophy that is "the" philosophy of natural law and, perhaps because of that premise, it also implies that natural law philosophy is especially in need of defense. Both of these suggestions may, perhaps, reflect Continental views of natural law philosophy. In fact, however, there are currently several natural law philosophies and, of course, "nature" is a very ambiguous term. But theories that have had the support of many of the keenest philosophical minds from Plato to Morris Cohen and numerous distinguished living scholars hardly seem to be in need of greater defense than other theories of law.

It is only necessary to recall Frederick Pollock's classic remark that natural law is "a living embodiment of the collective reason of civilized mankind," to formulate the current problems of natural law philosophy in much more realistic terms than the above assumptions allow. In these terms, it is far from evident, for example, that John Dewey was an unmitigated opponent of natural law philosophy, as was intimated in the discussion. Although Dewey criticized natural law philosophy based on a priori or transcendental values, abstract reason, or God, especially when it was employed as a reactionary ideology, he also recognized that "natural justice means that which commends itself to the best judgment of the most experienced or to the collective common sense of the race, as over against the conventional and technical justice of inherited legal rules"; [1] and he pointed out that the "identification of natural and rational, and the equating of both with the morally right has been at various times a source of great improvements in law." [2] These references to Pollock and Dewey would be considerably amplified in any adequate account of twentieth-century legal philosophy, because many legal philosophers, especially since World War II, have been constructing value-oriented theories of law.

Any meaningful discussion of current versions of natural law philosophy must recognize, next, that they reflect theories that make sense of value judgments as such; perhaps the terms "value-cognition" and "rationalist" may serve to indicate the character of these ethical theories. My preference is to restrict "natural law philosophy" even more, namely, to theories that hold that there is objective truth in moral valuation: (1) that there are objectively better and worse answers to moral problems and (2) that men are able to discover the better ones, the relevant moral truths. Much of Ross's and Ewing's work represents the kind of ethical theory that seems to me to be most germane to present issues in natural law philosophy, but Aristotle, Hartmann, Dewey, and other scholars have also written about ethics in ways that are likewise suggestive.

Natural law philosophy, as I view it, originates in distinctive personal experience connoted by such terms as "obligation," "right," "freedom," and "responsibility." The relevant quest is for the most persuasive explanation of this experience and for the soundest elucidation of the ideas expressing it. In particular, the present-day natural law philosopher defends the significance of his moral experience and the validity of thoughtful value judgments against naturalistic attacks upon them that, in one way or another, would reduce them to desires, ejaculations, commands, or decisions. In sum, legal experience is a kind of moral experience, and the natural law philosopher therefore shares with the above ethicists the tasks of establishing the distinctiveness and truth of sound value judgments. The legal philosopher does not merely apply the indicated type of ethics to positive law—that common opinion is a gross and misleading oversimplification of the relations of jurisprudence and philosophy. Instead, he contributes to ethics as well as to other branches of philosophy when he deals with legally significant problems.

Natural law philosophers sometimes seem to speak in puzzling ways, as when they insist that all laws have value and even that "an unjust 'law' is not a law." To many present-day philosophers this smacks of fantasy or fanaticism and gives rise to the suspicion that an orthodox theology is lurking in the background as the "real issue." But if one reads the history of legal and political philosophy, this sort of "verbal behavior" on the part of natural law philosophers is understandable and, for reasons shortly to be discussed, it is fully warranted. If one attends to the origin of the word "law" and to the indubitable fact that natural law philosophers have been particularly interested in justice and "right law," one may still criticize this verbal habit, but one will so do on more sophisticated grounds. For "law" was first associated with God ("the laws of God") and the term thus acquired an honorific meaning. Thus, Socrates, ordered by the Thirty Tyrants to arrest Leon of Salamis, refused to obey, not the law, but the command of the dictators. Socrates withheld the term "law" from such commands, because he apparently thought that the ordinary language of the time, or at least that part of it that he approved, required his mode of speech.

But although the origin of "law" partly accounts for the usage of natural law philosophers, it does not justify the tenacity with which they have insisted on a restrictive use of the word, one that excludes the unjust or immoral "commands of the sovereign." To understand the reasons for this, one must distinguish the practical realm of problem solving from that of theory and, also, take account of the fact that natural law philosophy, a practical discipline, draws upon theoretical discipline whose subject matter is the social reality of law.

In the realm of practical legal problem solving, the most important values, it is widely agreed, are order and justice; and there is frequent, sometimes obvious, tension between them. Order is essential to the survival of any society, and the relevant implication is that authority must be obeyed. Political authority is expressed in the commands of the sovereign, which should be clear and easily located and identified. Because of the inevitable ambiguity of the commands, however, certain persons are chosen and designated officials, and their interpretation of what the rules mean must be accepted as what the law is, hence, *ignorantia legis neminem excusat*. All of this follows from the basic premise of the value of order and the implication that the commands of the sovereign must be obeyed—they are "laws."

The equally insistent voice of justice demands that the sovereign's commands be morally valid; the eternal quest is for "right law," not any kind of order. This is expressed in our constitutions, especially in provisions that the sovereign's commands—or, if one prefers, his prima facie laws—that violate the minimal conditions of civilized life are not laws. The inevitable tensions between the demands of justice and the requirements of order, as felt and articulated from the diverse viewpoints of many interested persons, defy easy generalization concerning the relationship of the two values, when and to what extent the one should be sacrificed for the other, and the like. Generalizations purporting to express relevant canons are vacuous because circumstances and conditions are infinitely varied. It may be the case that the ultimate implication of the above clash of values is that of order versus anarchy; but it must suffice here to note that in particular situations the preservation of both order and justice depends upon an inevitable degree of fiat and a corresponding sacrifice of right.

But the above does not warrant the continued restrictive use of "law," even when one also takes account of the origin of "law," its traditional honorific sense, and the ideological functions of the natural law preference in the practical realm. One might, of course, submit that it is arbitrary to insist that the inherited linguistic slate be wiped clean and that natural law philosophers adopt the linguistic preference of legal positivists. But more than these considerations are required if the central thrust and the terminology of natural law philosophy are to be understood: certainly in ordinary speech, especially in democratic states, laws may be good or bad; nor are lawyers who challenge the constitutionality of prima facie laws apt to use the restrictive natural law terminology.

The required answers are to be found, as was suggested above, in distinguishing theory from practice and in the relations of theoretical knowledge, especially social science, to the practical disciplines of natural law philosophy and juridical science (legal positivism). When philosophers discuss legal problems and when scientists seek the most meaningful definitions of their data, their perspective is theoretical. There are various other limitations, especially resulting from the required uniformity of the subject matter of a science or discipline, which determine usage in this context. In this perspective, the conditions of free, informed problem solving are decisive so far as cogent description and analysis of the congruent subject matter is concerned. "Law" must, therefore, be given a meaning that does not include irrational commands in the same field of data as the norms discovered or invented in correct problem solving, including that expressed in a sound judicial process. Unfortunately, scholars who engage in debates on legal positivism versus natural law philosophy do not always articulate the premises of their position, and the results are inconclusive, since both order and justice are valuable.

To discover the theoretical reliance of the most promising version of natural law philosophy as currently viewed in this country, one most focus first and most, not on the commands of sovereigns, but instead on the social reality of law, on what has rather vaguely been referred to as "customary law." One must attend to the long stretch of the legal history of many societies, viewing their survival and development in relation to the legal norms that were spontaneously and rationally discovered or invented in answer to daily needs; and one must also study similar data among subgroups such as the family and other associations that are less extensive than the political society. The indicated social reality has been referred to, also, in terms of the "internalization of norms," "law as a cultural fact," "law-in-action," "living law," and so on. The social reality of law, thus viewed, is a "natural" artifact in the sense that it is produced spontaneously in informed, uncoerced social problem solving.

For the philosopher and social scientist seeking and elucidating significant generalizations, the rationality and justice of the natural artifact of law—the social reality of law—must guide the construction of an apt terminology. Once the subject matter of their disciplines is found to be a distinctive social reality, the knowledge of that subject matter is not a question of choice, nor is ordinary language apt to be very helpful. For here we are in the realm, not of practice, but of theory and science. Here, the purpose is solely to understand, not directly to influence action, as in adjudication. And, just as the physical scientist must limit the definition of the data subsumed by his scientific laws and specify certain "conditions," such as "perfect vacuum," so, too, the legal theorist cannot generalize most significantly (that is, other than formally) regarding a field that includes both the commands of an insane dictator and the norms spontaneously discovered or invented in free, thoughtful inquiry by persons living together and actualizing the values of their common life in and through a just legal order. The experience of normal social life and the knowledge of the character of a just order, of course, influence practical problem solving. For philosophers and scientists intent on maximizing knowledge of law, a restrictive definition of "law," limited by significant social and ethical criteria, is the desideratum—indeed, it is a necessity.

In the practical perspective of order, emphasis is apt to be placed on "command of the sovereign" and the importance of certainty; in that of justice, ethical values are emphasized. Much of what is called "legal positivism" is analytical philosophy applied to the practical solution of legal problems, and might preferably be called "juridical science." An adequate philosophy of law, a theoretical discipline, takes account of the various perspectives and purposes of the participants in practical legal problem solving, whereas these draw upon whatever knowledge they find in the theoretical realm to aid their purpose of directly influencing action. Thus the practical perspective of the citizen vis-à-vis his ruler, including that of a litigant seeking justice, interacts with the theoretical perspective of the legal scientist in various ways.

It would take much more space than is permitted here to give an adequate account of the social reality of law, distinguish it from official law, and interrelate them. It must suffice here to add that the social reality of law is, in this writer's view, a distinctive kind of social conduct. Specifically, it is conduct expressing norms and implying values, deviation from which causes harms (determined in a judicial process) to which sanctions are and must be applied (sanctions process). Official law, the so-called "command of the sovereign," is initially an abstraction from the social reality of law, that is, from "law as conduct"; later, it is amplified by legislation, including judicial law-making in interstitial spaces, by the logical extension of the abstracted rules, and, occasionally, by sheer arbitrariness.

In terms of the above theory, the "value of law" connotes the value of certain social conduct, not that of words or concepts. How, indeed, can value be found in formulas except in a marginal or hypothetical sense, resting finally on the assumption that the formulas somehow guide human conduct? It is the social action discussed above—law as conduct—that has value; and it is that paramount datum that limits significant definition of "positive law," validates natural law philosophy, and provides the subject matter of a humanist sociology of law.

The normativity of law is thus the normativity of certain conduct; and this cannot be adequately described in factual terms. The implication is that human conduct is, to a significant degree, free. Thus, law as conduct may proceed toward a selected objective, it may stop short of that, or it may take quite other directions. The interrelationships between the social reality of law and the traditional conceptual law (official law) call for a much more detailed discussion than can be given here.[3]

What can and must be noted here is that the "value of law" is employed differently in the practical and in the theoretical spheres. Natural law philosophy, a practical discipline, uses the value of the social reality of law, especially as articulated in a sound legal system, in criticism of the sovereign's commands. But the purpose of the social scientist who participates in spontaneous legal problem solving to understand the moral experience of the actors in selected events is description and explanation, not criticism. This implies that at least two very different "oughts" must be distinguished—the ought employed in criticism in practical problem solving and the ontological ought employed in theory in cogent description of the social reality of law. There are, accordingly, important links between natural law philosophy and a humanist sociology of law.

It follows from what has been said above that an adequate philosophy of law must recognize the important functions of both natural law philosophy and the sociology of law. Indeed, much more than that is required to construct a realistic, coherent configuration that takes due account of the fullness and variety of juridical experience. Thus the logic of law is, also, an indispensable part of an adequate jurisprudence, and there are basic conceptions to be discovered, invented, and elucidated in an integrative jurisprudence that seeks to bring into significant interrelationship the concept, value, and fact of positive law.[4]

NOTES

1. Reprinted in Jerome Hall, *Readings in Jurisprudence* (Indianapolis: Bobbs-Merrill, 1938), p. 231.

2. *Ibid.*, p. 230.

3. See Hall, *Comparative Law and Social Theory* (Baton Rouge: University of Louisiana, 1963); Hall, "Integrative Juris-

prudence," in *Interpretations of Modern Legal Philosophies,* ed. P. L. Sayre (New York: Oxford University Press, 1947), and revised and reprinted in Hall, *Studies in Jurisprudence and Criminal Theory* (New York: Oceana Publications, 1958); and Hall, "Reason and Reality in Jurisprudence," *Buffalo Law Review,* VII (1958), 351.

4. See sources listed in footnote 3.

7

Rule and Case

RICHARD KUHNS
Columbia University

THE CRITICISM directed to Professor Rommen's paper exhibits the antagonism aroused in some quarters by the idea of natural law. Perhaps most upsetting to the critics was Professor Rommen's assertion that there are "metaphysically necessary *bona,* or values" that social life is organized to realize. Without acknowledgment of such ultimate values, he contends, the highest goods, temporal felicity and the fullest development of this person, are impossible. It is the aim of the positive legal order to promote and preserve these values; positive law can be corrected if measured against natural law.

Here the dispute arises: even if all men, in a vague way, agree to a set of ultimate goods, the positive means employed to realize the goods would be the object of contention. Positive law must always fall short of the ideal that it presumably defends. Even though positive law is "in peaceful times . . . much more often an approximation of *jus naturale* and justice than not," it has many other aims in addition to the realization of natural law, and "peaceful times" is a difficult norm to define. Among the many conditions positive law must meet are the needs of the state and of individuals within the state; the demands of war and of man's unreason. The many needs positive law must meet are considered by Professors Levi and Freund (pp. 263 and 282), and in so doing they present a picture of how complex the job of law is in meeting the exigencies of social life in the state. Their contributions make it clear that one of the great problems for natural law theories, as well as for positivist theories, is the relationship of rules to cases.

As Plato pointed out, law is possible only where there is a willingness to generalize, and this willingness will resist the need to treat each case as individual. Natural law theories seem far too eager to generalize; positivist theories, too eager to scrap the generalizations for the individual case. Professor Freund attempts to describe and understand how the rule and the case are related and how, since the rule can never exactly fit the case, the two may be adequately (that is, justly) dealt with. He suggests a conception of justice that is not contrary to the tradition of natural law theory, but that, in being critical of that theory, may permit a restatement of its necessary contribution to the process of judicial decision.

There are two principles involved in the working out of general rules and their application to cases: legislation and precedent. In ancient legal theory the second was associated with the ancestral, the first, with the civic. Both ancestral and civic made demands on the individual that had to be met; but satisfying the claims of both often led to conflicts. Indeed, these conflicts provide the subject matter for much of our greatest literature. The conflict exists today, though we do not think of precedent as ancestral. But the claim of precedent compels, because of a special sanction, the power of ancestral tradition. In each of us, judge or citizen, there is a felt demand for consistency with traditional ways, and at the same time there is a recognition that reason must constantly re-examine the traditional to discover what is fair and just.

Therefore, the application of rules to cases is more complex than we at first realize. For judges and for those who must recognize an obligation to accept the judges' decisions there is a conflict between the sanction of the traditional and the sanction of the reasonable. However, once rules are applied to cases and decisions reached, there is also a practical need to resist fresh considerations every time action is taken, for in every society there is "the need for certain rules which can, over great areas of conduct, safely be applied by private individuals to themselves without fresh official guidance or weighing up of social issues, and the need to leave open, for later settlement by an informed, official choice, issues which can only properly be appreciated and settled when they arise in a concrete case." [1] When decisions have to be made in concrete cases, the confrontation occurs of traditional, accepted, and perhaps unself-conscious rules with cases that do not answer to the rules. Then a judicial decision is forthcoming, but on what principles is it formulated?

The defenders of natural law see the principles as fixed and established in reality, and therefore may present argument to strengthen the claim of the traditional, for there is a profound tendency to believe that the way our ancestors acted is somehow sanctioned by moral certainties. (The natural law position is not always conservative; reference is to the criticisms heard in this discussion.) But the drift of legal theory since the rise of utilitarianism has been to seek the foundation for such principles in social and psychological conditions. There is a conflict between the belief, descended from natural law theories, that if you only could discover the right rules, you could decide all cases; and the belief, descended from utilitarian doctrines, that if you could calculate welfare nicely enough, you could decide without prejudice or need for precedent.

The comments made by Professor Freund suggest a way out of the conflict, a way that does not foolishly try to annihilate either position, but rather sees what each contributes that is of value. Whatever principles a judge stands on, however he arrives at his decision, his judgment has a claim upon us. One reason why it has a claim, Professor Freund argues, is because the judge is guaranteed a unique position in society. He is at once bound and free, conservator and innovator. Natural law theories find it difficult to allow for innovation; positivist theories find it difficult to allow for conservation. This is so because the model that each assumes is but half of the social situation as it actually exists. Positivist theories tend to consider the application of the rule to the case as it redefines the sphere of allowable action of the individual; natural law theories tend to consider only the application of the rule as it realizes universal principles in the sphere of the social or communal. In moral terms, positivist views emphasize justice as an expression of self-interest, natural law theories emphasize justice as the right. Both aspects of justice are involved in judicial decisions and have consequences for the individual in applying rules to himself—as well as to the community in its enforcement of decisions through official agencies.

Professor Freund suggests that to move beyond the acceptance of the decision by the individual according to his private interest to the acceptance of agencies to enforce decisions on behalf of a social good requires the recognition on the part of the individual that it is right to be just. It is this further development that is most difficult to attain and that passionately concerns the defenders of natural law theories, for they fear that without the recognition of an obligation to obey grounded in universal moral principles, there can be no recognition of a claim made by the law and enforcing agencies. The defenders of positivism fear that there is, as Hume put it, "a principle of human nature, which we have frequently taken notice of, that men are mightily addicted to *general rules,* and that we often carry our maxims beyond those reasons, which first induc'd us to establish them." [2]

When the two positions are so considered, the lawyers' contributions to the discussion appear to be an appeal to recognize the legitimacy of these fears, but also to resolve a traditional conflict that rests on a misunderstanding of the process of judicial decision. Professor Freund points out that only if men begin with what is prudential can they conclude with what is moral. The judge must be guided by both prudential and moral considerations. The prudential caution is well expressed by the positivistic interpretation of decisions: it warns against being systematically misled by rules that, however skillfully deduced from "first principles," can never adequately meet the demands of the individual case. The moral is well expressed by the natural law theories that remind us that there is a cunning of the passions, more dangerous perhaps than the cunning of reason: we can be systematically misled by our own interests into thinking they are the demands of reason. Each position, as representative of a social force springing from a deep temperamental warrant, is a restraint upon the other; neither can be or ought to be given up.

NOTES

1. H. L. A. Hart, *The Concept of Law* (London: Oxford University Press, 1961), p. 127.
2. David Hume, *Treatise,* Book III, Part II, Section IX.

8

Law, Decision, and the Behavioral Sciences

PAUL KURTZ
Union College

I

The central problem in law is, in a sense, that of decision-making: Is there a decision-making procedure for law? What constitutes adequate grounds for a decision?

This methodological question has been much discussed in the philosophy of law and jurisprudence. It has sometimes been framed in this way: To what extent is scientific evidence applicable to decisions concerning the law? Writers, especially since Bentham, have attempted to found a science of jurisprudence and legislation. In the twentieth century successive waves of legal reformers—Pound, Holmes, Dewey, Bentley, Llewellyn, Frank, and others—have criticized traditional approaches to the law and have advocated instead sociological jurisprudence, legal realism, and pragmatism or experimentalism. Recently behavioral science research has extended into all sorts of legal processes. Moreover, decision-making theorists have attempted to apply game theory, operations research, linear programing, computer techniques, systems engineering, and other newer techniques to the field of law.

In view of this, it is unfortunate that few participants in this institute (except Professor Levi, and then only briefly—see p. 264) referred to the application of the behavioral sciences to law, even though the issue is relevant to their topics. Surely any meta-analysis of fundamental issues should deal with the role of scientific evidence in the law. This is what I propose to do.

II

Professor Rawls analyzes the relationship between law and morality, and he focuses on the question of whether one's decision to obey the law is justified by reference to the principle of fair play. He presents a model of *homo legalis* and seeks a "rational" justification for obedience to the law, even where the law appears to be contrary to one's advantage. Rawls's procedure is not unlike that employed by the classical economists of the nineteenth century who constructed a model of rational *homo oeconomicus*. Behavioral scientists at length have criticized this idealized version on the ground that it deviates from actual economic behavior. Similar considerations, I think, apply to Rawls's approach to the law. Can we talk in general terms about a fictionalized situation? Must we know more about the concrete circumstances, specific laws, and alternative courses of action before we can say whether a decision to obey the law is based upon the principle of fair play? In other words, conjecture about the relevance of basic moral principles to the case hardly seems an adequate substitute for empirical inquiry. To me this objection appears central—though I might add that I do not see why Professor Rawls rejects the principle of utility. Obeying the law may sometimes not be to our immediate advantage, but it will be, we envision, to the long-range advantage of maintaining the whole structure of law.

Professor Rommen discusses the classical doctrine of natural law, which is predicated on a "quasi-empirical" or "rational" theory of human nature. Yet how this prebehavioral and prescience conception of man relates to what we now know is never even raised. Of course, most advocates of traditional natural law doctrine reject scientific methodology altogether for a philosophical-theological approach. Professor Rommen seems to shuttle between his "rational" theory and revelation: he defends monogamy, for example, presumably because of Biblical interpretation. Yet Aristotle, Hobbes, and other natural law writers maintained that natural law was thoroughly compatible with the teleological or mechanical sciences of their day. I doubt if Professor Rommen's theory of man can be held in the light of contemporary behavioral science. As Professor Nielsen suggests in the last part of his critical paper, a demythologized natural law theory might be possible, but it would have to be based upon some empirically identifiable data, anthropological and other. Even such a revised natural law theory has a basic logical mistake: a law cannot be considered both descriptive and normative at the same time and in the same sense.

Professor Levi's paper does attempt to deal with the procedures of legal decision making that are performed; philosophical discussion more often than not seems to deviate fundamentally from actual behavior. Though, again, one wonders whether Levi's kind of legal reasoning fully describes behavioral processes (I doubt it), or whether it is partly a recommended normative ideal.

III

To what extent do the recent behavioral sciences help us in the area of decision? What are the prospects and the limitations of the behavioral sciences for the law? There are, I submit, at least three basic kinds of questions that careful scientific inquiry can help to settle.

First, there are analytic questions. Logical analysis is an essential tool of scientific inquiry; basic to analysis is the problem of definition. What do we mean by our key legal terms: "law," "statute," "ordinance," "precedence," "*stare decis*," "equity," "dictum," and so on. We now see the failure of classical attempts to find a "real" or "essential" definition for "law": legal terms are used in many different and changing ways. Recently the Oxford school has helped to uncover the subtleties and vagaries of legal usage.[1] One appropriate question is: How do people actually use legal language? This kind of descriptive linguistics is important for scientific inquiry. Generally, "law" refers to any system of rules that is held to be obligatory or is enforced. Clarifying legal language provides us some understanding of human social behavior, of which law is a living part. This does not prevent behavioral scientists and philosophers from criticizing the old uses of terms and stipulating new ones (in terms of operational criteria); however, if they want to be understood, their reconstructions must not diverge too far from existing uses.

Second, and perhaps more important to the science of law, are problems of empirical description and explanation. Presumably the task of the behavioral sciences—political science, psychology, sociology, economics, anthropology, history, and so on—is to formulate descriptive generalizations and causal explanations of legal processes; their goal is to predict behavior. This is consistent with Holmes's famous statement that "law" is "the prophecies of what the courts will do in fact." [2] It assumes that law is a form of behavior, that it is dynamic, and that legal behavior is a body of data to be inquired into in the same way as that of the physical sciences. The focus in this method is on the *transactions* of those involved in legal processes, rather than on the formal aspects of law. Inquirers can take a court decision and cut through its dialectic and legal statutes until they arrive at a group of behaving men who produce a series of decisions.

One point needing emphasis is that there are various kinds of legal behavior and decisions: judicial (the judgments of courts, judges, and juries), legislative (the enactments of legislators), executive (the regulations of administrators), and the whole body of quasi-legal rules (such as common law) in the society at large. To concentrate solely on judicial law or decision is a mistake.

To what extent can the behavioral sciences expand understanding of what actually goes on in whole areas of legal behavior? In the past most of the research in jurisprudence was library oriented: individual scholars examined and criticized written law, court decisions, legislative enactments, and the writings of others. A recent change in methodology involves the use of research teams and the application of the newer behavioral fields. Research projects, influenced by experimental, realistic, and sociological jurisprudence, have been organized to study the operations and the effects on society of specific laws or legal institutions. Teams of experts, for example, cooperating with jurists, have attempted empirical studies of the operations of legal devices. Such inquiries involve gathering data in the field and descriptive accounts of the phenomena under study (and also recommendations for legal correction and change).[3]

The interrelations of jurisprudence with the other behavioral sciences is clear today.[4] Law cannot be considered independently of political science inquiry into public opinion, power, or the political context; and it is related to economics and economic interest groups. Similarly, law is directly linked to sociology; jurisprudentists need to understand the social purposes and functions of legal rules within the broader community. The connection between modern psychiatry and criminal law is also apparent.

Third, the above kind of inquiry is basically descriptive; but still another kind is prescriptive and directive. The end here is not to describe or explain behavior, but to interpret, apply, or change it. The distinctive character of legal processes and institutions is their *imperativeness*. Law is a special illustration of a decision process, and those connected with the law have long faced a number of dilemmas in decision making.[5]

What does science say about the decision-making process? What is the relationship between (1) analytic and descriptive linguistics and (2) descriptive behavioral science, on the one hand, and (3) decision making on the other? First and foremost, descriptive research contributes detailed knowledge of *how* and *why* decision making occurs in many different institutional settings. In addition, it can increase understanding of the facts, conditions, techniques, means, and consequences of all sorts of decisions, and this should facilitate the ability to make decisions.

Reference to empirical data as part of the decisional base is widespread in the law. For example, courts, legislative bodies, and governmental agencies in the United States and elsewhere have drawn upon empirical studies in framing, inter-preting, and applying laws concerning drugs, public health, vaccination, milk purification, and water fluoridation. Public safety and traffic-control laws have been based upon extensive statistical studies of causes of accidents and ways to prevent them. Various scientific tests have also been employed to de-termine paternity, drunkenness, insanity, and truthfulness. Sci-entific evidence has been used effectively in city planning, criminology (crime detection and control), building codes, standards of weights and measures, area regulation, water re-source development, conservation, aviation control, and so on. Thus an experimental approach has progressively developed.

Important empirical methods are constantly employed in the judicial process itself. Judges have the responsibility of ap-plying general statutes, ordinances, and laws to particular cases. This involves not only deductive processes, reasoning by analogy, reference to precedence, and so forth, but also in-terpretation of whether a general law applies to a particular case. Judicial decisions may involve detailed empirical in-quiry, such as testimony by witnesses and experts to ascertain the facts. The judge may also consider the probable effects of the law upon the parties concerned and the interests and needs of the community.

The applications of scientific inquiry to the law, however, are far from complete and have profound deficiencies. Our judicial process is unusually archaic. Professor Levi points out (p. 267) that the adversary system operates under litigation where conflicting parties present opposing interpretations and claims. Our jury system as our chief fact-finding device is not always efficient. Many legal decisions seem based on neither evidence nor reason. Judges are all too human; whim, caprice, or sociological prejudice prevail. Some judges are conservative, others are innovators. For many lawyers the primary considera-tion in a case is not logic, but the fee that they can command and how to win!

Workers within the field of legislative decision making refer constantly to empirical conditions and to the effects of legislation on social interests and needs. A good deal of legislative activity, however, is drenched with noncognitive rhetoric and persuasion; and the legislative process is often a battleground of interest and pressure groups, with a piece of legislation nothing more than a workable compromise. Much of this is no doubt inevitable and the price of working in a democratic system, rather than in more "efficient" totalitarian systems.

Factual inquiry also directly applies to executive decision making—whether it be momentous (as was President Kennedy's policy decisions over Cuba) or trivial (as might be the ruling of a minor bureaucratic official). The administrator, too, must contend with all sorts of public pressures. If his decision is to be effective, however, it must, to some extent, be grounded in experimental inquiry.

IV

Factual considerations thus brook large in the decision-making process. But I do not mean to imply that decision making is simply or solely a factual matter. The naturalistic fallacy also applies to the law; and prescriptive or evaluative judgments cannot be deduced from purely factual premises. Of course, included in the facts of the case to be considered there are, in addition to technological or physical facts, what we may call "value facts"; that is, the judge, legislator, or executive will want to know and to take into account the *de facto* norms and interests of all within the community who are involved. Moreover, standards of relevance, procedures governing the admissibility of evidence, and so on, are also part of the decisional base.

Most of these rules have developed gradually out of historical traditions, and they are still growing. The truth of the matter is that there are many different forms of legal reasoning —Anglo-Saxon traditions are not the same as Continental or Oriental law—and these are dependent upon different legal systems and different social contexts. I do not know whether one can talk about *the* logic of decision making in the law or *the* nature of legal reasoning as it were there awaiting discovery, a "transcultural" system of ideal law, such as the natural law theorists envisioned. Rather, reasoning in the law is closely connected to the traditions and standards that are embodied in a political and legal framework. A decision is, in the last analysis, always concrete, institutional, historical, and factual.

Philosophers quickly enter the moral issue at this point: What should be our "ultimate" moral principle: natural law, common law, utility, or some other principle? I know of no solution to the problem of justifying "first principles," but is it a genuine question? We begin, it seems to me, in the middle, with a body of rules, procedures, principles, methods, laws —as various forms of existing human behavior—and we try to understand what is involved, how the system operates. This does not deny legal reform nor the efficacy of moral criticism from outside a system, but such criticism, unless it is in terms of an actual system, is hardly relevant or meaningful.

The chief point of this paper is this: If in meta-analysis of the law we are concerned with how judges, legislators, officials, and lawyers decide, then basically this is an empirical question and is contingent upon future behavioral research. I am not satisfied that any one has accurately accounted for what goes on. We need and are witnessing an enormous expansion of inquiry of this kind. If, on the contrary, we are concerned with a normative recommendation of how a rational being ought to decide, then any decision-making procedure, if it is to have complete significance, should be related in some sense to actual empirical conditions.

NOTES

1. See especially H. L. A. Hart, *The Concept of Law* (Oxford: Clarendon Press, 1961).
2. O. W. Holmes, "The Path of Law," *Harvard Law Review*, X (1897), 461.
3. Pioneer work of this kind was initiated by Walter C. Cook

and his associates at Johns Hopkins. Sheldon and Eleanor Glueck, a jurist and a sociologist, plus a staff of physicians, anthropologists, sociologists, and others, have studied criminal behavior and have published a series on adult and juvenile delinquency. The predictive tables developed have been used with some effectiveness in the treatment of juvenile offenders. See their *Predicting Delinquency and Crime* (Cambridge: Harvard University Press, 1959). The Chicago Jury Studies, another joint study of jurists and social scientists, has culminated in published reports. (See especially Hans Zeisel *et al.*, *Delay in the Courts* [Boston: Little, Brown, 1959].) The Columbia University Project for Effective Justice is another such project. (See Maurice Rosenberg and Michael I. Sovern, "Delay and Dynamics of Personal Injury Litigation," *Columbia Law Review*, December, 1959, pp. 1115–70.) For a recent work on experimental jurisprudence, see Frederick Beutel, *Some Potentialities of Experimental Jurisprudence as a New Branch of Social Science* (Lincoln: University of Nebraska Press, 1957).

4. For a review of the behavioral sciences as they relate to jurisprudence, see Rollo Handy and Paul Kurtz, *A Current Appraisal of the Behavioral Sciences* (Great Barrington, Mass.: Behavioral Research Council, 1963), Chapter VI, "Jurisprudence." (Reprinted in *The American Behavioral Scientist*, VII, No. 4 [1963]). There are several recent studies that relate the behavioral sciences to law. In political science: Heinz Eulau *et al.* (eds.), *Political Behavior; A Reader in Theory and Research* (Glencoe, Ill.: The Free Press, 1956); John C. Wahlke and Heinz Eulau (eds.), *Legislative Behavior; A Reader in Theory and Research* (Glencoe, Ill.: The Free Press, 1959); and Jack W. Peltason, *Federal Courts in the Political Process* (New York: Doubleday & Co., 1955). In sociology: William M. Evans (ed.), *Law and Sociology* (New York: The Free Press, 1962) and F. James Davis *et al.*, *Society and Law: New Meaning for an Old Profession* (New York: The Free Press, 1962). In psychiatry: Sheldon Glueck, *Law and Psychiatry: Cold War or Entente Cordiale?* (Baltimore: Johns Hopkins Press, 1962).

5. Some recent illustrations of the application of decision theory to legal behavior are R. Duncan Luce and Arnold A. Rogow, "A Game Theoretic Analysis of Congressional Power Distributions for a Stable Two-Party System," *Behavioral Science*, I (1956), 83–95; and Glendon Schubert *et al.*, "A Psychometric Model of the

Supreme Court," *The American Behavioral Scientist*, V, No. 3, (November, 1961), 14–18. Thomas A. Cowan reviews the uses of decision theory, computer techniques, systems engineering, and information retrieval in contemporary law, pointing out their limitations and potentialities, in "Decision Theory in Law, Science, and Technology," *Science*, 140 (1963), 1065–76. See also Lee Loevinger, "Jurmetrics: Science and Prediction in the Field of Law," *Minnesota Law Review*, 46 (1961).

9

Essence and Concept in Natural Law Theory

FREDERICK A. OLAFSON
The John Hopkins University

THERE IS a latent circularity in traditional natural law theory that receives no attention in Professor Rommen's paper, but which must be reckoned with in any general appraisal of the strengths and weaknesses of the position he seeks to defend. I propose to show how this circularity arises and why it can be removed only by scaling down quite drastically the claims that natural law theorists have typically made and thus substantially reducing the interest of their theory.

The natural law argument, in its classical form, undertakes to show that certain kinds of human actions are morally right and others morally wrong by exhibiting the relationship in which these actions stand to a common human nature. The latter is defined teleologically in terms of the distinctive ends to which human activity is allegedly directed; and it is then shown that morally right actions are actions that are either immediately included in the special function of man *qua* man or are necessary to produce the conditions in which that function can be satisfactorily exercised. In such arguments it is often tacitly assumed that the concept of human nature to which appeal is made is more or less coextensive with the concept of "human being" or "man" that is in use in the community to which the parties to the discussion belong. When this assumption is justified and the applicability of the proposed concept of "human being" is not contested, there is a clear, if somewhat trivial, sense in which the natural law argument may succeed in establishing its conclusion. Considered in the light of such cases, "natural law theory" is simply a way of exhibiting our most general moral beliefs as being implicit in the very concept by which we identify one another as human beings.

There can, of course, be no guarantee that such happy unanimity will prevail with respect to the content of the concept of human nature. When it becomes apparent that there is no such consensus and that arguments from human nature cannot simply rest their claims on the authority of common acceptance of a given concept of human nature, reasons must be given why persons who do not currently use that concept *should* do so. This new argument, in turn, takes us much closer to the heart of natural law theory, for, no matter how frequent the appeal to the maxim *quod semper, quod ubique* has been in the history of that doctrine, it is not primarily based on the fact of consensus or on the linguistic-conceptual articulation of that consensus. Instead, it purports to justify a certain concept of human nature by showing its ultimate basis in the real essence of man; and classical expositions of natural law theory, like that of St. Thomas, have accordingly been unshakably ontological and "translinguistic" in their mode of formulation.

It is at this point that the circularity alluded to at the outset begins to appear. To demonstrate that a certain concept of human nature is the "true" concept and that it should be adopted by persons or communities that do not already use it, the selection and ordering of human functions that it proposes must be shown to be uniquely valid or—what is much the same—it must be shown that certain human activities are essential and constitutive of what it is to be a human being, whereas others are not. But how is this segregation of human activities into categories of essentiality and nonessentiality to be carried out? The distinction cannot be made by reference to the criteria for the application of the concept of a "human being" itself, since what is at issue now is precisely the validity of the claim that these criteria are the ones we should use. Similarly, all arguments based on the historical authority accumulated by a given concept of what it is to be a human being or on the extent of our practical commitment to such

a concept are ruled out, since the question is directed to an
ordering of human functions that is alleged to be independent
of such considerations as these and must, therefore, be capable
of being established on other grounds.

But what are the other grounds to be? How, for example,
is it to be shown that rationality and sexuality, considered as
human attributes, are, quite apart from any conceptually stipulated relationship of moral priority of the one over the other,
so related as to make just that mode of conceptualization the
only correct one? At bottom, the difficulties raised by attempts
to justify the use of a concept by showing that there is a corresponding essence *in re* are much the same whether it is real essence of gold that has to be defined, as in Locke's famous example, or the real essence of man. It is not surprising, therefore,
that in both kinds of cases an appeal is frequently made to intuition. But the notion that the essentiality of certain attributes
of a thing can be simply "seen" and that it is this intuition of
their essentiality that justifies their use as criteria for the application of the corresponding concept presents great difficulties.
Since attributes do not come with labels attached that identify
them as "essential" or "nonessential," it is not clear how the
metaphor of sight is to be interpreted; and it seems a good deal
more plausible to argue that it is *because* certain attributes are
in fact criteria for the application of a given concept that we
are inclined to say that we just *see* that they are essential attributes of the things to which that concept applies. Once all appeal to the logical conditions for the application of a concept
has been ruled out as a means of explaining what "essential"
means in these contexts, nothing seems to be left, either in
gold or in human beings, that could uniquely validate one selection of traits as essential attributes of those things.

I submit that what all these attempts to provide an ontological foundation for some special concept of human nature
amount to is no more than an emphatic reassertion of the superior importance of the human activities to which that concept
assigns a privileged position. The ontological dimension of
such arguments consists in the claim that the things themselves

are so constituted as to make just this mode of conceptualization uniquely appropriate to them; but this claim turns out to be uninterpretable when it is not the presence in the things of the criterial properties of a concept that is at issue but the status as criteria of these properties themselves. What is effectively conveyed by the ontological mode of statement is simply a claim that we ought to use such and such a concept of human nature if we do not already. Unfortunately, this makes the whole natural law argument circular, since in effect we are being told that we ought to act in certain ways because it is our nature to do so and also that this concept of human nature is the concept we ought to use. The moral "ought" thus rests on what might be called a conceptual "ought," and the latter rests on nothing that is admissible for the purposes of the argument. The argument in behalf of the proposed concept of human nature turns out to be itself a moral argument and what is more, a moral argument that lacks the kind of ontological support that on natural law principles such an argument is required to have if it is to be authoritative. Instead of being told directly that human beings should act in a certain way, we are now being told that we should adopt a concept of human nature from which a rule of conduct directing us to behave in that way is then extracted. But anyone who is disposed to challenge the undisguisedly moral "ought" will presumably be willing to challenge the correlative conceptual "ought," so it is not clear in what sense the former receives any support from the latter.

If the above analysis of natural law theory is correct, then its claim to have provided an ontological foundation for the concept of human nature and for the moral principles implicit in that concept must be rejected. Its plausibility would appear to be due to a failure to distinguish two very different theses from one another. One of these is the claim, which has just been examined and rejected, that it is possible to compare our concept of human nature with the objects it denotes—human beings—and to find in the latter an ordering of functions that corresponds to the priorities stipulated in the concept. The other is the claim that it is precisely by virtue of the priorities that receive partial expression in this and other concepts that human beings are—or, more correctly, have become—what they are. The difference between these two claims lies in the fact that in the one case, the concept of human nature is held to reflect an order that is independent of, and ontologically prior to, human history, considered as the gradual working out of a minimum scale of priorities among human activities, whereas in the other, that concept and human nature itself in the relevant respects are the result, or deposit, of that evolution. To say that morality is grounded in human nature is both important and true if what is meant is simply that our conception of what it is to be a human being has developed *pari passu* with the working out of certain fundamental moral priorities; but this truth is only very obscurely reflected and to a considerable degree distorted when this relationship is interpreted, as it is in natural law theory, as a simple correspondence of our concept of human nature to a real essence. This way of putting the matter inescapably suggests that human nature is something that is distinguishable both from the way human beings actually behave and from the concept of human nature; and that just as the moral quality of the actual behavior of human beings can be determined by its correspondence (or noncorrespondence) with the norms implicit in the concept, so the concept is validated or justified by its correspondence to the real essence of man. If the second kind of correspondence presents unresolvable difficulties, as I have argued it does, then whatever relationship may hold between the other two terms— our concept of human nature and the way we actually behave— it can hardly be construed in such a way as to make the one the ultimate basis of the authority of the other in the sense contemplated by natural law theory. It seems much more plausible to view them as coordinate and interdependent elements in a system of moral practice rather than as subordinate and superordinate levels in a vertical hierarchy of justification that has, in any case, lost its bottom story.

It is interesting to note in this connection that there has recently been a certain revival of interest in some natural law

ideas among analytically inclined philosophers, and that what
has dropped out of natural law theory in this new incarnation
is precisely the ontological translinguistic claims that have been
shown to give such difficulty. As described by Sir Isaiah Berlin
in a recent essay, this new respect for "the kernel of truth in
the old a priori natural law doctrines" is inspired by a recognition that "an ability to recognize universal values enters into
our analysis of such fundamental concepts as man which are
usually thought of as descriptive and not evaluative." Other
writers have urged that there are some rules governing human
behavior the recognition of which is so fundamental to the
existence of anything we would be willing to call a society
that it makes better sense to treat an acceptance of them as
constitutive of the nature of man as a social being than as an
artificial convention. Perhaps this new and restricted version of
natural law theory might best be described as "conceptualistic"
to indicate that although its definition of man is a real—that
is, nonconventional—definition in the sense that it expresses
the only set of reciprocally applicable priorities that most people are really prepared to live by, no other kind of privileged
ontological status is being claimed for it. Its authority is simply that of the unwillingness or practical inability of the human
beings who use a certain concept of human nature to accept—
not just verbally but in actual practice—the implications for
conduct of an abandonment of that concept.

The force of a natural law theory reformulated along these
more modest lines might still be considerable, particularly
against the ethical skeptic who goes on living in a society whose
basic rules are implicit in a certain concept of human nature
that he thus tacitly recognizes in practice at the same time that
he repudiates in theory the obligations they impose. The strategy of such a rebuttal would be much the same as the one so
often used in meeting skeptical doubts about other rational
procedures, such as inductive reasoning, and would consist
in showing that the critic who repudiates the use of a certain
concept or rule of inference can do so consistently only on pain
of abandoning a whole sector of human activity and discourse,

which in this case would be the enterprise of cooperative social living. But even if it is conceded that some degree of moral consensus is implicit in our concepts of man and human being, it is hard to see how this line of reasoning, which is at bottom a sophisticated conceptualistic version of the *quod semper, quod ubique* argument, could be very effective either in cases of ethical disagreement that do not touch the core of agreement that is expressed in the concept or in the cases in which individuals or societies really and consistently break with some element in that consensus. In fact, this kind of argument from human nature would seem to have real force only in cases in which there is a demonstrable inconsistency between what a man does and what he says. These cases may be both numerous and important, but it would surely be an error either to think that all cases of ethical disagreement can be reduced to these terms or to tailor reality to fit the logical powers of this method of argumentation.

No doubt this danger can be avoided, but if it is and the limitations of a conceptualistic natural law theory are really accepted, it is not just the a priori mode of the older versions of that doctrine that will have gone by the board. By admitting the possibility of ultimate moral disagreement and a corresponding plurality of concepts of human nature, none of which has any more ontological foundation than any other, it will have been conceded that natural law theory is incapable of transforming moral disagreements into disagreements about the true nature of man in any sense that makes this question more than a question-begging paraphrase in pseudofactual terms of the original moral conflict itself. The claim that this could be done was central to traditional natural law theory, and, if it is given up, it seems scarcely worthwhile to recast our moral views in the form of concepts of human nature, since the historically established expectations aroused by such a mode of presentation are bound to be disappointed.

10

The Metaethics of Natural Law

FELIX OPPENHEIM

University of Massachusetts

I WISH to demonstrate that both the natural law thesis and its denial are theories of metaethics, and that controversies between adherents of these philosophies are pertinent only if fought on the metaethical level.

I. THE NATURAL LAW THESIS

The following assertions may be considered the common core of the various theories that make up the history of natural law.

A. The term 'natural law' refers to those normative principles of political and legal behavior that are objectively valid, independently of anybody's subjective value commitments, and independently of any given system of positive law.

B. There are such principles of natural law, morally binding on citizens and government officials, especially on legislators and judges.

C. Natural law "is the foundation for legitimate authority," in the words of Professor Rommen; that is, political authority is morally legitimate only to the extent that its legal enactments reflect the rules of natural law.

D. Positive laws that conflict with the objective moral order as stipulated by natural law are considered either "unjust laws"—legally but not morally binding—or "not laws at all"—pronouncements that lack legal as well as moral validity.

II. THE NATURAL LAW THESIS BELONGS
TO METAETHICS

Proponents of the natural law thesis are often deceived by the grammatical appearance of their own pronouncements and hence fail to realize (1) that they speak about *normative* statements, (2) that they speak *about* normative statements.

A. Principles of political ethics claimed to belong to natural law are often couched in the indicative mood; for example, "We hold these truths to be self-evident, that men *are* created equal, that they *are* endowed by their Creator with certain inalienable rights. . . ." Surely, the framers of the Declaration of Independence did not mean to assert that all men do in fact have the same physical or mental capacities and that their basic rights are in fact always protected. Rather, they meant to exhort governments to give citizens equal legal rights. Similarly, when Maritain states that "man *possesses* ends which necessarily correspond to his essential constitution," [1] he expresses the norm that man *ought* to pursue certain ends.

B. The Declaration of Independence does not merely *proclaim* a principle of political ethics, but also *claims* that this norm is "self-evident." It is this latter feature that makes this document one of natural law. Every proponent of the natural law thesis is concerned, explicitly or implicitly, with the logical status of those normative statements that he regards as belonging to natural law, and Rommen errs when he considers natural law "part of social ethics." Another common mistake is to contrast natural law with utilitarianism, even though the former theory belongs to metaethics and the latter to normative ethics. Although, as a matter of historical fact, utilitarians have tended to oppose natural law, it would be perfectly consistent to regard the normative principle of utility itself as a natural law command. Both "pro" and "anti" natural law theorists often accuse each other of being necessarily committed to a particular doctrine of political ethics, usually of an antidemocratic type.[2] In this they are both mistaken, since any metaethical theory is logically compatible with any theory of normative ethics. In fact, one and the same political doctrine has often been adopted by both proponents and opponents of the natural law theory, just as conflicting norms of political ethics have been interpreted as commands of natural law by different philosophers.

III. THE NATURAL LAW THESIS BELONGS TO VALUE COGNITIVISM

The metaethical theory of value cognitivism claims that there exist certain intrinsic value judgments that can be objectively validated. This is precisely what every proponent of the natural law thesis affirms with respect to certain normative principles of politics, whether or not he uses the term 'natural law.' Thus Plato should be included among the natural law philosophers, even though this expression was introduced after his time. Indeed, the future guardians in the *Republic* "must lift up the eye of the soul to gaze on that which sheds light on all things; and when they have *seen the Good itself,* take it as a pattern for the *right ordering of the state* and of the individual, themselves included." [3]

To side with natural law is to side with value cognitivism. Does value cognitivism entail the natural law thesis? Some natural law philosophers conceive of the norms of natural law as encompassing the whole of morality, individual as well as social. Thomas Aquinas, for example, refers to natural law as "the light of natural reason, whereby we discern *what is good and what is evil.*" [4] This view implies that any norm of either individual or social ethics that is discernible as valid constitutes a rule of natural law.

There are, on the other hand, value cognitivists who explicitly oppose the natural law thesis. For example, Bentham and J. S. Mill regarded utility as a demonstrably valid principle of "morals and legislation," but denied that it is a principle of natural law because they considered it too general to be directly translatable into a system of positive law. They viewed the relationship between positive law and utility as one between

means and end. There is only one objective principle to which
the legislator is morally bound to conform, namely, the pursuit
of the greatest happiness of the greatest number. Which laws
are best suited to implement this ultimate goal in any given
situation is a question to be determined empirically. It is thus
possible to affirm value cognitivism and to deny natural law.

Like theories of value cognitivism in general, theories of
natural law in particular may be classified broadly into those
of an intuitionist and those of a naturalistic type. According to
the former view, the validity of rules of natural law may be
demonstrated by appeal to revelation: "right reason" or "self-
evidence" or "moral conscience" or "rational insight into the
theological structure of the universe." Naturalists consider
natural law principles empirically true because they are deriv-
able from allegedly empirical laws concerning "human nature,"
or from "the spontaneous self-understanding of myself as a
human person," as Professor Rommen has noted—or, to take
another recent example, because they constitute "universally
recognized principles of conduct which have a basis in elementary truths concerning human beings, their natural environ-
ment, and aims." [5]

Many advocates of the natural law thesis do not seem to
realize that they have committed themselves to the metaethical
theory of value cognitivism, and that they have, therefore, the
burden of proving the validity of those norms that they claim
to be of natural law. Instead of attempting to demonstrate
them either deductively or inductively, they merely proclaim
them.

IV. THE DENIAL OF NATURAL LAW

Since proponents of the natural law thesis are necessarily
value cognitivists, it follows that value noncognitivism implies
the denial of the natural law thesis. Again, we should not be
misled by the terminology of opponents as well as proponents
of natural law. Although value cognitivists like Plato belong to
the natural law school without using natural law terminology,

Hobbes, a value noncognitivist,[6] speaks of a "law of nature, by which men are commanded to endeavor peace." [7] However, it becomes clear from the context that Hobbes means by a law of nature, not a rule of *ethics* that is *valid,* but a rule of *decision* that it is *rational* to adopt in view of the goal of self-preservation.

It is often claimed that to reject natural law is to affirm that all law is positive law—and hence to deny that laws may be considered either just or unjust.[8] The first part of this allegation is true, but not the second. The view that there is no natural, but only positive, law is perfectly compatible with the claim that a given legal provision, although legally valid, is morally wrong. All the critic of natural law is bound to deny is that statements of the type 'This law is intrinsically unjust' can be considered true or false in a scientific sense. As a value noncognitivist, he interprets such statements as expressions of the speaker's value commitments. They cannot be proved valid or not valid, but they can be shown to be rational or not rational, that is, consistent or inconsistent with some other normative principle that the speaker may have adopted.

While value noncognitivism is incompatible with the natural law thesis, we have seen that the denial of natural law is in principle compatible with value cognitivism. In fact, however, philosophers often criticize the natural law thesis precisely because of its value cognitivist aspects and then adopt, in turn, a value cognitivist metaethics. It seems to me that Bentham and Mill are consistent in their denial of absolute individual natural *rights* against the government, independent of the principle of utility. But after having used naturalistic arguments in support of the principle of utility itself, they have come at least close to adopting the very theory of natural *law* that they criticize.

To me, the question as to whether it is plausible (and not merely consistent) to affirm value cognitivism and to deny natural law is not an important one. For reasons beyond the scope of this paper, I hold value cognitivism to be mistaken in the first place. This is a sufficient reason for me to deny the natural law thesis. It is the only pertinent argument against natural law. If it succeeds in destroying value cognitivism as a whole, so much the worse—or so much the better.

NOTES

1. Jacques Maritain, *Man and the State* (Chicago: University of Chicago Press, 1951), p. 86. Italics in all quotations are mine.

2. For examples, see Felix E. Oppenheim, "The Natural Law Thesis: Affirmation or Denial?," *The American Political Science Review*, 51 (1957), 41–53.

3. F. M. Cornford (trans.), Plato's *Republic* (New York and London: Oxford University Press, 1945), p. 262.

4. Thomas Aquinas, *Summa Theologica*, I–II, Q. 90, A. 2. Plato holds a similar view (see footnote 3).

5. H. L. A. Hart, *The Concept of Law* (Oxford: Clarendon Press, 1961), p. 189. "Such universally recognized principles . . . may be considered the *minimum content* of Natural Law." (*Ibid.*; italics are Hart's.)

6. *Leviathan*, Chap. XV: "Good and evil are names that signify our appetites and aversions."

7. *Ibid.*, Chap. XIV.

8. See, for example, Leo Strauss, *Natural Right and History* (Chicago: University of Chicago Press, 1953), Chap. 2.

11

Either-Or or Neither-Nor?

KENNETH STERN
New York University

MUCH OF the discussion during the second session of the conference followed lines drawn by Professor Nielsen in his criticisms of Professor Rommen's paper, which supported natural law. In his attack Nielsen argued that the traditional theory of natural law was "myth-eaten" even when (as it did do in some versions) it did not suppose some theology and instead was based on some belief about the function or role of man. In so saying, Nielsen agrees with existentialists that there is, in fact, no peculiar function associated with man *qua* man.[1] So Nielsen denies that "man has a function or some final cause that, like a robot, he was programed to achieve." But, Nielsen claims, even if it were shown that there was some peculiar function associated with man, still the advocate of natural law who tried to base law on such a function would run head on into what Nielsen calls "Hume's Hurdle" namely, that no normative conclusion can be drawn from any factual premise. Nielsen explicitly tells us that any ascription of function or purpose to man, even if true, would be "simply facts about man and about 'what there is'; hence, Hume's Hurdle." This point was echoed by Professor Nagel (among others) who remarked to the effect that if anyone were to try to draw what seemed a plausible normative conclusion from some statements about the capacities of man, Nagel would immediately suspect that this person had "smuggled" an evaluation into his premises.

I

In the course of these remarks I wish to question this normative-descriptive dichotomy that appears to have been accepted as a kind of revealed truth by a good many philosophers whose experience with that other great divide, the analytic-synthetic, ought to have taught them better. After all, if empiricists do not learn from experience, then who on earth should? But first it is worthwhile to raise some questions about Nielsen's implicit assumption (which he also shares with existentialists) that a normative conclusion can in some sense be based on the notion of function in the instance of "artifacts," objects manufactured for a certain purpose, because whether or not such an artifact is a good or desirable one of its kind is a question of whether that artifact efficiently performs its function. By saying that since man is not an artifact and so (1) has nothing that can be called a function and (2) cannot have any normative conclusion about him based on this nonexistent function, Nielsen implies that in the case of artifacts there is some important logical relation between the statement, "This A performs its peculiar function F efficiently," and the statement, "This A is a good A" where A stands for some artifact. It is, of course, still not clear just what the relation between the two statements is and, indeed, to what extent it runs up against Hume's Hurdle. What we have here is, of course, Aristotelian naturalism, and I know that Nielsen accepts the Hume-Moore argument against naturalistic ethics. Certainly he would not accept any intensional equivalence between the two statements in question, and I doubt whether he would even accept an extensional equivalence between them. From what he says further on in his paper I expect that Nielsen would accept some "good reasons" interpretation of the relation between the two statements such that the first would constitute a "good reason" for the second, but there would not be any deductive relation between them. I myself find the 'good reasons' approach an obscure one, but this is no place to discuss this issue, and neither would it be fair to ask that Nielsen ought to have explained exactly what he means in the paper he wrote. But even so, without bothering very much about just what the relation is between a statement saying that an object has performed its particular function efficiently and saying that it is good, it is possible to examine the question whether the relation is even so strong as Nielsen appears to think it is.[2]

A mousetrap would seem to be an excellent example for anyone who wished to establish a strong relation between the notions of efficient functioning of an artifact and its value or desirability. The peculiar function of a mousetrap, unlike even a knife or Aristotle's flute, is plainly manifested in the name of the article. There is no dispute, I should hope, that its peculiar function is to catch mice. It would function efficiently if it caught mice efficiently. It would, I suppose, follow from this that if one mousetrap X is better than another mousetrap Y, that X performs its function (in this case, catching mice) better than Y does. Very well, then, let us put this to a test. Suppose I am in the market for a mousetrap. The shopkeeper shows me one which he assures me is a most efficient mousetrap. Indeed, it is the most efficient mousetrap he has. But, when I tell him to wrap the article up, he informs me that he has a still better mousetrap to show me. How can this be? Has he not already said that the mousetrap already shown me is the most efficient he has? Yes, but the other, better, more desirable, and indeed more expensive mousetrap has a safety-catch, an attachment that ensures that the setter of the trap will not catch his finger while inserting the cheese. I think it must be agreed that it is no part of the proper function of a mousetrap not to catch my finger. In telling a child what that object (a mousetrap) was for I should not think to say in my description, "It is for not catching my finger." And if anyone did try to argue that it was part of the proper function of a mouse-trap not to catch my finger, I should then simply contend that such a person was arguing just for argument's sake, or, as Aristotle once put it in the course of commenting on Plato's contention that virtue is a *sufficient* condition for happiness, no one would so argue "unless he were maintaining a thesis at all costs." [3] Or take the instance of a tie clip. One tie clip may be judged better than another because of its ornamental value or because it was bought at Brooks Brothers.

It might now be thought that it could be argued that, although the thesis I have been arguing against has been shown to be mistaken, a somewhat weaker substitute for it was indeed correct. It might be said that although the efficient performance of a function is not, indeed, a sufficient condition for holding an artifact desirable, still it is at least a necessary condition. This weaker thesis is more plausible, but some counterinstances can be found even here. Here is a simple one: a bread knife that is so sharp that it is dangerous to have in the house is surely less desirable than a less sharp and, thus, less efficient one that would not cause worry.

I have already indicated that a philosopher may, if he wishes, so extend the notion of efficient functioning so as to include in its scope every contingency, very counterinstance that can be thought up. What he would accomplish by doing this is obscure to me, for all that he could accomplish would be to create a very large and very useless tautology, pointless and uninformative.

Here two caveats need mentioning: (1) In the consideration that I posed above, I might be interpreted as arguing that there is no relation at all between something's efficient functioning and its value. This would be a misinterpretation. What I have pointed out is that the relationship that is there must be approached with caution. I have indicated that it is not already, as it were, set out in advance just what people will consider worth having and valuable—not even in what seems to be the simple case of artifacts. (A supplementary point is that the notion of "function" needs to be understood further, —especially the question as to how functions can be identified *independently* of our judgments with respect to the value of the object in question). (2) More important, I might be misinterpreted as having simply given additional support to the normative-descriptive dichotomy: it might be argued that what

I have shown is that even in the case of artifacts there is no
transition between the factual or descriptive and the evaluative
or normative. But to interpret what I have said in that way is
to assume the distinction that I think is questionable: that in
the case of any statement (which is not analytic), it can
always be classified as either normative or descriptive or, perhaps, as a combination of elements of both, so that ascribing
a function to something would be to say something "factual" or
"descriptive"—and thus the problem of what Nielsen terms
Hume's Hurdle. But it might be that when I ascribe a function
to anything (whatever that might be), I am not engaging in
either making a factual *or* a normative claim. I do not, that is,
believe that the normative-descriptive dichotomy is a clear
one, nor do I believe that even if it were clear it would exhaust
the complexity of statement making. Not every statement is
either normative or descriptive, and to think so seems to me on
a par with the rather superficially primitive political classification spoofed by Gilbert in *Iolanthe*: "Nature does contrive that
every boy and every girl/that's born into the world alive/Is
either a little Liberal or else a little Conservative."

II

I have contended above that the normative-descriptive
dichotomy is neither clear nor exhaustive. I think that most
philosophers (and Nielsen has admitted this to me in private
conversation) would allow that the distinction is not a clear
one: that there are borderline cases, that there are cases in
which both elements are intermixed, and so forth. But very
few philosophers have been willing to allow that it might
even be true that some judgments fall into neither classification. When I suggest that some judgments might fall into a
classification that is sui-generis, philosophers with whom I
have spoken have become very puzzled and then challenged
me to name these other classification(s) into which the other
judgments might fall and to give examples of such judgments.
I shall presently comply with the latter challenge, but the

former challenge seems to me to be an odd one. After all, "normative" and "descriptive" are terms of art, and upon pressure I suppose that I could invent some others, but why should *that* be an issue of any importance? If I can provide plausible examples of judgments that fall into neither category, then what further would be gained by providing some new classifications? There may be, I suspect, a good many kinds of judgments that are neither normative nor descriptive in any straightforward sense,[4] but would anything particular be gained by inventing new terms for all of them—or worse, stretching old terms to provide room for them? Here I am unable to resist an *ad hominem* thrust. It seems to me that the need for names that I have described above is a kind of primitivistic superstition well known among anthropologists who do field work among primitive tribes. There, knowing the name of something is believed to give the knower a special power over the bearer of the name, human or nonhuman. An atavistic relic of this occurs when the detective thrills to the realization that the name of the culprit is Richard Deadeye and not John Doe, although this adds nothing more to the ability to catch the criminal. (Indeed, it seems to me that such wholesale enthusiasms for dichotomies, sense data versus material objects, and analytic versus synthetic, smacks, as Austin has suggested, of primitive thought and the need for simplification.[5]) These superstitions cannot be refuted; they must, in psychoanalytic jargon, be "worked through."

III

I remarked above that it would be possible so to employ the notions "normative" and "descriptive" as to make certain that all judgments fell into one or the other category. I also remarked that it seemed to me that this would be pointless. After all, in the final analysis, the question that arises is regarding the utility of any set of categories. If a dichotomy (or trichotomy, and so on) masks important differences among different things, if it masks important connections, and if it raises problems as difficult or more difficult to solve than the problems it is constructed to solve, then it seems to me that there is justification for questioning the classification in question.

I now wish to suggest some examples that it does not seem to me fit plausibly into either category. (I do not suggest, however, that they cannot be *made* to fit into either category.)

One class of examples that I should want to maintain, does not fall neatly or plausibly into either the normative or descriptive category has already been suggested by Stanley Cavell,[6] who has pointed to the sorts of sentences (and Cavell is willing to call them *statements*) found in *Hoyle's Rules of Games,* such as, "The opponent at declarer's left makes the opening lead. . . . Declarer's partner then lays his whole hand face up on the table with his trumps, if any, on the right." Do these say what ought to be done by bridge players (normative), or do they say what *is* done (descriptive)? Cavell says that this depends upon how they are taken. But what *that* means I find most obscure. Another very interesting set of judgments that seem to feel, not to fall, into either category concerns needs. Suppose I say that Johnny needs a new coat. Is that normative or descriptive? It might easily be analyzed as either. For instance, normatively: "The child ought to have a new coat"; descriptively: "The child will suffer cold unless he gets a new coat." Which of these is correct?—or is it, as I should suggest, that neither gives an analysis of what the original "need" judgment meant (although either might be in some sense "implied" by the need judgment)? A third class of judgments that I suggest falls into neither classification are judgments about feelings and emotions, either those of other people or one's own. If I claim to feel hungry, for instance, it is possible for someone else to challenge my self-description by saying something like, "But you couldn't feel hungry; you finished eating an enormous meal only a little while ago"; It seems to me that such a challenge, in the circumstances, would be in place, since many mental words describing feelings or emotions have recognized causes or are directed toward ob-

jects. One hopes for or expects this or that. One hungers because one has not eaten. These are inexplicit presuppositions of
our utterances. Sometimes, some of these will be lacking. When
they are, the situation is ripe for a challenge of even a self-
description. Seldom, however, unless the challenger suspects
downright insincerity, will he challenge with the wholesale
denial "You are not hungry," "You are not bored," or the like.
This is rude and implies deceit. Instead, locutions less drastic
will be used, locutions such as "But you can't (really) X that,"
"You couldn't (really) X that." Such challenges seem to me
not to fit with any comfort into either category. If a child
claims to want something outrageous or outlandish or dangerous, and I then say to him, "But you cannot want that," am I
saying something that is either normative or descriptive? Am
I, that is to say, saying that he *ought* not to want it, or am I
saying that people do not want that sort of thing?

Finally, I wish to turn to another class of judgments,
those we make upon the abilities of others to perform certain
actions or certain sorts of actions. Suppose I am watching a
man playing a simply rotten game of chess. He leaves his
pieces *en prise* all over the board. In short, he is, in the parlance of American chess players, a "fish." Suppose, now, that I
remark to another onlooker, "That man cannot play chess" or
even, "That man simply isn't playing chess." Am I describing
or am I evaluating? A philosopher who maintains the dichotomy that I am questioning may here argue that I must be
evaluating, since in a strict sense the man is certainly playing
chess, and therefore he can play chess. He would say this on
the grounds that chess is a rule-governed game, and if the
man is doing nothing illegal (for instance, moving a knight
like a bishop), then no matter how bad his moves are, the
man is certainly playing chess. Such an argument would raise
at least two interesting questions: (1) If, in playing chess, the
object is to win, then is a man who is making moves that
could only lose playing chess? Should we say that a man who is
making legal moves, but making them purely *randomly*, is
playing chess? (2) Why, then, do we, to make this allegedly

evaluative judgment, fall so easily into what seems a descriptive idiom? What both these questions seem to suggest is that it is not an easy matter to draw the line between atrociously bad playing and not playing at all. But even if my opponent is right—since there is no denying that chess does have its rules set down by the International Chess Federation, and we ought to say that so long as no illegal moves are made, the man is playing chess—then what would he say about an activity that is not rule governed as chess is? Take dancing, for instance. I point to someone on the ballroom floor and remark, "That man simply cannot dance. He is falling all over his partner's feet and his own as well," or even, "That man isn't dancing . . . ." Do we have *here* a description or an evaluation? Note that there is no International Dance Federation that sets up what dance steps are legally mambo steps and which waltz. There are, of course, some general dance steps that do constitute a particular dance, but there are an indefinite number of individual variations on these. There are no definite sets of steps to follow, but, indeed, if there were, then anyone who confined himself to these only would be considered not only an uninteresting dancer, but also a rather poor one. (Consider the notorious tyro who, as he dances, counts "one-two-three, one-two-three, . . ."). As in music, the importance of innovation and variety in dancing is admitted by everyone. If what I say is true, then it does not seem to me that "He cannot dance" or "He is not dancing" can be classified with any comfort as either descriptive or normative in the circumstances cited above.[7]

III

It is time to draw a few threads together. To what extent, it may be asked, do the arguments that I have adduced above tell against what Nielsen has called Hume's Hurdle, which appears to be what is called "the naturalistic fallacy"?—for it may be argued that even if I have shown that there are judgments that are neither fish nor fowl, neither normative or descriptive, this does still not touch the point that is made by the advocates of the naturalistic fallacy. This fallacy is simply that of drawing normative conclusions from descriptive premises. But this remains a fallacy even if I have shown that there are judgments that are neither normative nor descriptive. This counter is clearly quite right. In this version I have shown nothing that would enable a philosopher to clear Hume's Hurdle. However, there is, I believe, another version of Hume's Hurdle that is undermined by my arguments if they are valid. This version assumes that the normative-descriptive dichotomy is exhaustive. Is there such a version? Am I hitting out at a straw man? It seems to me that I am not, and that much of the force of the charge of the naturalistic fallacy does stem from the belief that the division is indeed exhaustive. Many philosophers have, indeed, argued as if when an argument is presented that has a normative conclusion, there must, in the premises, be at least one normative statement. But I wish to argue that a normative conclusion may be drawn from *non-normative* premises, and that here the class of nonnormative statements need not include descriptive or factual judgments. I have no general argument for this, but then what is the argument on the other side? So far as I can see the assumption embodied in the argument for the other side is something like this: Statements that imply other statements must be of the same type as the statements that they imply. Therefore, if a normative statement is inferred, then the statement(s) from which it is inferred must also be normative. But I really see no reason to assent to the premise of the argument that produces this assumption.

If I am right, then my arguments undermine at least one version of Hume's Hurdle. Am I, however, right? Some members of the conference seemed to think so. Professor Danto, for instance, remarked that, after all, if someone said that Hitler was scarcely a human being, it would not be obvious that he was either contradicting himself or that "human being" contained an evaluative element. It may be, I suggest, that certain kinds of attitudes and tendencies to action are connected with those biological elements that make up our notion of a person

or human being. This is, at least, how we do think and talk.
("Act like a man," "He is behaving like an animal," for example.) Professor Hook (oddly, in view of his naturalistic trend
in philosophy) supported Nielsen in the discussion when he
said that it seemed to him that any kind of behavior was
compatible with the biological description of man. The notion
of "biological description" is anything but clear, but I think I
know what Professor Hook means. But I suggest that his remark
really begs the question. For can we assume that a biological
or scientific description gives a complete account of what is
meant by the notions "human being" or "man"? It may be
that if there were such a thing as a "complete account" or
"complete description" of human nature, it might have to include in it certain capacities and characteristics, and some
of these might be what we should say were, in some sense,
moral. In any case, Professor Hook's remark seems to me to
embody the same sort of mistake embodied in the seventeenth-
century belief that, inasmuch as physics did not need to take
qualitative facts into account in its calculations, but only had
to take quantitative facts into account, the former (colors and
tastes, for example) were "secondary" qualities and had no
real existence. The truth that for some purposes certain facts
need not be taken account of does not imply that these facts
are somehow nonexistent. That any conduct is compatible with
the "biological description" of man need not imply that any
conduct is compatible with our concept of man or human
being. Here an analogy may be illuminating.[8] If we just consider the rules of chess "neat," as it were, then we may get the
idea that *any* strategy or *any* set of tactics was compatible with
the rules of the game. But when we further consider that, after
all, the object of the game is to *win* (as already mentioned),
then, *caeteris paribus,* there are some strategies (like moving
at random) that do not jibe with playing the game. It is certainly not enough for someone not to make illegal moves for
us to allow that he is playing chess. To use another analogy,
there may be a wide range of possible interpretations that are
acceptable interpretations of a Chopin sonata, and some of

these we may grade as good or bad or indifferent. But the range is not utterly unrestricted. Surely there are some interpretive attempts that we should simply reject as not being within the range of interpretations whether good or bad or indifferent.

It is not clear to me whether what I have been arguing, if true, supports any doctrine of natural law. After all, the notion of natural law is not the name of anything very clear. Certainly it needs reexamination, and it cannot be overthrown by one or more rapid rubrics of the kind I have been stricturing.

NOTES

1. Although he would no doubt deplore the language, Nielsen agrees that in the case of man, "existence precedes essence." Another confirmation of something that Richard Bernstein points out in a perceptive review of Aiken's *Reason and Conduct:* "Although in temper, emphasis and concern it [analytic ethics] has been radically different from existentialism and there has been practically no communication between these two approaches, they end in basic agreement." "Post-Wittgenstein Dilemmas," *Commentary,* June, 1963.

2. The following criticism of the notion in question was, in its main outlines, suggested to me by some remarks made by J. L. Austin a number of years ago in Oxford.

3. *Nichomachean Ethics,* Book I, 5.

4. Naturally, it is as easy as it is unprofitable to use these classifications in order to make quite sure that all judgments fit in; that is why the two challenges above are not so independent as they might seem.

5. In, for instance, *Sense and Sensibilia* (Oxford: Oxford University Press, 1962) Austin once remarked that it was philosophers, not the facts, that were simple.

6. "Must We Mean What We Say?" *Inquiry* (Autumn, 1958), p. 183.

7. Cf. R. M. Hare, "Philosophical Discoveries," *Mind* (April, 1960), pp. 145ff. The argument above is, in part, making use of some suggestions I find in Hare's article. Hare would, no doubt,

deplore the use I am making of them. "Descriptive" and "normative," are not, of course, the only terms used to describe the kind of dichotomy I am trying to prick. "Evaluative"-"factual" and "prescriptive"-"descriptive" are others. It would no doubt be valuable to analyze the differences among these terms.

8. Suggested to me by Professor Max Black. I am also indebted to Professor Nielsen for a number of sharp questions that forced any clarity here, and to the Editor for suggesting the title of my contribution.

Judicial Reasoning

A

The Nature of Judicial Reasoning

EDWARD H. LEVI
University of Chicago Law School

IN THIS paper I shall attempt (1) to describe some attributes of judicial reasoning that give uniqueness to the process and concern to those who use it; (2) to examine to some extent the process itself and the relationship between it and the articulation of neutral principles; and (3) to examine once more the uncertainties of judicial reasoning in the light of the importance of time and place and changing function.

I

The topic of judicial reasoning evokes the memory of countless after-dinner talks given by members of the judiciary and a kind of entourage of lawyers and law professors. This is not all it evokes, of course. In any case, many of the talks are good, and it would be churlish to mention this except to suggest one point and to ask a first question. The point is somewhat difficult to make. It involves questions of emphasis and degree and qualification to such an extent that I cannot help but have doubts about it. Yet to put it in the large it would be this: It would be difficult to think of another scholarly profession that speaks as little of the consequences of its acts or the discoveries it has made and as much about the circumstances of its own behavior. Surely these public expressions of wonderment at the difficulties and niceties of the judge's behavior are not to be dismissed simply as orgies of narcissism or flattery. I am not, of course, speaking of the judicial opinion, although there is a relationship between the opinion itself and the talks about how opinions get to be written. A facet of the point is that, as I believe, the literature about judging is an American, possibly an Anglo-American, phenomenon.

I have put the point that I am suggesting in terms of a concern with judging and a lack of inquiry into the effects of judging. This must be qualified. Inquiries into judicial behavior are related to inquiries into effect. A shift in constitutional interpretation can have obvious consequences, suggesting questions as to the relationship between judging and the justi-fication for the shift. Perhaps it should be said that the effect of the shift so far as the judge or lawyer is concerned is pri-marily on the fabric of the law. The lawyer's or the judge's function may be sufficiently self-delimited so as to exclude from the realm of their professional competence the larger social consequences, for example, of the school desegregation decision or the recent reapportionment case, even though the lawyer or judge will know or believe what others in that kind of segment of society will know or believe. For the judge or lawyer the relevant effects are upon the web of the law, the administration of law, and the respect for law. These are large items, and the priest who only keeps his temple in good repair is not to be condemned on that account. Yet with all these qualifications, and even with the difficulties that analogous il-lustrations suggest, the point, though battered, seems to me to persist. Is the analogy to be to the man of medicine who describes not what the virus does and how it is to be counter-acted but rather emphasizes the difficulties and virtues of his diagnostic art? Is it to be to the scientist who cares less about his discovery and more about how he made it? Again, is it to be recognized that perhaps the discovery is more the way and less the result? Perhaps the analogy should be to the novelist who thinks his reactions and growth are matters of importance to an understanding of the craft. I think the analogies on bal-ance emphasize the point that there is, indeed, unusual con-cern with the decision-making processes of judges, and the question to be put is whether this unusual concern, if it does exist, points to a uniqueness in the judicial process itself.

The uniqueness does not appear to arise in any simple way from the importance of the items ruled upon by the judge. Much of what a judge decides, if you look at the situations with which he deals, is no more or less important than what a plumber does, to speak of the plumber as the symbol of the worker on everyday items without whose skill matters could be uncomfortable, annoying, and at times catastrophic. Of course there is a difference, since the judge, even though the case before him may involve price fixing on plumbing items, is dealing with rights and duties imposed or acknowledged by the state, and he is an instrument of government. But this is true also of the legislator, the policeman, and the prosecutor. Behavioral scientists do attempt to study the decision-making processes of these occupations. We know these groups do make important decisions, yet the literature of the wonderment and agony of the road to determination does not really pertain to them. A comparison between the judge and the legislator seems particularly suggestive, because even though we were traditionally told that the judge only applies old rules through specific determinations to cases brought before him, whereas the legislator changes the law, we know that to a considerable extent the judge and the legislator perform the same function. By this I mean that the legislator, also, must have points of reference to basic doctrines that justify the determinations of changes he makes. Yet the differences in the American practice between judge and legislator are there to be seen. First, there are many legislators, and although appellate judges are more than one, the comparison is not so much between individual judges and individual legislators as it is between a judge and the legislative body. The legislator is champion of a point of view. If all points of view are to be represented it is because the debate, if that is what it can be called, has brought them out and the legislator is but a participant, although a later voter, in that debate. On the contrary, the judge who writes an opinion has the task of reflecting the outlines of the debate, to show that he is aware of the different voices and that his thought processes have traveled through an inner debate prior to determination. In short, although this is honored in varying degrees, the judge, although he may feel strongly, does not appear as an advocate. Second, although we know that both judges and legislators change the law and both refer to immutable principles, the emphasis in the court in the American system is not only on the prior or stated rule but on its application in other cases, creating for the judge the problem of showing how an old equity can be preserved and better and new justice be done. Third, the assumption for the judge is that the process of determination is one of reason. There is almost a claim to infallibility if the system works properly. The result is not one of indifference or bias, but one that follows from inner thought processes that bring the right result implicit in the rule. Judicial reasoning no doubt is like any other kind of reasoning that involves the use of a moving classification system. But here a moral judgment is frequently involved in the conclusions reached by the judge. Moreover, as I will indicate later, the integrity of the process in which the judge is engaged depends not only on distinctions that he may make reasonably, but also on his own belief in the legitimacy and decisiveness of these distinctions. Thus there is an astonishing combination of compulsions on the Anglo-American judge: the duty of representing many voices, of justifying the new application in terms of a prior rule and the equality of other cases, the assumption that reason is a sufficient and necessary guide, the responsibility for moral judgment, and the importance of sincerity—all these do tend to give uniqueness to the institution of judicial reasoning in our system and in our society.

II

I come now to the second point, which is that the technique of judicial reasoning is admirably adapted to a moving classification system and has a built-in device for the exploration and creation of ambiguities. At the same time, the process tends to obscure the problem of the relationship between equality and change. Equality seems to be the moving principle that justifies, indeed compels, the reference to the handling of similar cases once this material is readily available. I realize the reference to a similar specific instance could be considered solely as a means of supplying or clarifying a definition of a key concept in a rule. I do not meant to suggest either that the sole style of legal reasoning is from case to case to the creation of a rule. Styles change and the structure of the opinion at any given time and with a particular judge may appear to be from the general proposition downward. The problem of the determination of the application of the general proposition to the cluster of facts still remains, however. The adversary system, which is closely related to the idea of a fair hearing, creates a forum in which competing versions of the factual situation can be explored, and this is another way of saying that competing propositions are being advanced. And it is a little difficult, even under the most static and simple view of law, to see how competing versions of the same fact situation can be avoided. The briefs of counsel further the idea of the comparison of situations by their citation of cases. Yet it is true that the cases may be cited more for the statement of general propositions and less or not at all for any close scrutiny of similarity of factual situations. A judge with strong convictions and an authoritarian view as to good and bad cases and a well-formed, logically held structure of the law in mind may cite only those good cases that reflect his view as to the appropriate and correct application of the right terms—much as it appears the early casebooks tended to do. One could then conceive of the process as laying down an understood logical structure of terms illustrated through cases that in their function with respect to the system are quite passive. Thus I would not want to say here that what is usually called reasoning by analogy is the sole judicial technique in opinion writing, nor even that it is the concealed starting point for the judge's own working out of the problem. But I do think that a closer look at how reasoning by analogy or example works in the judicial process will reveal some interesting problems.

The Anglo-American legal system has as one of its comfort points the idea of dictum. The system is not very precise as to what "dictum" is. In some sense the idea undoubtedly is a necessary one, since otherwise the judge could write a treatise as an opinion and accomplish an unacceptable codification of the law. So we say loosely that the judge's observations on matters not before him for decision, or that are perhaps not necessary for the conclusion which he reaches, are only dicta and not binding on future judges. At one extreme the doctrine suggests that the particular views of a given judge on propositions of law can be decisive on future cases, and indeed must be, if these views are given with cogent reference to the precise issues he had to decide. At the other extreme the doctrine contends that we need not permit the prior judge to overreach and establish law by his own exaggerated view of the issues or the relevance of what he feels called upon to say. At the same time, as we all know, in the web of the law one can find the compelling influence of repeated doctrine, even though close scrutiny would show that, for all the appellate cases that have discussed it the doctrine could be called only dictum. But the phrase "close scrutiny," although it may indicate diligence and the bringing to bear of an expert mind, does not disclose the rules of the game. I suggest as a starting point for inquiry the question of how pivotal the position taken by a prior judge is made to be by the inner discipline of the system. I believe a view of the system through the structure of reasoning by example is helpful in this connection.

From the standpoint of reasoning by example, the circumstances before the court are compared with a number of somewhat similar circumstances that have been classified in terms of opposing categories. These categories would result in opposite or at least different legal conclusions and different although presumably compatible rules of law. The fact cluster before the court could be included within either category. After enough successive fact clusters have been added, the probability is that it will be apparent that the original rule of law has changed its meaning, and this may be reflected in a change in the name of the determining concept, and therefore in the language of the rule. If it is correct that the fact cluster could be classified equally well under the categories of opposing concepts and rules, this must be because no authoritative definition has removed ambiguity. If reliance is to be on the authority of a prior case for the scope and effectiveness of an announced rule of law now to be applied, then the similarity and difference between the present fact cluster now up for decision and the fact cluster of the prior case are decisive. What power does the judge in the prior case have to establish for all time the compelling and, in the future, decisive aspects of the case before him, including (1) a determination of what is irrelevant and, therefore, would make no difference if present or absent, and (2) a determination of what cannot be done without? Thus what is to be the result if the first judge forecasts similarity when the second and later judge finds a reasonable difference?

I think the answer in Anglo-American law, although some English writers have suggested this is only true of American and not English practice, is that the second judge, where only case law is involved, is free to make his own determination of decisive similarity or difference. This, of course, gives the law a great deal of flexibility and capacity for growth. I am not suggesting that the inner discipline of the system permits the later judge to create distinctions that he regards as irrelevant. If the judge reworks the system and has a new classification, he is under compulsion to supply reasons for reworked old cases in order to project a pattern that can guide later cases. The distinctions that he makes must appear reasonable to him. Under one view of the judge's restricted power, the amount of change is limited by the judge's ability to encompass it within a logical structure that explains all prior cases, albeit the judges of the prior cases would have rejected the explanation. Under this view there is a sense in which the system is engaged, not in change, but in explication. At best, this view of the constraint upon the judge is somewhat idealized. It is recognized that cases are discarded and are explained in terms of the now inoperative ideas of their time rather than in terms of any present pattern. Particularly in those areas of the law where reported cases are so numerous, the present judge is really not compelled to organize them all. Yet the compulsion upon him is real and effective, even though it does not require him to make sense out of every case that has ever occurred and even though now and then he may recognize a shift in the law so that he is not required to take account of an older view. If the views of the prior judge and the distinctions he made were decisive, the system would be much more rigid and change more frequently would have to come about through legislation.

When English commentators describe their system as one in which the second and later judge is bound by the determinations of the first judge, they appear to have reference to cases in which the question is one of statutory interpretation. They thus do not distinguish between common law cases and cases in which the issue is the meaning of legislation. I believe that, to a considerable degree, it can be shown that in this country also the second and later judge finds himself much more bound by the prior court's views when the prior court is construing a statute. In such situations the prior court's views, even when broadly stated as dictum, frequently determine the direction of future statutory construction. I state the matter too simply of course, but I think there is this basic difference in the freedom of the judge in case law areas as contrasted with the case law-statutory interpretation fields. The explanation may be that dictum places a gloss upon the statute; it is a kind of communication to the legislature as to how their words will be interpreted, and since the legislature has manifested an interest in the area, anyway, if the gloss is not to its liking it can change the statute. This line of argument is not fully satisfying, since it can be said that court and legislature should be considered in a partnership, even in the absence of legislation. It may be that subsequent court interpretations of legislation reveal less leeway for the second court for the very reason that interpretation must focus on specific language and its meaning, and there may be a natural inclination to assume that the document takes on and keeps the meaning assigned to it. One way the restriction of the second court in statutory matters manifests itself in our country is in the plea of a judge that he is free of the restraints of the previous case because this is a case involving basic or constitutional issues. The written constitution and the insistence that it, and not its interpretations, must prevail, in marked contrast to the situation in which legislation is involved, make it possible in constitutional matters to change from the even flow of common law-case law accretions or from the more rigid following down the path in statutory interpretation to an abrupt, although usually foreshadowed, change in direction.

I do not deny that there are difficulties in the way of the application of this analysis. For example, the United States Supreme Court in 1922 held that the antitrust laws did not apply to baseball, since the exhibition, although made for money, was not to be called trade or commerce. In subsequent years, as a matter of constitutional interpretation, the scope of the commerce power of the United States was greatly increased. In 1953 the Court was again asked to rule on the application of the Sherman Act to baseball. Quite apart from the point that the Sherman Act is so vague that it may be regarded less as legislation and more as common law, one can argue that if this is a matter of statutory interpretation, then the 1922 opinion, assuming the basic facts of baseball are the same, must be adhered to; if it is a matter of constitutional interpretation, then presumably the wider impact of federal power would be acknowledged to exist. As we know, the way the matter was handled compels us to distinguish between baseball on the one side and theaters and boxing on the other, leading to the interesting argument, which failed when football was considered, that football was a team sport like baseball and unlike boxing and therefore should be exempt also. The point is that the jurisprudential question of the leeway in the law for particular categories really decided these cases.

This analysis of judicial reasoning is rudimentary and could be made more elaborate, paying more attention to those cases in which there is a mixture of legislation and case law interpretation, or cases in which legislation is persuasive as indicating a shift in policy or, perhaps, is to be treated much as an analogous case for reasoning by example to work upon. It is surprising, however, that a judicial reasoning system that places such great store on the correct analysis of cases should have as little doctrine as ours does upon the crucial question of whether the judge's own explanation of the decisive features of the case, a successor judge's rationale, or perhaps the underlying structure as seen by some commentator, are all equally available methods for finding or justifying the law. To the extent that there is any general assumption about this, I would suppose that it is that the first judge's language, when not dictum, is decisive—a view that is not only unclear but wrong. This in itself suggests that for the effective operations of the system it is not necessary to be either clear or correct about such matters.

The compatibility of judicial reasoning, which relies heavily on reasoning by example, to a moving classification system is, I think, clear. The movement in the system frequently will not be apparent. When it is apparent, it is often justified obliquely on the basis that this policy step was taken some time ago and is reflected in prior decisions. The system permits a foreshadowing of results and therefore has built into it the likelihood of a period of preparation so that future decisions appear as a belated finding and not a making of law. The joint exploration through competing examples to fill the ambiguities of one or many propositions has the advantage of permitting the use in the system of propositions or concepts saved from being contradictory because they are ambiguous, and on this account more acceptable as ideals or commonplace truths; it has the advantage, also, of postponing difficult problems until they arise and of providing an inner discipline for the system by forcing an analysis of general propositions in terms of concrete situations. The avoidance of explicit policy determinations by referring to prior and selected examples appears as a substitution of the idea of equality for a head-on examination of issues of policy. Undoubtedly some of the magic of the judicial process stems from this fact, and also some of the doubt that has given rise to the literature of self-examination.

III

Against this background it seems to me that a third point is at least tenable; it is this: The caliber of a court's opinion, even in a constitutional case, is not to be made dependent on its announcement of a principle that is fully satisfying in reason and that will indicate for us how future cases are to be decided. I put the matter this way in reaction to Professor Wechsler's observations on neutral or articulated principles and upon the basis that the caliber of an opinion is to be seen in terms of the governmental function it performs. What Professor Wechsler said was that the courts, in exercising their duty to review the actions of the other branches of the government in the light of constitutional provisions, must act as courts of law and not as naked power organs. The determinations of the court, then, to have legal quality, must be "entirely principled," and a "principled decision . . . is one that rests on reasons with respect to all the issues in the case, reasons that in their generality and their neutrality transcend any immediate result that is involved." The emphasis throughout his superb essay is on "standards that transcend the case at hand" and upon "principles articulation." I have heard it suggested that the use of the "neutrality" concept is unfortunate, since it seems to give the impression that the values about which the judge feels deeply may not be the appropriately articulated reasons for decision. And this has thrown the essay into a kind of maelstrom of discussion as to whether judges should be neutralists or umpires or social reformers. I would suppose that all would agree with the answer

I think is suggested by Professor Wechsler's essay; namely, that a judge who makes changes in the law must take seriously the duty of reworking the pattern of the law. The distinctions that he makes must be genuine, articulated, and sufficiently acceptable. But granted the description of judicial reasoning as the working or reworking of a moving classification system, to what extent must the judge have worked out the full impact upon future cases of conflicting values and legal concepts? And to what extent is it appropriate or necessary for a judge to plot out in the written opinion, as contrasted with the inner process of decision, the future course of the law as to those instances and future distinctions that seem foreseeable to him?

Surely there are several meaningful ways in which the Constitution is something more than what a court says it is. In our country, in any event, the Constitution is a written document embracing basic and sometimes contradictory values and using both very broad and sometimes rather specific concepts. The freedom that the court has to abandon its prior reading of the Constitution is a recognition of primacy of the document. Granted the right and duty of the court to interpret the document, it has not been given the duty or the opportunity to rewrite the words. It can decide cases on the basis of its interpretation of the words, but if the analysis of reasoning by example means anything, it means that a later court can accept the results in those cases but justify it on a different theory. And the value of court action as opposed to action by a constitutional convention or a legislature is that the matter can be taken one step at a time. This does not mean that the steps can be taken without justification—the discipline requires a justification that will explain the way prior cases and this case have been handled, and may even be a justification that latches onto a shift in constitutional interpretation. But I do not think this is equivalent to demanding a fully satisfying theory that projects a line to the future and steers a safe course for future conflicts. Particularly where a constitution is involved with its conflicting values, such a demand seems unobtainable. In addition to the point that it is one of the values of court action that it can deal with the case at hand and avoid the broad reach, there is the more central complexity that with conflicting values a political system has to decide some things on the basis of specific decisions approaching a dividing line that, in fact, may be a moving line and not one that can be grandly fixed through articulation. Because the Supreme Court has ventured into an enlarged circle in which primaries are protected from racial discrimination does not, I think, require it or make it desirable for the court to attempt to leap to a determination of whether under any and all circumstances political parties should be prevented from being organized on racial or religious grounds in the United States. An attempt to make a judicial pronouncement on this subject might be more fraught with mischief than a wrong decision crossing a line that it should not cross and resulting from the misapplication of a more standard principle that a governmental function must be carried on without that kind of clear discrimination. And so for the opinion of the Supreme Court in the segregated schools case, I would not suppose it would be desirable for the court to have attempted to articulate its adjudication upon the basis of a resolution of the conflict between the right of freedom of association and the right to not associate—a conflict that Professor Wechsler has suggested he would like to see come out on the side of association, but where he indicates there are certain difficulties, and, as he said, he has "not yet written the opinion." It is because Professor Wechsler has not yet written the opinion that I am dubious that others can. But it does not follow that segregation in schools should be allowed to persist. It is possible that the Brown case should have been decided with the same result, but with less of an immediate jump and on the partial basis of an old and accepted theory.

The recognition and preservation of future leeways in the law, until the time for decision has been reached, is, of course, not a new thought or a new value. The doctrine that constitutional matters should not be decided until their resolution is necessary to the case at hand is in part a reflection of that thought. Of course, it is virtuous in terms of the legal process to be willing to deny the legitimacy of desired results that cannot be reached through appropriate reasoning. But the process of judicial reasoning is frequently, perhaps basically, retrospective, taking advantage of situations that have been met. This in itself involves some projection into the future as well, going beyond the case at hand, but it can also involve care not to foreclose the consideration of further distinctions and further relevance. This is in recognition that time has its advantages, that the constitutional or legal posture of later cases may be doctrinely different, situations that seem the same now may appear otherwise under a new light, and situations and doctrine may be more interrelated than is earlier realized.

Having said this much I hasten to add that I realize that a call for responsible, articulated reasons does not mean that a judge must shoulder the responsibility for deciding all future cases. And probably the articulation of reasons in the opinion is of greater or at least different importance in constitutional cases to the extent that the court's overriding authority has to be justified. The course of common law cases in which one can find inchoate theories, incomplete expressions of new views, and then finally the better expression of the theory is well known and includes the best judges as the writers of opinions. Shocking as it may be, even the case that has no articulated theory to support it, but seems right and is treated as a kind of unique incident, has a place in our jurisprudence. Perhaps one's point of view on the importance of the completed theory depends upon whether one sees the theory in some sense as prior to the determination of result or as arising out of the same process of seeing similarity and difference. If it is the latter, then the completed theory is less important than the description of the process of comparison (which, of course, includes a statement of what are the crucial points of comparison), for, after all, it is that process upon which we must rely. I trust that the category of articulated neutral principles is broad enough to permit this approach.

IV

I have to describe some of the strains inherent in judicial reasoning that perhaps have contributed to the literature of self-examination, and to describe also the process of this reasoning that is adapted to a moving classification system. I have urged that the articulation of neutral principles be regarded in the light of a process of judging in which the direction of perceived standards and the comparison of situations both play a part, but one in which it is not always possible or wise to anticipate the inevitable collision of important values too far beyond the case at hand. But of course the choice of the preferred way of judicial reasoning depends upon a judgment as to the functions that judicial reasoning is to perform. Clearly these functions are not always the same. They depend in part upon the needs of a society at a given time and the availability of other and possibly better ways of fulfilling these needs. The classic function for judging is to redress a wrong caused by a violation of a sufficiently understood, legally authorized standard. The clearer the standard and the more acceptable that standard is to elements within the community, the greater the moral judgment carried by the decision. Because rewards and punishment are involved and the relationship to moral judgment very close, judging is an important educational and changing factor. The interpreter of the standard becomes the creator of the standard, and the standard or law that is applied may become, in varying degrees, no more than, but as much as, the changing customs or value systems of the community as seen through a particular mechanism. As we know, there need not be an institutional separation of judging from executive or legislative authority. The functional lines between them can become exceedingly blurred, in part because even naked power hardly ever is that simple. We can begin with a skeletonized view of the judicial process: the received standard, the adversary proceeding, the focusing on a single situation, and the exemplification of the standard in similar actual or hypothetical cases. But these are the broad outlines, and the working of the process will change as needs are felt differently.

It is, perhaps, relevant to remind ourselves that law as regulated by the judicial opinion operates within a literary tradition. One function of the opinion has been to map out the contours of the law, much as a text writer would do, and in this sense the reasoning of the judge as dictum has been quite important. But the view of the judge on the effects of laws or on the quantity and types of cases and issues that may arise within the legal system itself may be quite limited. I do not know whether it is worthwhile, but modern methods of research could tell us a great deal more about the operations of the legal system itself—that is, the frequency with which particular types of cases arise, the relationships among issues, the likelihood of recovery, and similar questions—than can be handled appropriately in legal opinions. This limitation of judicial reasoning to an examination of the facts that arise in the particular case, an acceptance of enlightened or sound social views, and an intense scrutiny of the intellectual issues thought to be involved in the case is, no doubt, regarded as a positive value by members of our craft. Judges are not behavioral scientists. The point is, however, that there was a time when no one else was, and the sphere of the judge as social philosopher was less limited or threatened. Today the organization by the bar of various instruments for mapping out the law and, also, for such collaborative research as can be done both on the operations within the legal system and the effect of laws on social problems—all these suggest a certain limitation on the need for formal judicial reasoning as words on high to fill these gaps. We still want to know what the judge thought was relevant in deciding the case, but the thought that he might do some research on his own in matters economic or sociological fills us, no doubt correctly, with dread.

But we still think of the judge as appropriately law reformer and also as wise man or political scientist for the community. The meaning of the image of the judge as law reformer is clouded because, in part, it refers only to the re-

stating and remaking of the case law as the pattern of the law.
But the fact is that in our society the law court is a powerful
instrument for effecting changes that the legislature will not
enact or for preventing, for some time, at least, the changes
that legislatures do enact. And the defense of judicial action
against the charge that its behavior is simply legislative, and
therefore the assumption of naked power, is frequently but not
always that where action is prevented, the matter is so great
as to go to the essential spirit of institutions, and where change
is effected, that the amount of change is so small that a comparison of other situations will show it has already occurred.
It would be comforting to think that an analysis of proper
judicial reasoning would show which actions were appropriate. I do not think an articulation of powerful reasons and
serious concern is sufficient to separate proper judicial from im-
proper judicial, or essentially legislative, behavior—or wise
from imprudent judicial behavior. It seems to be a question
partly of time and place: the acceptability of what is done and
the need for it. It can be plausibly argued that all great judges
have recognized this, and that it is one of the tragedies of
judging that, with this recognition and, perhaps, because of it,
misconceptions of felt needs can make for unwise decisions.
Of course a court that operates in areas where there are
strong differences of views runs great risks, but in our system
it is supposed to do so somewhat. The analysis of jurisprudence
that makes much of the difference between the "is" and the
"ought" does not seem to me to be helpful at this point. A
judicial system that makes this distinction and eschews the
ought will have lost both the spirit and symbol of justice. In
effect, it will have made the "was" the "is."

Yet it can be asked whether at a particular time and place
it is valuable for a court to become the main forum for basic
political debate. It is somewhat anomalous in a highly developed political society that lawyers in court and lawyers in
robes should have to discuss matters of political power, which
certainly as appropriately come within the province of lawyers
in the legislature, but which presumably are inadequately

treated there. The fact of the anomaly is not necessarily a criticism of the court's behavior. The fact is that in our society, although some may disapprove, the court has advantages as a forum for the discussion of political-moral issues. In a broadly based vocal and literate society, susceptible to the persuasion of many tongues and pens, and with inadequate structuring of relevant debate, the court has a useful function, not only in staying time for sober second thought, but in focusing issues. It is sometimes the only forum in which issues can be sharply focused—or appear to be so. It has the drama of views that are more opposing and less scattered, because its procedures require a certain amount of relevance. It operates more within a structure of logical ideas, and yet a structure into which current views may be infused through new words that must find a relationship to the old and through new meanings. It has the drama of a limited number of personalities who are called upon to explain their views. It has the advantage of beginning with certain agreed-upon premises to which all participants profess loyalty, and thus it can force concentration upon the partial clarification of ambiguities. It must reach a conclusion that has the force of a moral judgment upon the particular situation. The court operates from a base in which the identification of its members is explicitly to the higher ideals of the entire community. This freedom and responsibility minimizes that kind of double standard between public and private convictions that cannot so clearly be said to be inappropriate in other areas. This does not mean that the price for such participation by a court does not come high nor that there are not substantial weaknesses in its fulfillment of these functions. A basic insecurity in the foundation for a court's approach to such issues is that the court must proceed with a standard of constitutionality, including problems of distribution of powers, or a rule of minimum fairness that may distort the lesson. This would make for poor public education, even though it might be the best available. Finally, without regard for the technical propriety of what the court does, there is no doubt that the court's influence as an acceptable objective force is diminished the greater the controversy. This easy and customary point, however, must be corrected by an awareness that it is the court's appeal to our better selves, connoting some controversy, that is the source of its moral power and persuasion.

In this setting the function of articulated judicial reasoning is to help protect the court's moral power by giving some assurance that private views are not masquerading behind public views. This might lead to the conclusion that the more controversial the issues, the more the court should endeavor to spell out the future rules of the road. But I doubt if this conclusion follows. I do not ignore the obligation of higher courts to give directions to trial and intermediate courts, the need greater in some areas than in others to guide private transactions, the special duty to enforce rules of fairness when court procedures are involved, and the requirement that law not be segmented but be a continuing pattern. But the existence of controversy on public issues may speak for a less decisive and far-reaching determination by a court that can have the advantage of taking the law a step at a time. The commentators' happy and useful lament that the reasoning is unclear and that ambiguities and uncertainties remain is, in itself, no cause for alarm; future courts can and will take advantage of such learning and hindsight in the process of taking advantage of their own. What is needed in the judicial opinion is an indication of the points at issue, a narrowing of the determinative factors, and to some extent care not to take unnecessary steps until they can be taken, in a sense, retrospectively. This is not an argument for the thoughtless decision. It is, rather, an argument that the decision must bear witness that it was reached through the discipline of the pattern of the law, which provides both restrictions and leeway. It is, indeed, the recognition of the present and future leeway, as much as of the prior restrictions, which compels the thoughtful decision and makes of judicial reasoning something more than arrangements to be projected on a computer or predicted from the bias of a judge.

B

An Analysis of Judicial Reasoning

PAUL A. FREUND

Harvard University Law School

PROFESSOR LEVI's paper—sensitive, sagacious, and suggestive—
takes as its prelude the theme that there is a special fascination
among lawyers and judges with their own behavior, their own
processes of thought, as distinct from the products of their
labors. To ask why this should be so may cast some light on
the nature of judicial reasoning itself.

If there is something distinctive in this phenomenon of
concern with method, it lies not in the concern itself but in
the preoccupation of the practitioners of the discipline. In
other areas the concern is evidenced by philosophers, whether
of science or mathematics, language or history. One explanation of the disparity may be a very practical one, that while
these disciplines are part of a general education, shared at
least on a basic level by philosophers, the study of law has by
and large not been infused into a liberal arts curriculum and
remains an esoteric specialty.

Is this, then, the full explanation, that lawyers and judges
simply fill the gap in an analysis of their own activities, filling
it, to be candid, generally in a parochial and superficial way?
There is, I believe, a more significant reason. There is something central to the enterprise in legal and judicial method.
What earns approval or disapproval is bound up with the
processes of decision as fully as with the outcomes. In the
enterprise of judicial decision there is, at least, to borrow a
phrase of Lionel Trilling, a morality of morality. It is not
merely that the judge's task is prescriptive; a moral teacher

would also fulfill that role. Rather, the judge performs a role full of ambivalences: he is conservator and innovator; impersonal and individual; authoritarian and suppliant; bound and free. No annual Nobel Prize is awarded for the most revolutionary decision of the year. If there were a prize, it might well be bestowed for excellence in resolving the ambiguities of the role.

The elements of judicial reasoning are by no means unique. They have been described compendiously by Professor Levi as a moving classification system, which implies coherence, rules and categories and their application to a set of facts, and a built-in capacity for change. This suggests a process of scientific reasoning with ethical concepts, problems, and criteria. But to this description must be added the institutional framework of the process, not just a framework like the fraternity of scientists, but a delegated mission, a received set of offices, procedures, responsibilities, and limitations in administering the moving classification system.

Now to a closer look at the system. Before attempting to explain its secular "moving" feature, it is useful to consider the system in its more diurnal operation; it spins on its axis, so to speak, as well as traveling through space. So viewed, the judicial process may help to illuminate the meaning of a "rule," of "application," and of justice.

A rule is what it does: the guarantee of the privilege of habeas corpus means what habeas corpus is deemed to do. The meaning is indeed the use. Interpretation is not an inert verbal exercise, as the baggage conductor was painfully learning when he mused, "Dogs is dogs, and cats is dogs, but this 'ere tortoise is a hinsect!" Suppose, to take a simple case, that a notice is posted at the entrances to Washington Square: "No vehicles allowed." If interpretation were a fathoming of intrinsic meaning, we might first select the seemingly crucial word "vehicle" and then determine its meaning by looking for paradigm cases and marginal cases of that entity. We might posit automobiles and bicycles as paradigms, and toy trains as outside the definition, with, perhaps, baby carriages in between. For purposes of the rule, however, difficulties arise at once. Is a bicycle being pushed or carried a "vehicle"; is a racing car in a stationary exhibit a "vehicle"? If a baby carriage is held not to come within the definition, what of a commercial pushcart, physically quite similar? The interpreter will be impelled to look for the purpose or purposes of the rule in order to answer these questions; a vehicle may be one class of thing in a tax statute and quite another in a park regulation. Indeed, the interpreter will have to look not only at the context in the rule itself but at the context of neighboring rules. In deciding the question of the stationary racing car, it would be relevant to know whether the subject of exhibitions was separately regulated; if, for example, exhibitions were allowed on official permits, it would be anomalous to single out vehicles as an impermissible form of exhibit. Not only this, but in the act of interpreting the rule the institutional setting has its place. A judge might very probably decide that a pogo stick is not covered despite its danger and annoyance, because the common usage of "vehicle" sets limits to interpretation. But suppose that the city charter authorizes the park commissioner to make rules and regulations for "vehicles" in public squares, and that he issues a notice barring pogo sticks along with bicycles and other aids to locomotion. I can imagine that the same judge who had declined so to interpret the general ban on "vehicles" might sustain the commissioner's order, for in two respects the problem of rule-interpretation has been altered: now the interpretation has been made in the first instance by an official vested with large responsibility and discretion in management; and his interpretation is not applied retrospectively to violators of a general notice, but is spelled out in advance so that those charged as violators cannot complain of lack of specific guidance in their conduct.

This analysis of the "meaning" of a rule has been labored, but it can hardly be said to be laboring the obvious. There are those who would interpret the First Amendment guarantee "Congress shall make no law abridging the freedom of speech . . ." by rejecting all "balancing of interests," insisting that "no" means no, and explaining laws punishing, for example, incitement to riot as control over behavior that is not "speech." The delusive nature of that approach ought to be evident enough by putting the case of the formally parallel guarantee that no state shall pass "any law impairing the obligation of contracts" and asking whether this means that a minimum wage law may not supersede an existing labor contract for substandard wages.

The meaning of a rule, whether about vehicles or speech, is thus shaped in its application, which is a dialectic process that sharpens our appreciation of the rule and the facts alike. Of course, some rules may be highly detailed and precise, like the rules of a game to be enforced by an umpire, but these are hardly the most interesting or representative analogies to legal rules. Despite popular assumptions, it is not very useful to consider judges as umpires in this sense, though umpiring has, to be sure, its philosophical, even metaphysical, aspects, as is made evident in the fable of the three baseball umpires. The first, explaining his actions, said "I call them as I see them." The second: "I call them as they are." And the third: "Until I call 'em, they ain't nothing."

The distinction commonly drawn between interpretation and application is really a reflection of differences in the specificity of terms in the rules. The interpretation of "vehicle" or "speech" entails a set of applications of the rules in which the terms are embedded. As rules become more general, with fewer denoting terms, and are in the form of standards or principles, we are accustomed to speak of application rather than interpretation.

The spectrum of interpretation and application is illustrated by a problem referred to in Professor Levi's paper, drawing on a question posed by Professor Wechsler: whether the Supreme Court's outlawing of the so-called "white primary" election would not require a similar holding, if consistency and neutrality of principle are respected, precluding a religious (for example, a Catholic) party. We start with the constitutional provision dealing most explicitly with discrimination in the suffrage, the Fifteenth Amendment, which declares that no state shall deprive any person of the right to vote on account of race, color, or previous condition of servitude. With respect to a primary election in which the party has confined participation to white persons, the question is whether the amendment is inapplicable because it is not the "state" that has decreed the discrimination. After a period during which the Supreme Court so held, the decision was overruled, because of the state's involvement in the whole electoral process, including the primary as an integral phase. A tempting conclusion would be that the primary is legally cognate to the general election and that the qualifications for participation must be the same. But this is clearly too hasty, for surely Republicans can be excluded from voting in a Democratic primary, though not, of course, from voting in the general election. The party primary is, in truth, a hybrid of private and governmental elements, so that the regulations made by the party are for some purposes, but not for all, ascribable to the "state."

We have taken the first ambiguous step toward answering the question of the legitimacy of a religious party. If, as we have assumed, Republicans cannot be excluded by the state from voting in a general election, this proposition must rest elsewhere than on the Fifteenth Amendment, which deals only with race and color. The most appropriate support would come from the more general standard of the Fourteenth Amendment, declaring that no state shall deny to any person the equal protection of the laws. We are here, if you will, "applying a standard" rather than "interpreting a rule." If, then, the Fourteenth Amendment comes into play in cases of discriminatory suffrage, and if primary elections are to some extent subject to the restraints on state action, we have to consider why a Democratic primary is different from a white primary. What is the difference, in this context, between the excluded groups, Republicans and Negroes? The glaring difference is that Negroes occupy an immutable status, whereas Republicans do not. If we follow up this distinction, we would conclude that a native-American party is forbidden, but a farmers' (or Catholic) party is not. Perhaps a more refined distinction would start from the legitimate function of a primary, to select candidates who will most effectively represent a certain political ideology. From this point of view immutable status would again be rejected as a test, and beyond this the relevant criterion would be whether the qualifications for voting in a given primary were based on a community of political belief or objectives. In this view a Catholic party or a farmers' party might again qualify if, in a given state, a political program were in fact identified with such a grouping. But there is one further constitutional consideration: the guarantee of free exercise and nonestablishment of religion, which may override what would otherwise be a relevant classification. Thus the court has struck down a state requirement that public notaries must avow a belief in God, even though such an avowal might be deemed a reasonable test of the applicant's belief in the solemnity of the oaths he must administer. (John Locke, it will be recalled, excluded atheists from his circle of toleration because they did not appreciate the binding quality of an oath and were therefore a threat to civil society.) The upshot is that a religious party might be accepted without impugning the consistency or neutrality of a court that has rejected the white primary, but that for additional reasons deriving from religious guarantees the result might well be to bracket religion with color as an impermissible criterion for participation.

This illustration of rules and standards in operation suggests the element of ultimate choice when the relevant considerations have been explored and narrowed. It would be easy to indulge in cynicism and insist that the judge in resolving a question of this kind is at large, freewheeling, and only creating an illusion of rational principle. But to discern the element of choice is only the beginning, not the end, of sophistication in an understanding of the judicial process. Surely a bias for or against religion, or a particular religion, has no place in the decision of the issue of religious parties. The conscientious judge may, indeed, have to guard against an overcompensating counterbias in an effort to achieve neutrality. On the other hand, a bias against splinter parties because they would prejudice the working of our political system might stand on a different footing at the point of ultimate decision: *ut res magis valeat quam pereat* is a respectable maxim of interpretation. The obligation to articulate the reasoning entering into a decision is itself a safeguard. Not infrequently, we are told, a judge changes his vote because the opinion he is preparing "won't write." Once more, there may be danger that a conscientious judge will measure the soundness of a result by the relative ease with which a supporting opinion can be constructed. As the corruption of the best is the worst, so an identification of facility with soundness, in the name of reasoned articulation, may produce an excessive conservatism in which the familiar is enshrined. Opinion writing may be downhill or uphill, and the fact that an opinion "doesn't write" easily is not necessarily an impeachment of the endeavor.

It remains to consider the factor of change in Professor Levi's moving classification system. Change by virtue of judicial decision may be of two kinds: in new subsumptions under constant categories or in the formulation of new categories or concepts. Often the second is an outgrowth of the first, since new subsumptions implicitly alter the categories themselves, and it becomes a matter of judgment when and whether a more explicit reformulation should be essayed. Changes are made because of shifting mores, new ethical standards, or a demonstrated need for more economical or workable or fruitful formulations. The process of change in concept formations is not unlike that employed in science. A striking example in the law is the emergence of the concept of privacy. When Louis D. Brandeis was at the bar he sought some legal basis for imposing liability on the publishers of gossip and scandal sheets; the law of libel was inadequate because the truth of the revelations would be a defense. Among the analogies afforded by the law was the offense of eavesdropping. This was readily extended to shadowing on the streets, perhaps metaphorically still eavesdropping (as

both that and shadowing are themselves metaphors). The leap
to the gossip sheet was too great for metaphor, involving no
physical intrusion or proximity, but not too great for simile.
But there were other legal categories that recognized injuries
to feelings, such as the violation of confidential relationships,
and it seemed desirable to generalize and unify under the
new rubric, the right of privacy. In time the common elements
had to be compromised to meet certain special claims of
privilege on the part of the press, in the light of the public
interest in knowing about public figures, and so after a period
of unification there has set in a tendency once more toward
fragmentation, but without loss of the insights gained from the
overarching concept. Some parallel may be seen in scientific
thought, in, for example, the union and disunion of celestial
and atomic mechanics.

Science, too, may furnish an analogue to the overruling of
precedents. As every experiment tests in principle, according
to Duhem's theorem, not only the hypothesis under direct
scrutiny but the whole antecedent pattern of which this is a
part, so in the law a reexamination of antecedent rules and
principles is, in principle, open when a new set of facts is
presented for decision, and it becomes a matter of judgment
how radical the reexamination shall be. Such a judgment must
take into account the special function of a legal system to
maintain stability and continuity in the midst of change. It
must take account, too, of the judge's limited role in the legal
process as a whole, limited by the scope of admissible evidence, by rules of procedure such as presumptions and burden
of proof, and by the difficulties of administering decrees and
imposing unfamiliar sanctions. The judge is not a legislator,
not an Ideal Observer, much less God. In his acceptance of
his limitations as well as his powers he may find it tolerable
to hold sway over the lives and fortunes of others and possible
to alleviate the existential agony and absurdity of choice. In
his constraints he may find liberation.

C

The Nature of Judicial Reasoning

HERBERT WECHSLER

Columbia University Law School

PROFESSOR LEVI's account of the nature of judicial reasoning is concerned with the situation in which the court is, by hypothesis, vested with something less than the authority to make a free decision; that is, in which the issue to be determined is governed by law, be it the common law, a statute or administrative regulation, or a constitutional provision. It is worth noting, preliminarily, that this is not by any means the universal situation. Often, and increasingly in modern times, a court is granted broad discretion in an area, which means that it is competent to make the decision it considers the expedient or just determination of the issue posed.

Should a convicted criminal be sentenced to death or to imprisonment or, as the question is faced more frequently, to imprisonment or to probation; and how long should the prison sentence be? Should an injunction be awarded or the plaintiff left to some less peremptory and less effective remedy? Should the Supreme Court grant a writ of certiorari to review a lower court's decision? Examples without number could be given of such delegation of discretion unaccompanied by the prescription of authoritative norms. Even when the system does articulate a norm to guide adjudication, it may be so cast that it amounts to little more than an authority to make *ad hoc* evaluations in the process of its application, as in passing upon claims of negligence or reckless driving, to confine the illustration to the most familiar fields. One can point, finally, to situations in which the function of decision is essentially a type

290

of mediation or, perhaps, of arbitration; the goal, to find an answer that will reconcile the disputants or will, at least, assure that they go hence in peace.

As I read Professor Levi's paper, he is not concerned with cases of this order in which the judge can frankly view his task as that of doing justice, facing issues not intrinsically different from those posed to all of us in judging what is just or right in any given situation. His purpose, rather, is to show that even when the judge's function is admittedly to judge according to the law, his task has inescapably a certain legislative aspect, which the system deems legitimate and quite deliberately maintains. The role of courts in our polity is not, in short, confined to application of a set of antecedently established legal norms, but extends also, within limits, to the adaptation and the renovation of those norms. This is, of course, most clearly so in situations wherein the issue calling for decision is untouched by written law, and such authoritative data as there is consists of past decisions. It is, however, true as well, although the limits are much subtler, when a statute or a constitutional provision governs and the issue calls for its interpretation.[1] Especially in constitutional adjudication—since the difficulty of amendment is so great—our system relies heavily upon the courts for adaptation through the processes of reinterpretation.

I have nothing but admiration for the way Professor Levi locates and delineates this element of freedom in the function of the judge in our system and for his discriminating treatment of the claims of precedent in different situations—echoing and supplementing the analysis presented in the brilliant book he wrote some years ago.[2] He goes beyond this subject in the latter portion of his paper and deals with the extent to which a court, insofar as it exercises freedom of decision, is obliged to announce "a principle that is fully satisfying in reason and that will indicate for us how future cases are to be decided." Some of his comments in this connection are responsive to my contention that a court is obligated by the nature of its function to confine itself to principled determinations.[3] Professor Hook has directed me to deal with this position, a command I shall endeavor to obey.

The paper of mine to which Professor Levi refers was concerned with the judicial function in interpreting the Constitution and, particularly, with the nature of the courts' authority to pass on the validity of legislative and administrative action when such issues arise in litigation. In the Holmes lectures of the year before, Judge Learned Hand had stated his considered views upon this subject,[4] endorsing the judicial function as we know it only within very narrow limits. The limitations he advanced would, in substance, confine judicial intervention to cases in which the language of the Constitution, read in the light of its "historical meaning," shows that the legislator or administrator has transcended his authority. Conceiving the First Amendment and the due process clauses of the Fifth and the Fourteenth, as well as the equal protection clause of the latter, to be "cast . . . in such sweeping terms that their history does not elucidate their contents," judgments of invalidity based on these provisions would be barred. Such judgments would, in Judge Hand's view, inevitably call upon the courts to function as "a third legislative chamber," opposing their own conceptions of competing values to those reflected in the challenged acts of legislation or administration— a course Judge Hand thought neither authorized by the text of the Constitution nor desirable upon balance, notwithstanding some advantages to be perceived. That element of freedom of decision that Professor Levi rightly has discerned as an intrinsic feature of the system would accordingly be drastically narrowed, at least when it would pose a barrier to action of the other branches of the government of the United States or of a state.

I made bold to differ with Judge Hand upon the major points. To begin with, I defended the traditional conception of judicial review as a doctrine firmly grounded in the language of the Constitution, especially the declaration in Article VI that "This Constitution and the Laws of the United States which shall be made in Pursuance thereof; and all Treaties made, or which shall be made, under the authority of the United States, shall be the supreme Law of the Land," and the provision of Article III including within the scope of the federal judicial power "all Cases, in Law and Equity, arising under this Constitution." On this premise I could not accept the proposition that the courts have a discretion to abstain or intervene when constitutional infringements are averred in cases properly before them in the course of litigation. Their duty in this situation, I submitted, is to govern their decisions by the law, including the Constitution as the supreme law supplanting any inconsistent norms derived from lesser sources. Thus they cannot escape the obligation of interpreting the open-ended concepts framed as limitations upon government, like the guarantees of "the freedom of speech and of the press," "due process of law," or "equal protection of the laws," even though it involves passing upon action of the other branches resting on a choice of values, as invariably action does.

These affirmations forced me to consider whether there are any standards to be followed in interpreting such open-ended clauses, criteria that both the Supreme Court and those who undertake to praise or to condemn its judgments are morally and intellectually obligated to support. Noting that the history of our politics is rich with illustration of the way in which opposing factions have felt free to manipulate their constitutional positions to advance or hinder interests they supported, be it those of capital or labor, shipping or manufactures, slavery or abolition, radicals or businessmen, I asked if something else is not required of the courts, whose only competence to intervene derives from their sworn duty to apply the law and to regard the Constitution as the supreme law. Putting the question differently, I asked how determinations that do not derive from any true compulsion of the text or even of its earlier interpretation can be asserted to have a legal quality.

My answer was "that the main constituent of the judicial process is precisely that it must be genuinely principled, resting with respect to every step that is involved in reaching judgment on analysis and reasons quite transcending the immediate result that is achieved." Granting that "the courts decide, or should decide, only the case they have before them," I suggested that they must "decide on grounds of adequate neutrality and generality, tested not only by the instant application but by others that the principles imply"; and that it is "the very essence of judicial method to insist upon attending to such other cases, preferably those involving an opposing interest, in evaluating any principle avowed."

Reverting to Judge Hand's contention that a constitutional interpretation based on any other ground than the historical intendment of provisions having ascertainable specific content casts the courts in the role of a third legislative chamber, I asked if there is not a vital difference between legislative freedom to appraise the gains and losses in projected measures and the kind of principled appraisal, in respect of values that can reasonably be asserted to have constitutional dimension, that alone is in the province of the courts. I argued that there is a difference; and, moreover, that the difference yields a middle ground between a judicial House of Lords and the abandonment of any limitation on the other branches—a middle ground consisting of judicial action that embodies what are surely the main qualities of law, its generality and its neutrality.

If I had been content to put this general position without testing it by concrete illustration, I doubt if I would have provoked substantial disagreement, since few among us really think it proper for the courts to act by fiat rather than as organs and expositors of law, in a sense that implies a limitation of this kind. But deeming it important to delineate the point of the position by some challenging examples of its application, I selected three great cases in which the Supreme Court sustained egalitarian contentions, with which I am deeply sympathetic, upon grounds that seemed to me deficient in the quality of principled neutrality and generality for which I asked. The cases all involved the interpretation of the clause of the Fourteenth Amendment that forbids a state to deny to any person within its jurisdiction the equal protection of the laws, and each involved the overruling of an earlier decision. The first was the decision that a Negro voter excluded from the Democratic party and declared ineligible to vote in the party primary election by a resolution of the party was denied equal protection by the state. The second was the holding that a state denies equal protection if the state courts enforce a racially restrictive covenant against an owner or successor who attempts to break it. The third was the decision that state segregation of the public schools violates equal protection because it discriminates against the Negro, even though the schools for Negroes equal those for whites in every other way except the color of the students.

I shall confine myself to dealing with the covenant, where it is easiest to make the point involved. The Court's opinion rested the decision on the simple ground that the covenant embodied a discrimination and that the enforcement order of the court is action of the state. Both of these propositions are correct. Yet I submit that it is clear that they do not suffice to uphold the judgment, unless it is affirmed that a private discrimination becomes a discrimination by the state whenever it is legally enforced. But such a proposition is absurd and would destroy the law of wills and a good portion of the law of property, which is concerned precisely with supporting owners' rights to make discriminations that the state would not be free to make on the initiative of officials. Hence, I suggest that this was not a principled decision in the sense that is demanded of the courts.

In saying this, I do not, of course, deny that it would be entirely proper for a legislature to enact a law forbidding the enforcement of racially restrictive covenants, or even for a court with general jurisdiction over the reshaping of the law of contracts or of equitable remedies to declare the covenant invalid or to deny its enforcement by injunction. I not only consider such a statute or decision permissible; I consider it entirely proper. But the Supreme Court had no authority to enact such a statute or to deal generally with the law of contracts or of remedies. It claimed no such authority. Its sole competence was to give meaning to a general provision forbidding a state to deny the equal protection of the laws. Nothing in that provision accords relevance to the particular impact of restrictive covenants concerning land as distinguished from other kinds of discriminatory agreements or discriminations in the use or disposition of property. If the enforcement of the owners' discrimination made it that of the state in the case of the covenant, the tenement owner's refusal to lease, the store owner's refusal to sell, the testator's discriminatory devise must equally become the discriminatory action of the state if enforced by a state court. That is, indeed, precisely what has now been argued in the sit-in cases—that a state discriminates against Negroes if it enforces the general law of trespass against persons excluded by an owner upon racial grounds. If that proposition is unacceptable, as I believe it will prove to be, can the covenant decision be defended—or is it an *ad hoc* determination, as I argued, lacking the generality required of decisions of the courts?

This brings me back, at long last, to Professor Levi's paper and his treatment of the issue I have tendered. I must say that I am grateful to him for his understanding reading of my lecture, which has variously been regarded as propounding a mechanical formula for the determination of constitutional controversy, demanding blind adherence to precedent, excluding value judgments from interpretation, ignoring the significance of experience, and applying "an inadequate and rudimentary notion of the philosophy and methods of systematic thought." [5] One who has been the subject of canards of this dimension welcomes a restatement that perceives in his position no more than the suggestion that "a judge who makes changes in the law must take seriously the duty of reworking the pattern of the law," that the "distinctions that he makes must be genuine, articulate, and sufficiently acceptable," and that granted "the right and duty of the court to interpret the document, it has not been given the duty or the opportunity to rewrite the words." These are, indeed, elements and basic elements of my position, and it is agreeable to see them stated in these mild and untendencious terms. But when Professor Levi puts it as "at least tenable" that "the caliber of a court's opinion, even in a constitutional case, is not to be made dependent on its announcement of a principle that is fully satisfying in reason and that will indicate for us how future cases are to be decided," I find myself uncertain if we actually do agree or, at least, how far we may disagree.

My uncertainty turns first upon the weight to be accorded the word "fully" in the phrase "fully satisfying." Judicial opinions, like other appeals to reason, will be more or less successful or persuasive, but I should suppose that their success or their persuasiveness in reason does afford a measure of their caliber and that, indeed, no other and no better measure of their caliber can be proposed. The case "which has no articulated theory to support it but seems right" would seem to me to have "a place in our jurisprudence" only when there is a theory that becomes apparent on reflection, though it may not be articulated by the court. If the point is that courts may reach correct decisions by accident or intuition, I should readily agree, while noting that correctness turns on someone else's statement of the reasons that the court has sensed but has not stated in its judgment. But if it is contended that there is a measure of correctness distinct from the existence of such reasons, I must say that I am forced to disagree.

I have a similar difficulty on the other aspect of the problem, namely, how far the court's reasons must "indicate to us how future cases are to be decided." In one sense, I agree entirely that this is unnecessary and to be avoided, that the court decides the case at hand and not the cases that have not arisen; in constitutional adjudication this, indeed, is one of the important principles that governs the entire process. But it is one thing to anticipate such future cases that perhaps may be distinguishable, without now deciding the sufficiency of the distinction. It is quite another thing to judge the instant case in terms that are quite plainly unacceptable in light of other cases that it is now clear are covered by the principle affirmed in reaching judgment and indistinguishable upon valid grounds. That was the situation, I must say again, in the case of the restrictive covenant, unless the court was ready to adjudge the same result in dealing with the sit-in or at least could state the terms in which that case might be distinguished, in which event appraising the sufficiency of the distinction might perhaps be postponed to another day.

To put another illustration, those who defended the school decision on the ground that equal protection precludes any action by the state based on a racial classification surely were required to anticipate the problem of benevolent quotas, which would be outlawed by the principle that they avowed, and indicate if they considered them distinguishable. Without so doing they could not responsibly declare the principle that race is outlawed as a basis of official action.

Whether Professor Levi would agree with me on this, I must declare I cannot tell from his analysis. He recognizes that "a call for responsible articulated reasons does not mean that a judge must shoulder the responsibility for deciding all future cases." How much weight is carried by the reference to "all"? I would say that the principle of the decision must be viable in reference to applications that are now foreseeable; and that viability implies a similar decision or the existence of a possibly acceptable distinction. Nothing less will satisfy the elements of generality and of neutrality implicit in the concept of a legal judgment as distinguished from the fiat of a court.

Professor Levi recognizes this in dealing with the obligation of the court to make a rationally coherent pattern of the new decision in relation to the past adjudications. Why is the obligation to the future smaller than the obligation to the past?

Were I to criticize my view myself, I would not cast the critique in Professor Levi's terms; I would, rather, inquire whether there may not be situations in which the courts can do no better than perform the function of an arbitration, for the reason that no principles can be developed to govern the adjudications to be made. That may be true, for example, in passing on state burdens upon commerce, where no one has improved upon Reed Powell's statement of the operative proposition: "The States may burden interstate commerce but not too much." How much is too much is, perhaps, beyond the possibility of principled decision. This is an area, however, where the courts do not now speak the final word, and it is possible to view their function as a delegation of authority to make an arbitral determination, subject to the overriding action of the Congress, which may authorize state burdens that the Court has held excessive. That is a special case of free decision with which I admit I did not deal.

In closing, I perhaps should say that I have never thought the principle of neutral principles offers a court a guide to exercising its authority, in the sense of a formula that indicates how cases ought to be decided. I assumed all the difficulties of that august function, including the problem of the weight to be accorded to the text, to history, to precedent, and to the case for a reformulation of the operative norm. That an adjudication be supported or at least supportable in general and neutral terms is no more than a negative requirement. A decision is not sound unless it satisfies this minimal criterion. If it does, but only if it does, the other and the harder questions of its rightness and its wisdom must be faced. But minimal as the submission is, I do not hesitate to say that I believe it has a special relevance and importance in our time.

NOTES

1. See, for example, Charles D. Breitel, *The Courts and Law-making* in Monroe Paulsen (ed.), *Legal Institutions Today and Tomorrow* (New York: Columbia University Press, 1959), p. 1; and the illuminating comments by Henry M. Hart, Jr., *ibid.*, p. 40; and Roger J. Traynor, *ibid.*, p. 48.

2. *An Introduction to Legal Reasoning* (Chicago: University of Chicago Press, 1949).

3. See *Toward Neutral Principles of Constitutional Law*, 73 Harv. L. Rev. 1 (1959), reprinted in my *Principles, Politics and*

Fundamental Law (Cambridge: Harvard University Press, 1961), p. 3.

4. *The Bill of Rights* (Cambridge: Harvard University Press, 1958).

5. The quotation is from E. V. Rostow, *The Sovereign Prerogative* (New Haven: Yale University Press, 1962) p. 39. See also, for example, Mueller & Schwartz, *The Principle of Neutral Principles*, 7 U.C.L.A. L. Rev. 571 (1960); Miller & Howell, *The Myth of Neutrality in Constitutional Adjudication*, 27 U. Chi. L. Rev. 661 (1960); Wright, *The Supreme Court Cannot Be Neutral*, 40 Tex. L. Rev. 599 (1962); Clark, *A Plea for the Unprincipled Decision*, 49 U. of Va. L. Rev. 660 (1963). For relatively sympathetic treatment of the thesis, see, for example, Henkin, *Some Reflections on Current Constitutional Controversy*, 109 U. of Pa. L. Rev. 637 (1961); Pollak, *Constitutional Adjudication: Relative or Absolute Neutrality*, 11 Journ. Pub. Law 48 (1962); Bickel, *The Least Dangerous Branch* (1962) 49–65; Golding, *Principled Decision Making and the Supreme Court*, 63 Colum. L. Rev. 35 (1963).

1

"Neutral Principles" and Future Cases

LOUIS HENKIN
Columbia University Law School

PROFESSOR LEVI's fine paper on "The Nature of Judicial Reasoning" is sound in conception and spangled with insights. His remarks in avowed difference with Professor Wechsler, however, seem to mistake Professor Wechsler's point as I see it, creating an issue where there is none and diverting the issue that may be. Professor Wechsler can speak for himself, of course. But since Professor Levi's remarks in this regard reflect a prevalent confusion about an important aspect of constitutional jurisprudence, I offer these paragraphs in hope of clarification.[1]

Professor Levi's third point, "at least tenable," is this: "The caliber of a court's opinion, even in a constitutional case, is not to be made dependent on its announcement of a principle that is fully satisfying in reason and that will indicate for us how future cases are to be decided." Later he puts the question: "to what extent must the judge have worked out the full impact upon future cases of conflicting values and legal concepts?" To what extent should he "endeavor to spell out the future rules of the road?"

All these statements are apparently directed at Professor Wechsler's thesis in support of "neutral principles." In fact, in these statements Professor Levi is saying and asking several different things, some of which, at least, are beyond disagreement. No one has ever suggested that the Supreme Court, in constitutional cases or elsewhere, should or can decide any but the case before it. In constitutional cases, indeed, the Court has made a principle of *not* deciding any but the case before it, and even that only if it cannot avoid the constitutional issue, and then on the narrowest grounds.[2] Surely in constitutional cases, then, the judge is expected *not* to spell out the future rules or the full impact upon future cases. Neither is there any requirement in sound judicial process that a judge work out *for himself* "the full impact upon future cases"—although one might hope that judges, like others, might be aware of the impact of their actions as far as the wise eye can see. One begins to approach the area of difference when Professor Levi addresses himself to the *principle of decision* announced in a court opinion; even there one may not necessarily disagree with him that "the caliber of a court's opinion is not to be made dependent on its announcement of a principle . . . that will indicate for us how future cases are to be decided."

If, in the quoted statements, Professor Levi thinks he is disagreeing with Professor Wechsler, I believe he is mistaken; in any event, Levi's statements are not inconsistent with my view of the Wechsler thesis. The confusion arises from the impression that Professor Wechsler was asking the Court either to decide cases in addition to the one before it, to indicate how they would be decided, or to tailor its present decision to future needs. This is error. Mr. Wechsler's reference to other cases is one element in a broader context—the need for principle in judicial decision.

Perhaps the Wechsler thesis, as here relevant, should be briefly stated. He pleads for "neutral principles" of decision. (I hold no brief for the phrase—"neutral principle" may involve a tautology—although no clearly better phrase has been suggested.) Professor Wechsler is insisting that the process of decision satisfy intellectual, analytic scrutiny, that decision be "principled," that it be based on reason, not *fiat*, on doctrine impartially applied, not on *ad hoc* intuition or whim. Professor Wechsler criticized the Court for failing to act in accordance with doctrine and reason, and he invoked important cases in which, in his view, the reasons given by the Court for reaching its results do not satisfy the demands of principle and reason.

Inadequacies of principle and reason in judicial decision may take varying forms: courts have been charged, for example, with unacceptable readings of constitutional language, with logical fallacy, with failure to heed their quality as courts (rather than legislatures), with capricious preference for personal values. Such inadequacies are included in Professor Wechsler's bill of complaint against the Supreme Court. His principal complaint, perhaps—and the one that concerns us—charges a special inadequacy: the principles asserted, in one or two of the cases he cites, are not adequate as princple in that they do not have that indispensable quality of a principle —general applicability. They are not of general applicability, we know, because the Court has not been willing, and quite clearly is not now willing, to apply the principle to other indistinguishable cases.

Here is the root of disagreement and of confusion. All agree that there must must be principle, doctrine. All agree, too, that principle implies general applicability. Professor Wechsler insists that an announced doctrine is not viable as a general principle if it is now quite clear that the Court is not ready to apply it generally. Professor Levi—and others—seem to reject the suggestion that the Court must, or should, examine whether the doctrine it is announcing has general applicability. They may be saying that it can never be clear now that a principle will not be applied to other cases; they may be asserting that the Court is entitled to postpone that question until the other cases come before it. Professor Wechsler might reply that he agrees, in general, but that in some cases—including the cases he cites—the inadequacy of the doctrine as general principle is immediate and blatant and cannot be disregarded. At least, he would say, where the principle is prima facie deficient, the Court must examine its doctrine to be sure that it is indeed viable.

One difficulty with judging this disagreement is that Professor Wechsler's critics on this point have maintained that disagreement on the plane of the abstract. They have not looked at his cases to examine whether in those cases the doctrine announced is or is not generally viable. They insist, apparently, that in no case can an announced doctrine be deemed deficient for lack of generality. If so, I think their position is difficult to defend. They seem to overlook that principle and doctrine have, *ipso facto*, a predictive quality. They neglect, too, that as concerns the Supreme Court of the United States in particular, it is accepted that the Court's role is not primarily to see that a case before it is correctly decided, but to lay guidelines for the future.

One may disagree with Professor Wechsler's conclusion that in the cases he cites, or in any other specific instance, the principle is indeed not viable as a general principle. Sometimes it may be a relevant and complete answer to criticism of a decision to recall that qualifications, distinctions, the drawing of lines, and the measuring of degrees are inherent in principled adjudication. One may suggest, then—perhaps closer to what bothers Professor Levi—that qualifications not immediately relevant need not be anticipated or indicated when the principle is announced. The Court decides the case before it on a basis that at the time of decision it believes will have general and continued applicability. Later cases may require qualification, but the principle as then qualified is also a principle of general applicability. As modified, the principle still governs the earlier case. If not, the earlier case was mistakenly decided. (Whether it must therefore be overruled is a different question.) But it seems clear that a court should not announce a principle if it is immediately and obviously deficient, because it clearly is not intended to be applicable in a general area in which no legitimate distinctions are apparent. It is not principle if it is now clear that the "similar case" will require a rejection of this principle as soon as the Court can be compelled to look at it.

In any event, it should be clear, the disagreement is about the predictive element in principle, and what obligations that imposes on courts that apply principle. Professor Wechsler questions the general applicability of the principles in selected cases on the basis of *present* constitutional jurisprudence plus

that limited *predictive* element that is *inherent in principle*.
He is not at all asking the Court now to decide any future case,
to "spell out the future rules of the road," or "to work out the
full impact upon future cases of conflicting values and legal
concepts." He is not even demanding a principle "that will
indicate for us how future cases will be decided," except to
the very limited extent that principle *ipso facto* has predictive
quality.

These abstractions may become more meaningful if applied to what is clearly the strongest of Professor Wechsler's
cases for his thesis—the opinion of the Supreme Court in
Shelley v. *Kraemer*.[3] In that case the Court held that the
courts of a state could not enjoin an owner of property from
selling it to a Negro, despite an earlier agreement that the
property would not be sold to Negroes. If the state courts
enforced this restrictive covenant, the state would be denying
to the putative Negro purchaser the equal protection of the
laws guaranteed him by the Fourteenth Amendment of the
United States Constitution. The Supreme Court reaffirmed
the long-accepted view that the Amendment governs only the
actions of the states. It does not then forbid a private person
to refuse to sell property to Negroes, to enter into restrictive
covenants, to require such covenants in their contracts, to live
up to such covenants, or to ask others to abide by them. But if
the state courts lend their authority and power to enforce such
a covenant, the state is thereby denying equal protection to
the Negro.

The Court's opinion, it has been widely recognized, leaves
too much to be desired. What concerns us here is whether the
principle set forth in the opinion is adequate to justify the
result. The Court reached its result by holding that a state
denies equal protection of the laws when its courts give effect
to private discriminations. This is the principle of decision. The
Court could not, apparently, reach its result without asserting
this principle as the meaning of the Constitution.

It is this principle that Professor Wechsler challenges as
unacceptable because the Court does not and cannot mean it

as a principle of general applicability. The Court, he says, cannot be asserting a general principle that a state may never, by its courts, give effect to private discrimination. State courts every day give effect to private discrimination, even private racial or religious discrimination, when they enforce discriminatory provisions in wills or apply the laws of trespass to persons excluded from private property. The Supreme Court does not intend to hold that judicial enforcement of those wills or those trespass laws is a denial of equal protection. If the Court is not prepared to apply its principle to those cases, it is no principle. The Court, then, has not given any rational justification for holding unconstitutional the action of the state in *Shelley* v. *Kraemer*.

This argument, I emphasize, does not ask the Court to decide the will and trespass cases when it decides the case of the restrictive covenant. It does not ask the Court to lay down a rule for those cases or to consider the impact upon them of the present decision. Professor Wechsler is saying, rather, that there is and can be no constitutional principle that a state may not enforce private discrimination because it is clear that such a principle has no predictive general applicability. We already know that these other cases have not been, will not be, could not be decided in accordance with such a doctrine. If so, there is no such doctrine, and one cannot assert it to support the result in *Shelley*.

Of course, Mr. Wechsler may be mistaken. If the Court were now prepared to apply this doctrine to the will and the trespass, this objection to the *Shelley* principle would fall. (There might still be argument as to whether the Court should have explicitly recognized the sweep of its doctrine to other fields, but that—Professor Levi's question—is a different question.) I have suggested elsewhere a basis on which the asserted *Shelley* principle can be applied to the other cases as well.[4] If I am correct, then *Shelley* v. *Kraemer* may not be a proper instance to support or illustrate Professor Wechsler's thesis. Philosophically, the thesis remains valid: the Court cannot properly decide a case on the basis of a "principle" that is not a principle because it is not intended and expected to apply generally to similar cases.

Behind the disagreement and confusion may also be a difference about the importance of judicial opinions. Professor Levi says, "the caliber of a court's opinion is not to be made dependent on its announcement of a principle that is fully satisfying in reason." With allowance for the fact that little is "fully satisfying," I thoroughly disagree. The caliber of an opinion may depend on many things; surely it is not an adequate opinion if it does not adequately satisfy the requirements of reason and principle. That seems to me a truism inherent in the process of adjudication, and in the writing of opinions. "To those who believe," I have suggested, "that the game has rules and the rules have purpose, that the process has reason, principle is the essential reason. One might do worse for the beginning of a definition than to suggest that judicial doctrine and principle are those reasons for reaching a result which can be stated in a judicial opinion. . . . Inadequate efforts to write adequate opinions cry for criticism, not least because they lend support to the cynics to purvey the impression that reason is unnecessary, that opinions have to be indulged but do not really matter." [5] One can argue persuasively that an adequate judicial opinion is essential to due process of law, at least to adequate performance of the judicial function. Surely, the *caliber* of an opinion does depend, *inter alia*, on its adequacy in reason.

This emphasis on the caliber of judicial opinion, however, has deeper implications. A decision is not necessarily wrong if a bad opinion is written. In regard to the three cases that Mr. Wechsler cites, I believe that the opinions are not all as inadequate as Mr. Wechsler thinks; I believe, too, that better opinions can be written that would support those results on the basis of general, enduring principle rooted in the Constitution and in constitutional jurisprudence. But courts and their critics must recognize that if an opinion is inadequate to support a new and important result, the result has not been justified. One may properly ask the Court to supply a more adequate justification. If none is forthcoming, and if students of the Court cannot supply the adequate justification, one may have to consider that the result is not justified because it is not justifiable. One cannot accept as a basis for decision either intuition, visceral reaction, or the private notion of the good, which cannot be justified and explained on the basis of the considerations relevant to determining the good in our system of constitutional adjudication. The inability to write a good opinion in a case would then require judicial "abstention," not because of some special view of the limited function of the courts, but because courts must always "abstain" from reaching a result if there is no basis for reaching it in the factors relevant to constitutional adjudication. For a court to say merely, in effect, "we like the result; the result feels right; therefore it is right; of course, we will write for it the best opinion we can," is inadequate and impermissible.

There are those who fear any criticism of the Supreme Court at this time. These are those who fear particularly criticism of the Court's handling of cases supporting racial equality. There may be those, too, who fear to face the possibility that if valid opinions in those cases have not been written, and cannot be written, one may have to conclude that the cases were erroneously decided. I do not share these fears. I believe the Court requires scholarly criticism and that its performance —in many areas—has not been above criticism, although those of us who disagree with Professor Wechsler about the cases he cited and think the opinions in those cases adequate or remediable may regret that by criticizing those particular cases his writing may have given comfort to those who reject those cases for ignoble reasons. But whatever one's regrets or fears, they should not obscure Professor Wechsler's important contribution and the obvious validity of his thesis and of his demand for principled adjudication.

NOTES

1. I have written elsewhere in general support of Professor Wechsler's thesis as I understand it, and in substantial difference from him in regard to the cases he invokes to illustrate his point. See "Some Reflections on Current Constitutional Controversy," 109 Pa. L. Rev. 637, 650–62 (1961); *cf.* "*Shelley* v. *Kraemer:* Notes for a Revised Opinion," 110 U. Pa. L. Rev. 473 (1962).

2. An entire jurisprudence has been developed, moreover, to enable the court not to decide even what is before it, including a largely optional jurisdiction as well as doctrines of standing, case or controversy, ripeness, and so forth.

3. 334 U. S. 1 (1948).

4. See "*Shelley* v. *Kraemer:* Notes for a Revised Opinion," *supra.* My suggestion briefly is that in all cases—including the will and the trespass—it is a denial of equal protection for the state to enforce private discrimination; there is, however, a countervailing freedom to discriminate that, in some cases, the Constitution prefers or permits the state to prefer.

There is no indication that the Court had any such suggestion in mind. In fact, it is far from clear that the Court is prepared now to accept this basis, or some other basis, for rendering the *Shelley* doctrine a legitimate doctrine applicable to judicial enforcement of all kinds of private discrimination.

5. 109 U. Pa. L. Rev. 654–55, 662.

2

Leges sine Logica Vanae

RICHARD M. MARTIN
New York University

TO SUGGEST that the logic of the law is *sui generis* or in some sense unique is at best misleading. Logic may be applied to diverse subject matters, the application being unique but not that which is applied. "One God, one country, one logic" must remain the underlying maxim.

The fundamental problem in applied logic is that of determining the predicates (including symbols for relations) required for the given subject matter. The choice of predicates goes hand in hand with determining the ontology (values for variables) admitted. In logical analysis the fixing of axioms or primitive sentences governing the predicates is rather secondary. Surely no satisfactory axiom—"satisfactory" here in the sense of being true or highly accepted when suitably interpreted—can be framed without clear-cut semantic rules for the primitives. Mathematicians tend to prefer the converse procedure: frame axioms no matter how, and hunt for an interpretation afterwards. And if none is forthcoming, make one up—hence the artificiality of many mathematical models and the forcing of actual data to fit them.

Logical analysis is sharply to be distinguished from constructing a mathematical model, then, in having *ab initio* suitable semantic rules of interpretation for the primitives chosen. These rules may be of the form stating that such and such primitives *designate* such and such classes or relations or *denote* such and such objects.[1] The classes and/or relations and objects must be available to start with—otherwise there is nothing, as it were, to analyze. Strictly the mathematician has nothing to analyze—he frames axioms and hopes that something will turn up to fit them. For him, obviously, the axioms are the crucial object of worry, and once chosen, their full parade of consequences must be reviewed. The logical analyst, on the other hand, will not worry over axioms needlessly to begin with. Usually there is sufficient difficulty in choosing suitable primitives. Once we are clear about these, there will then be ample occasion to explore alternative sets of axioms.

Interesting cases in point are, of course, modal and deontic logics. The former are concerned with such notions as "necessity," "possibility," and so on, the latter with "obligation," permission," and the like. These logics are usually constructed (as mere calculi) by framing axioms and exploring their consequences, and only secondarily does one seek to interpret them. And if no suitable interpretation at all is forthcoming, this does not seem to matter.[2] Some minor mathematical interest may perhaps attach to these logics. It is doubtful, however, that deontic logic has provided (to date at least) analyses of obligation, permission, and so forth, of sufficient subtlety and depth to be of much interest for the logic of the law.

If obligation and the like are to be handled in terms of one-place predicates, we are entitled to ask what the arguments of these predicates are. Straightaway some will tell us *propositions,* but it is doubtful whether such entities are suitable for clear, logical analysis. A better candidate for the arguments would be *action-kinds,* or *act-properties,* as Von Wright calls them.[3] But action-kinds may in turn be medadic, monadic, dyadic, and so on, depending upon the various factors involved in the action. To light a cigarette is clearly monadic, but to light a cigarette with a given match or lighter is dyadic. Also, action-types are performed *by* given persons *at* given times. Obligation, furthermore, is relative to a given legal code and, perhaps, to a given social group as well. Thus a predicate for obligation should have at least five arguments: a person, an action-kind, an object of the action-kind (if it is dyadic), a time, a social group, and a legal code. A full theory of obligation, it would appear, must incorporate analyses of each of these factors.

The approach to the theory of obligation via deontic logic is essentially that of the mathematician. Get axioms or deontic laws no matter how, and do not worry about codes, social groups, and the like. The logical approach undertakes rather painstaking analyses of these various factors and of the whole pragmatic context. There would seem little doubt but that this latter approach is of greater interest both for the philosopher and legal analyst than is the method of mathematical model building.

Similar remarks obtain concerning logic as a philosophical tool generally. Laws or axioms without a full analysis of their context and content are vain and sterile. Mathematical logic is, thus, often rightly viewed as philosophically irrelevant. But mathematics and logic are not the same, despite a fashionable view to the contrary. The mathematician is interested only in a body of laws in some fashion pertinent to the given subject matter, but without making it clear how or why or in what way. Logic in the broad sense of semiotic (syntax, semantics, and pragmatics together), on the other hand, may be thought to constitute the very core of philosophical analysis. Mathematics is a luxury for philosophy, but logic is its daily bread.

What seems needed now in the philosophy of law is a full semiotic analysis of the judicial process. There is, first, the actual language of the law that requires codification and syntactical and semantic characterization. Then there is human behavior—the performing of action-kinds—which must be interrelated with this language. Such study takes place as a part of the wider pragmatic study of the interrelations of language and action.

We have come a long way from the attitude expressed in Holmes's epigrams that "the life of the law is not logic but experience" or "a page of history is worth a volume of logic" (as though the two are even comparable). It is time now to reassess these views *au fond*. Modern logic is becoming increasingly useful for legal practice (witness the many interesting appications reported from the Yale Law School in the journal *Modern Uses of Logic in Law*), and the development of pragmatics promises elucidation of some of the intricate connections between logic and experience. After all, the two do not compete, any more than history and logic do. The one is a useful tool for the intimate study of the other.

Many of Holmes's comments on logic seem, in fact, rather wide of the mark. "The moment you leave the path of mere logical deduction you lose the illusion of certainty which makes legal reasoning seem like mathematics. But the certainty is an illusion, nevertheless," he writes.[4] Holmes does not deny that lawyers need logic, but "there is a fallacy in trusting too much to this tool." Of course logic must be embedded in the social context and viewed as an instrument *in usu*. But the theory of valid deductive inference does not give certainty where certainty is denied to the premises. Holmes seems to confuse these and hence most of what he says about logic is unsound. (Most uses of "logic" or "logical" in common parlance, in fact, if not actually incorrect, are either bad or misleading.) Of course Holmes has in mind the older logic, of which, however, the new is to be viewed as a continuation. Also inductive logic, the theory of confirmation and of inductive probability, which at the moment is undergoing intensive development, will no doubt have great interest for the law.

"Behind the logical form lies a judgment as to the relative worth and importance of competing legislative grounds," Holmes wrote, "often an inarticulate and unconscious judgment, it is true, and yet the very nerve and root of the whole proceeding. You can give any conclusion a logical form. You always can imply a condition in any contract. But why do you imply it? It is because of some belief as to the practice of the community or of a class, or because of some opinion as to policy, or, in short, because of some attitude of yours upon a matter not capable of exact quantitative measure and therefore [sic] not capable of exact logical conclusions." Now, it is not the case that one can validly infer any conclusion one wishes *quodlibet*, and Holmes seems here to be saying that it is. One cannot validly imply any condition in a contract. Implication is not a matter of caprice or social pressure or individual preference. This is not to deny, however, that comparative judgments and preferences of various kinds may enter fundamentally into the judicial process. But the study of preference itself, even quantitative preference, has itself received enormous impetus from recent decision theory. From this, also, important applications to the law may be expected. Once the preference is made, however, or the premise accepted, logical implication takes its course whether we will or no, and it is *this* that Holmes seems not to have taken adequate account of. Also "exact logical conclusions" may be founded on matters other than those "capable of exact quantitative measurement." The force of "therefore" in the last sentence of the passage just quoted is thus suspect.

These few remarks, it might be objected, do little to get at the really "substantive problems" in the logic of the law. But one must begin somewhere, preferably with a sound logic. There is all the difference in the world between a sound and a spurious logic, a difference not sufficiently realized. Also, the task of logical analysis is not primarily to solve substantive problems in various special disciplines. It "is, rather, of the essence of our investigation that we do not seek to learn anything *new* by it. We want to *understand* something that is in plain view. For *this* is what we seem in some sense not to understand. . . . It is as if one had altered the adjustment of a microscope. One did not see before what is now in focus." [5] Once the proper focus is gained, detail as well as general prospectus are seen anew.

NOTES

1. See the author's *Truth and Denotation* (Chicago: University of Chicago Press, 1958), pp. 99 ff. and 166 ff.
2. Compare the author's "Does Modal Logic Rest upon a Mistake?" *Philosophical Studies* XIV (1963): 8–11.
3. G. H. von Wright, *An Essay in Modal Logic (Studies in*

Logic and the Foundations of Mathematics, Amsterdam: North-Holland Publishing Co., 1951). See also the author's "Performance, Purpose, and Permission," *Philosophy of Science* 30 (1963): 122–37.

4. Quoted in Jerome Frank, *Law and the Modern Mind* (New York: Tudor, 1936), pp. 253 ff.

5. L. Wittgenstein, *Philosophical Investigations* (Oxford: Basil Blackwell, 1953), p. 42 e.

3

Legal Formalism and Formalistic Devices of Juristic Thinking

ILMAR TAMMELO

University of Canberra, Australia

THE PHRASE "legal formalism" has come into English juristic use as a term designating misapplication of logic, and an application of pseudologic, in the field of law. The ill fame of the term has dragged the word and the notion of "formalism" into disrepute along with it; and this is unfortunate. There is nothing intrinsically evil in what is formal, as there is nothing intrinsically good in what is nonformal. As far as human communication is concerned, it is rather that which is defective in form that is likely to produce difficulties in understanding and dissipation of energies in efforts to communicate. Although "formal" has acquired meanings that are disreputable, "an indiscriminate polemics against formalism is unjust, because in wanting to hit too many adversaries at once it hits also those it ought not to hit." [1]

In the field of law as elsewhere in the areas of essential human concern, what is formal plays a significant role. This role consists above all in providing patterns of thought by which juristic thinking can be organized, made coherent, and thereby disciplined; so that whatever material content is put into these thought patterns can be expeditiously handled for purposes of thought and its expression. The formalism here in question should obviously resort to principles and methods of the best available logic.

Formalism in juristic thinking, if appropriately and consistently carried out, would lead to an axiomatization of some parts of fundamental thinking about law. Thinking about law in terms and along the patterns of an axiomatic system may even produce strivings to axiomatize the systems of positive law. However inappropriate and impracticable this may be, such strivings should not surprise us, for—as Ulrich Klug has rightly observed—"legal science with all its efforts to systematisation has already long proceeded quasi-axiomatically."[2] It has tried to find hidden links in the law where there has been an apparent lack of connections; and it has assumed that the law is never absent but is always there, even though its discovery may require extreme ingenuity.

However it may be with quasi axiomatics of legal systems, it is highly questionable whether a rigorous axiomatisation can be even a conceivable future state of the law. But what could be achieved is organization of certain basic principles and methods of thinking *about* the law into a formally adequate framework of thought patterns. Even this enterprise may seem to many lawyers fanciful if not preposterous. Among the reasons for this attitude are the skepticisms produced by past misapplications of logic,[3] the failure of theories on the foundations of juristic thinking to offer a set of well-defined concepts and the lack of satisfactory terms corresponding to these concepts, the unfamiliarity of lawyers with modern logic, and their unreadiness to examine thoroughly and soberly relevant philosophical points of view. Thus there is no wonder that lawyers tend to suspect that any formalism in juristic thinking leads to a mechanical derivation of judgments.[4]

To provide an exposition of a formally rigorous system, it is indispensable to employ a symbolic language according to principles and methods of modern logic. When, in the exposition of a system of concepts that should be helpful for analyses of certain legal problems, we shall resort to such a language here, we believe that this is useful not only where there is a need for proceeding in the manner of calculation or where it is imperative to avoid ambiguities of ordinary language. We believe that such a language is useful also to promote sharply focused and easily controllable transparent thinking. Thus formalistic devices appear to be valuable even where parallel translations into ordinary language are supplied for formulas expressed in symbols.[5] Their value is not defeated by the fact that any worthwhile application of formalism requires an extra effort in making a detour of thinking by learning first the principles and skill of handling symbolism. Such an effort is likely to pay dividends, since through it minds are schooled for cogent and efficient reasoning.[6]

All this does not remove, of course, doubts about the actual significance of formally rigorous thinking in the field of law, but it may provoke questions like these: Has stringent logical reasoning any place at all in legal thinking on its *practical* level? Is not practical legal thinking purely "dialectical" in the sense that it proceeds toward the ascertainment of what is legally valid by way of confrontation of pro and contra arguments bringing forth reasons for making judgments, which are always essentially a matter of evaluation? In particular, has rigorous proof any place at all in the legal practitioner's thinking?

There is, indeed, a type of legal argument that can be contrasted, as a nonstringent (or rhetorical or dialectic) argument, with the logical argument characterized by formal stringency. For the present purposes it is not necessary to enter upon the problems that it involves. Here it may suffice to say that rigorous proof appears to have *some* application in legal thinking on its practical level. Logical consistency of norms presents problems in actual litigation, be it in the context of a single statute or treaty or in the context of the relations between various legislative acts—for example, state and federal laws. In most cases rather unsophisticated techniques of logic, even a sort of "common-sense logic," may prove quite adequate. But there are also complicated cases in which nothing short of rigorous logical proof would do to make their legal solutions convincing and conclusive. For such cases instruments of thinking adequate to them must be made available. It is the endeavor of our succeeding pages to give an idea what these instruments are and how they are built. Their value for actual and immediate use is not a principal consideration for us, for in the field of learning much labor is spent on matters that have no such use, but that prepare the requisite foundation for coping with problems that are likely to emerge in the future. It would be an unwarranted prediction that law will never present problems that require resort to techniques of stringent thinking and rigorous proof.

We propose to outline a system of formalistic devices by the aid of which the normatively closed (or normatively complete) legal systems [7] can be expounded. Thereafter we shall show what else is required for the exposition of normatively open legal systems. A normatively closed legal system is one in which all behavior that comes to the lawyer's attention is *ex hypothesi* legally regulated under the legal system of his concern. Such normative completeness is established, as it were, by a "sealing principle" that makes a legal provision for any behavior not regulated by an express legal provision. The only "sealing principle" that total legal orders have employed is the residual negative legal principle usually expressed as "Whatever is not legally prohibited is legally permitted." [8] It would also be logically possible for the "sealing principle" to be "Whatever is not legally prohibited is legally obligated," [9] but a legal order persistently resorting to such a principle would turn out most inconvenient to operate even for most resolute tyrants, it could not assert itself as an enduring legal reality.

The above wording of the residual legal principle is very much like a slogan. To communicate efficiently the idea that this expression purports to convey and to provide an adequate analysis of the deontic universe to which it belongs, we shall employ the following terms: "obligatory," "permissory," "licensory," "action," and "omission." In doing so, we are not bound to the meaning they may have in official legal texts or in current legal practice, which meaning may be considerably narrower than the one intended by us: for example, the ordinary legal meaning of "obligatory" may entail the possibility of enforcing what is said to be obligatory, and "action" may have a meaning that relates exclusively to procedural law.[10]

We are using the term "obligatory" to indicate that something *ought to be done or ought not to be done;* the term "permissory" to indicate that something *may be done or may not be done irrespective of whether or not there is an obligation to do or not to do it;* and the term "licensory" to indicate that something *may be done or may not be done without there being an obligation to do or not to do it.* We are using the term "action" to denote any behavior that from a certain point of view is conceived as *doing* something, and the term "omission" to denote any behavior that is conceived as *not doing* this thing.

The residual negative legal principle can be expressed in the above terms as follows: "Whenever a behavior is not a legally obligatory omission, it is a legally permissory action, and whenever a behavior is not a legally obligatory action it is a legally permissory omission." In this sentence there is no terminological correspondent to "prohibited," which would be the adjective "prohibitory." This term can be eliminated because "prohibitory action" means the same thing as "obligatory omission" (and "prohibitory omission" means the same thing as "obligatory action").

In the deontic universe we have here in view, there are the following deontic states of affairs: (1) obligatory action, (2) obligatory omission, (3) permissory action, (4) permissory omission, (5) licensory action, and (6) licensory omission. To express them in symbols, we shall use six lower case italicized letters as follows: b for "obligatory," p for "permissory," l for "licensory," a for "action," and o for "omission." By combining them into units ba, bo, pa, po, la, and lo we are providing formulas for the following deontic modalities: "X is an obligatory action for Y," "X is an obligatory omission for Y," "X is a permissory action for Y," "X is a permissory omission for Y," "X is a licensory action for Y," and "X is a licensory omission for Y."

These formulas we shall combine into further units by means of certain logical connectives expressed by the capital, italicized letters *N*, *K*, *C*, *E*, and *A*. The resulting formulas will express relations that obtain between the deontic modalities in a given deontic system.

To build up our system of deontic principles we have, first of all, to specify the rules according to which expressions are admissible in it as well-formed formulas.[11] A formula is well formed in our system [12] if and only if:

1. It is exactly a *ba*, *bo*, *pa*, *po*, *la*, or *lo*, or
2. It is the expression formed when an *N* is immediately followed by exactly one well-formed formula, or
3. It is the expression formed when a *K*, *C*, *E*, or *A* is immediately followed by two well-formed formulas.

Every well-formed formula in our system is conceived as having either the value "tenable" or "nontenable." We shall use the symbol *T* for the former and the symbol *O* for the latter. These values correspond to what is usually called "truth-values" by the logicians. The function that the capital letters specified above under the rules (2) and (3) have in our logical operations [13] we shall define below by the method of tenability tables, corresponding to "truth tables" by which the logicians define the function which the signs of negation, conditional (or material or Philonic implication), equivalence, and the like have in the propositional (or sentential) calculus.

x	Nx	x	y	Kxy	Cxy	Exy	Axy
T	O	T	T	T	T	T	T
O	T	T	O	O	O	O	T
		O	T	O	T	O	T
		O	O	O	T	T	O

In employing the appropriate logical connectives to express relations between the above deontic modalities, we can state the cardinal principles governing the deontic universe in the following formulas:

(1) *NKbabo;*	(2) *Apapo;*
(3) *Cbapa;*	(4) *Cbopo;*
(5) *Clapa;*	(6) *Clopo;*
(7) *Elalo;*	(8) *ElaKpapo;*
(9) *NEbopa;*	(10) *NEbapo.*

The formula *NKbabo* expresses that the statements "X is an obligatory action for Y" and "X is an obligatory omission for Y" cannot both be tenable, but either or both of them can be nontenable. In terms of traditional logic, there is a contrary opposition between the two statements.

The formula *Apapo* expresses that the statements "X is a permissory action for Y" and "X is a permissory omission for Y" can both be tenable or either of them can be nontenable, whereas the other is tenable but they cannot both be nontenable. In terms of traditional logic, there is a subcontrary opposition between the two statements.

The formula *Cbapa* expresses that the statements "X is an obligatory action for Y" and "X is a permissory action for Y" can both be tenable, can both be nontenable, and can be such that the former is nontenable and the latter is tenable, but cannot be such that the former is tenable and the latter is nontenable. In terms of traditional logic, there is a subaltern opposition between them. The formula *Cbopo* expresses the same about the statements "X is an obligatory omission for Y" and "X is a permissory omission for Y"; the formula *Clapa* expresses the same about the statements "X is a licensory action for Y" and "X is a permissory action for Y"; and the formula *Clopo* expresses the same about the statements "X is a licensory omission for Y" and "X is a permissory omission for Y."

The formula *Elalo* expresses that the statements "X is a licensory action for Y" and "X is a licensory omission for Y" can both be tenable and can both be nontenable, but they cannot be such that one of them is tenable and the other is nontenable. The formula *ElaKpapo* expresses the same about the statement "X is a licensory action for Y" and the conjunction of the statements "X is a permissory action for Y" and "X is a permissory omission for Y."

The formula *NEbopa* expresses that the statements "X is an obligatory omission for Y" and "X is a permissory action for Y" cannot both be tenable and cannot both be nontenable, but can be such that one of them is tenable and the other one is nontenable. In terms of traditional logic, there is a contradictory opposition between the two statements. The formula *ENbapo* expresses the same about the statements "X is an obligatory action for Y" and "X is a permissory omission for Y." Both formulas represent what was called above "the residual negative legal principle."

The formulas (1) to (10) are applicable only to the thinking about the normatively closed legal systems, but not to the thinking about the normatively open legal systems. These systems require for their exposition certain concepts and symbols not provided in the above formulations.[14]

To analyze normatively open legal systems, of which the international legal order seems to be the main instance,[15] the following additional concepts and symbols have to be introduced: the concept "legally neutral" and its corresponding symbol n and the concept "allowable" and its corresponding symbol w. Legal neutrality is a deontic state of affairs resulting from absence of the law, that is, it results from the situation in which there is no law by virtue of which it would be either obligatory to do or not to do something or licensory to do or not to do something; in other words, there is no legal basis for the statement that something is permissory in any sense (that is, either as an obligatory action, obligatory omission, licensory action, or licensory omission).[16]

In our system we conceive of legally neutral behavior and permissory behavior as two kinds of allowable behavior in the manner that an allowable behavior that is not legally neutral is permissory and vice versa. Since behavior can be either action or omission, we have now, in addition to the above enumerated deontic modalities, the following ones: "X is a legally neutral action for Y (*na*)," "X is a legally neutral omission for Y (*no*)," "X is an allowable action for Y (*wa*)," and "X is an allowable omission for Y (*wo*)." The formal relations here obtaining are these:

$$EwaNEnapa; \qquad EwoNEnopo$$

That is to say: "X is an allowable action for Y" is equivalent to "either X is a legally neutral action for Y or X is a permissory action for Y (but not both)" and "X is an allowable omission for Y" is equivalent to "either X is a legally neutral omission for Y or X is a permissory omission for Y (but not both)."

The formulas (1) to (10) can be made to represent the deontic relationships with respect to normatively open legal systems if at any place where the formula *pa* occurs the formula *wa* is substituted, and at any place where the formula *po* occurs the formula *wo* is substituted. Or, more articulately, if the substituting formulas are *NEnapa* and *NEnopo*, respectively.

Deontic relationships can be expressed in employing fewer deontic operators than we have employed. For example, we can eliminate "obligatory" through appropriate substitutions and express the deontic modalities in which it occurs in terms of "permissory" and "licensory" in normatively closed deontic systems and in terms of "allowable" and "licensory" in normatively open deontic systems. We can further eliminate "licensory" through appropriate substitutions derived from the equivalence of *la* and *lo* with *Kpapo*.

The deontic system here presented can be developed into a full axiomatic system by eliminating all the formulas that can be reduced to certain other formulas selected as axioms. Through introduction of quantifiers, it would be possible to express logical links also between *b, p, l, n,* and *w* on the one hand, and *a* and *o* on the other. These developments fall outside the scope of the present summary exposition.

The formulas we have provided may be found useful as instruments for inquiry into the formal structure of existing legal orders; they can also prove useful for working out matrices according to which formally self-consistent legal systems

can be created. The formulas may be found particularly helpful for ascertaining whether or not two or more norms relating
to the same legal situation are logically consistent with each
other in a legal system. Thus, if we want to find out whether
two such norms in a normatively closed legal system are logically consistent with each other, we must first identify the
deontic modalities that they stipulate as being one of the following: *ba, bo, pa, po, la,* or *lo*.[17] These norms are logically inconsistent with each other if the deontic modality stipulated
by one is *ba* and by the other *bo, lo, la,* or *po,* or if the deontic
modality stipulated by one is *bo* and by the other *ba, la, lo,* or
pa. There is no logical inconsistency between two norms belonging to the same legal system if the deontic modality stipulated by one is *ba* and by the other *pa,* by one *bo* and by the
other *po,* by one *la* or *lo* and by the other *pa* or *po,* by one *la*
and by the other *lo,* and by one *pa* and by the other *po*.[18] It
should be obvious that exact formulation of the conditions of
antinomies in the law and gaps in the law can take place only
in applying the principles and methods of modern logic.[19]

However rigorous the derivation of the formulas may be
by which deontic states of affairs are described and related to
each other today and however forbiddingly formalistic all
these formulas may appear to be, this rigor and formalism can
never impose rigidity and formalism on the actual operation of
the law that would conflict with the requirements of flexibility
and justness of the law, unless this is through the intervention
of some sort of misconception. To believe that application of
formalistic devices in legal thinking necessarily imports legal
formalism involves a regrettable misapprehension of the endeavor of modern logic, for which not logicians but their over-
zealous and unthoughtful adepts could be made responsible.[20]

NOTES

1. See Norberto Bobbio, "Sul formalismo giuridico" (1958)
1 *Rivista Italiana di Diritto e Procedura Penale* (N.S.) 977, at 998.
2. See U. Klug, *Juristische Logik* (2nd ed., 1958) p. 149.

Natural law systems have had even higher ambitions; they have sometimes striven for systems *more geometrico demonstrata*. For a number of instances, see N. Bobbio, "Diritto e logica," (1962) 39 *Rivista internazionale di filosofia del diritto* 1, at 13–16.

3. See J. Stone, *The Province and Function of Law* (London: Stevens & Sons, Ltd., 1946), Chapter 7.

4. *Cf.* F. Paradeis, *Die Technik des Rechts und ihre Logik* (1958). *Cf.* also R. C. Lawlor, "Information Technology and the Law" (1962) 3 *Advances in Computers* 299, at 309, who says that "the practical application of symbolic logic to law has been retarded because of the Tower-of-Babel, jungle-like . . . varieties of notations employed in symbolic logic, which impede the study and learning of symbolic logic by non-mathematicians, and partly because the symbolic logicians, being primarily pure scientists, are more interested in extending and developing theories than in finding everyday uses for them."

5. *Cf.* J. Michael and M. J. Adler, *The Nature of Juridical Proof* (private publication, 1931) v–vi, who, setting out to employ principles and methods of symbolic logic in their exposition of judicial proof, say that "the analysis which is here given of judicial proof could not have been developed without the aid of symbolic notation; or rather, without the symbolic notation the analysis would have become verbally so intricate and cumbersome, that it would have been impossible to write or read."

6. See M. R. Cohen, "The Place of Logic in the Law" (1915–16) 29 *Harvard Law Review* 622, at 638, saying that "the judge's feelings as to right and wrong must be logically and scientifically trained. The trained mind sees in a flash of intuition that which the untrained mind can succeed in seeing only after painfully treading many steps. They who scorn the idea of the judge as a logical automaton are apt to fall into the opposite error of exaggerating as irresistible the force of bias and prejudice."

7. This state of normative affairs is usually called "logical completeness." However, the use of the word "logical" in this context is not quite appropriate; for what is involved here is not a matter of logic but a matter of normativeness, namely, full covering or not full covering by the norms of a normative system of all the situations arising under it. It is to be noted that in his earlier writings, the present author has followed the general usage by employ-

ing the terms "logical completeness" and "logical openness" in referring to the states of affairs in question.

8. This principle is usually termed simply "negative legal principle." See, for example, K. Engisch, "Der Begriff der Rechts-lücke," *Sauer-Festschrift* (1949) 85, at 94. The more descriptive name employed here comes from J. Stone, *"Non Liquet* and the Function of Law in the International Community" (1959) 35 *British Year Book of International Law* 124, at 136.

9. Rigoristic systems of morals imposing unattainable moral standards can contain, of course, the corresponding ethical principle. See A. G. Conte, *Saggio sulla completezza degli ordinamenti giuridici* (1962), 21. Even "Everything is permitted" would guarantee the completeness of a normative system. See *ibid.,* 20, referring to Dostoyevski's *Brothers Karamazov* ("If God did not exist, every-thing would be permitted") and to N. Bobbio's reply to "8 domande sull 'erotismo in letteratura" (1961) 9 (No. 51–52) *Nuovi argomenti* 11–20, observing that the sole norm of the ethics of eroticism is "Everything is permitted."

10. Without the caveat that the actual legal usage of these words does not control their meaning for the purposes of talking *about* the law, the ambiguities of these terms would, of course, be dangerously misleading. The most appropriate way of avoiding confusions and promoting precision in talking about the law would be to provide artificial terms, as is done in physical sciences. But we must abstain from following this course, not only because in the present stage of juristic learning the majority of legal thinkers would feel repelled by unfamiliar technical terms, but also because even among the legal theorists who have addressed themselves to the problem of theoretical concepts applicable to law, no technical terminology for these concepts has so far emerged. To provide special jurisprudential terms for the concepts here employed would thus simply involve resort to an idiosyncratic language, which would scarcely promote the communicability of the present thoughts, al-ready subjected to communication hazards because of their con-tentual unfamiliarity.

11. For the concept of well-formed formula, compare L. E. Allen, "Logical Theory" (September 1959) M.U.L.L. 4, at 5.

12. For these rules *cf.* L. E. Allen, *WFF 'N Proof: The Game of Modern Logic* (New Haven: Wiff'n Proof, 1962), p. 7.

13. For the notation here employed, see Allen, *op. cit.*, and A. N. Prior, *Formal Logic* (2d ed.; Oxford: Oxford University Press, 1962).

14. See *infra*. Compare I. Tammelo, "On the Logical Openness of Legal Orders," (1959) 8 *American Journal of Comparative Law* 187, at 194–99.

15. See Stone, *op. cit.* Compare G. Sawer, "Substance and Form in the Relations between Federal and State Legislation in Australia" (1963) Beiheft 39 *Archiv für Rechts und Sozialphilosophie* 61, at 70, suggesting that there are reasons to believe that systems like the Anglo-Australian are also normatively open.

16. This raises the question as to whether legal neutrality is a deontic state of affairs at all (for it may be contended that it cannot be regarded as this just as unreality cannot be regarded as a kind of reality). In answer to this question (actually raised by Professor Norberto Bobbio of the University of Turin to the writer in a letter) it is to be said that deontic states of affairs are not here considered as something necessarily to be encountered in a given normative system, but as conceptual constructs created for analyzing normative systems. In so doing the "no-law areas," too, come into the field of the vision of the framer of a deontic system and find a conceptual accommodation in such a system. For a deontic system is not a map of a normative system, but a set of coordinates for mapping the latter. Its language with respect to a given normative system is a metalanguage.

17. This identification presupposes interpretation of the given legal material, which is an activity not exhausted by logical analyses.

18. The problem of inconsistency of norms, too, is not exhausted by logical analyses. There is also an inconsistency of feelings, attitudes, and the like, which seems to be logically intractable.

19. See Conte, *op. cit.*, *passim*, for a notable attempt of the formulation of these conditions along the lines of modern logic.

20. Perhaps it is fair to add that study and application of rigorous logic may have the psychological effect of predisposing lawyers to legal formalism. But this can be resisted if the proper meaning and scope of formalistic devices of juristic thinking are understood.

4

Comments

EDWARD J. BLOUSTEIN
New York University Law School

PROFESSOR LEVI has remarked on the "unusual concern [of judges] with [their] decision-making processes" and; in his discussion of Professor Levi's paper, Professor Freund has inquired into the explanation of this "special fascination." Both Professors Levi and Freund have offered suggestions in this regard. I would like to add another reason why judges are especially concerned with the nature of judicial logic; it is, I believe, an extremely important one, but it has been virtually neglected.

The fact is that there is a sense in which judges fashion or determine their own logic. The main business of judges is, of course, to decide the substantive issues that come before them; for example, may a person who was not a party to a contract for the purchase of a loaf of bread sue for an injury arising out of its unwholesomeness? Aside from deciding substantive issues, however, judges also decide what constitute good or appropriate reasons for their decision of substantive issues; for example, is a court bound by a prior decision that holds that privity of contract is a necessary requirement for a suit for breach of warranty of wholesomeness, or may the court revise this rule in the light of contemporary social, political, and economic factors?

To be sure, decisions that fashion the outlines of the judicial organon are relatively infrequent and very often they are made *sub silentio,* but they nevertheless abound. Thus, for instance, *Brown* v. *Board of Education* [1] is most significant for its resolution of the school segregation issue, but it is also an important precedent determining that the data of social sciences may constitute appropriate and legitimate reasons for appellate decisions. In *Woods* v. *Lancet* [2] the New York Court of Appeals abandoned a substantive precedent that barred recovery for injury to a fetus. This decision was much more significant as heralding a change in the Court's attitude toward precedent in the area of tort law, however. Thus in *Burg* v. *Thunig*,[3] in which the Court of Appeals abandoned the doctrine of charitable immunity, and in *Randy Knitwear* v. *American Cyanamid Corp.*,[4] in which that Court abandoned the requirement of privity of contract in suits on a warranty—the Court cited its earlier decision in *Woods* v. *Lancet* as authority for abandoning a rule of law that was not "in accordance with present day standards of wisdom and justice." Precedent was cited and relied on for a modification in the application of precedent.

Numerous other cases in which the courts have modified their way of judging are easy to hand. In fact, the entire trend in this country toward judicial lawmaking is illustrative of judicial control of the logic of the decision process. This is not to say, of course, that judges are "free" to abandon the syllogism, for instance, and invent a new system of deductive logic. Nor is it to say that judges have "complete freedom" in controlling the development of their logic; in fact, the restraints imposed on them in this area by precedent, tradition, and their role in the political process are undoubtedly much more stringent than those imposed in the area of the development of substantive law. I mean only to say that there is a common law of judicial logic and this explains, in part, why judges, in Professor Freund's apt terms, have a "special fascination with their own behavior."

NOTES

1. 347 U.S. 483 (1954).
2. 303 N.Y. 349.
3. 2 N.Y. 2d 656.
4. 11 N.Y. 2d 5, 181 N.E. 2d 399, 226 N.Y.S. 2d 363 (1962).

5

Comments

MICHAEL H. CARDOZO
Cornell University Law School

THE FOLLOWING thoughts were stimulated by two aspects of the discussions at the conference. The first arose out of Professor Levi's analysis of judicial reasoning, and the second out of the general discussion of natural law. It is my purpose merely to cite some relevant examples, not to discuss the issues at any length.

Professor Levi commented that "the function of articulated judicial reasoning is to help protect the court's power by giving some assurance that private views are not masquerading behind public views." One of the games frequently played by iconoclastic law professors has been facetiously labeled "gastronomic jurisprudence." The professor tries to draw from students "the real reason" why a judge decided as he did. Did His Honor eat not wisely but too well last evening, giving him a dyspeptic outlook on the importuning plaintiff's case? Is that gastronomic condition *the real reason* for his decision, his "private views," and the justification spelled out in the written opinion, the "public views," only window dressing?

More seriously, however, there has been wide recognition that the decisions and opinions of judges reflect "the likes and dislikes, the predilections and the prejudices, the complex of instincts and emotions and habits and convictions, which make the man, whether he be litigant or judge." A distinguished commentator has said that "we are constantly misled by our extraordinary faculty of 'rationalizing,'—that is, of devising plausible arguments for accepting what is imposed upon us

by the traditions of the group to which we belong." In applying this observation to the commitment of judges to the traditions of their groups, a distinguished jurist added, "Never will
these loyalties be utterly extinguished while human nature is
what it is."

It is interesting to weigh these ideas against the results
in specific cases. Instances abound in almost any field of law.
Within the past year or so, for example, two courts of high
repute in this country have rendered significant decisions re-
specting the enforcement of contracts having interstate features. In both cases observers, troubled by the outcome of
the decisions, have suggested that predilection was more in-
fluential than precedent in leading to the results. I will not
align myself with them or against them, but merely pose the
questions.

In the *Bernkrant* case, a statute of frauds was involved,
and the court found for the plaintiff despite the lack of a
written agreement. The operation of statutes of frauds has
long troubled legal scholars. Many suspect that they facilitate
fraud more than they prevent it. This doubt has led to the
added suspicion that judges, sharing the doubt, sometimes
search hard for means to avoid the requirement of a writing.
The peculiar uncertainties of the rules of conflict of laws lend
themselves readily to this search. How much did judicial dis-
taste for statutes of frauds contribute to the court's choice of
the law of the state that would enforce the contract? Do we
see in this situation the influence of "subconscious loyalties,"
some of "the predilections and the prejudices . . . which
make the man"?

In the *Haag* case a young woman was seeking an increase
in the amount the alleged father of her child was paying to
support the infant. The existing payments were based on a
written agreement between the man and the woman, who
lived in different states. The court applied the law of the state
that would enforce the agreement as written, giving as its reason the fact that the most significant contacts were located
there. Many commentators have felt that more significant con-

tacts were in the other state. Could the court, however, have been influenced by a desire to thwart the plans of a gold-digging plaintiff? The opinion states, "He has provided sums far in excess of his agreement; all told, we were informed on oral argument, the defendant has paid the complainant some $30,000." Facts revealed only on oral argument, not found in the record and not appropriate for judicial notice, are supposedly irrelevant to the decision. Indeed, nowhere does the carefully written opinion expressly rely on those extraneous facts. Are students of judicial reasoning, however, warranted in suspecting that the choice of law was made as much because of judges' "private view" of gold-digging as their "public view" of the rules of conflicts?

The discussion of natural law recalled to me various judicial opinions in which the judge either called upon principles of natural law to support his position or condemned another judge's opinion because, contrary to our traditions, it seemed to invoke some kind of natural law. Examples have appeared at all stages in our judicial history. Early in our national life, Justice Joseph Story found rights based on the slave trade unenforceable in United States courts because it was "an offense against the universal law of society." Soon after, Chief Justice Marshall said that the same trade, though "contrary to the law of nature," was sanctioned by the law of nations and, if carried on in foreign areas, had to be recognized as valid in our courts.

In later years we have heard further references to "natural justice" in connection with such matters as procedural due process. Justice Holmes once stated that the common law "required a judgment not to be contrary to natural justice." He also talked about the "first principles of legal thinking" as grounds for applying the law of the place of making to the question of the validity of a contract. Many years later, Justice Black objected to a criterion that tied the validity of a governmental act to "this Court's notions of 'natural justice.'" His opinion reflected a trend away from the older acceptance of a natural law that was supposed to guide all our judges. Still, judicial opinions continue to contain references to natural law and natural justice from time to time, sometimes using those very words, sometimes using synonymous phrases such as "it is fundamental."

An interesting example of the diverse contexts in which these references appear is the 1955 case involving the custody of the minor children of a separated couple. The judge, sitting in the Juvenile Court of Cuyahoga County, Ohio, stated that the parent-child relationship "was not created by law but grows out of natural law." Then he found that the return of the children to either of their parents in that particular case "would not serve the best interests of the children." He granted permanent custody to the County Division of Child Welfare. This is not a very unusual result, but it is unusual for the judge to invoke natural law as a guide to his decision. Does this lead him to apply and interpret the laws of nature according to his human wisdom?

Index